Dan Hardy is an MMA and UFC competitor and now commentator and analyst for BT Sport and Fox. *Part Reptile* is his first book. He lives in Leicestershire.

PART REPTILE
DAN HARDY
UFC, MMA and Me

with Paul D. Gibson

HEADLINE

First published in 2017
by HEADLINE PUBLISHING GROUP

First published in paperback in 2018
by HEADLINE PUBLISHING GROUP

1

Cataloguing in Publication Data is available from the British Library

Paperback ISBN 978 1 4722 4382 9

Typeset in Bliss Light by CC Book Production

Printed and bound in Great Britain by CPI Group (UK) Ltd, Croydon, CR0 4YY

Headline's policy is to use papers that are natural, renewable and
recyclable products and made from wood grown in sustainable forests.
The logging and manufacturing processes are expected to conform to
the environmental regulations of the country of origin.

For Grandad Derek

CONTENTS

ACKNOWLEDGEMENTS

It's hard to know where to begin when thanking people for a lifetime of help and support. Right at the beginning I had a mother and father willing to set everything aside and make me their priority. I had a waiting room full of people anxiously standing by for news of my arrival and every one of them has played an integral role in my development as a person. I have also encountered a lot of awesome people on my journey so far, and they too have helped me, guided me, lead me, and at times carried me in the right direction, and this book would need twice as much paper if I were to thank every one of them individually. I have made an attempt to name a few of the key people below, yet there are many, many people that may go unthanked in these pages, but they are far from unappreciated.

My family are amazing. I couldn't have wished for better parents and grandparents, they have been a constant and consistent support network from my first breath and I will be eternally grateful. My little sister, Gemma, has been a ray of light since she was born and continues to inspire me every day with her talents and work ethic. Aunties, uncles and cousins were always close by and have given tremendous support in a variety of ways, and have added to the foundation that is my family. I couldn't have had such a beautiful life so far without these people around me.

As I have travelled around the world training with some of the best martial arts teachers available, I have been equally as blessed to meet people generous with their time and expertise. They have shared knowledge with me and invested hours into my development, often for little or nothing in return, other than the satisfaction that they were a part of the chain that keeps the martial arts alive. I have to begin with Mick Rowley. The first person to really teach me what it is to be a martial artist. Hours of each week for years of my life were spent learning from and training with Mick, at Eagle Taekwondo. His obsession with combat was infectious, and his questioning mindset kept me realistic in my training, preparing me for many cage, ring, and, ultimately, Octagon confrontations. I owe him a lot and will always hold him in the highest regard for all he has done for me throughout my life.

Continuing along my martial arts journey chronologically, Master Lec is the next teacher I would like to mention. Never would I leave a training session without being as exhausted as I was exhilarated by his Muay Thai training. He also guided me to my first Thai boxing fight, and I have loved the sport ever since.

That leads me onto Owen Comrie.

Much like my training with Mick, Owen and I spent many hours working together over several years of competition. A lot of late night pad and bag sessions, and too many early morning circuit sessions, including the tradition of Christmas morning before everyone else is awake. He traveled around the world to corner me and we enjoyed a lot of success together. His singing along to the music in his headphones whilst working his way through the travel-stash of Ritz crackers and peanuts, was the soundtrack to many a fight week. Falling out with people in the crowd while cornering was his specialty, as was trying to steal something from the hotel or venue, sometimes with my Nanna Barbara as an accomplice! Regarding training though, Owen was exceptional. His skill at all ranges as well as his conditioning always set a high bar for his fighters to reach, even at half his age.

Nathan Leverton comes next. Still one of my go-to guys if I have questions or want a high fight IQ to bounce ideas off. It must have been a nightmare trying to get through to us at times, but I recall many instances on fight day or before my way out where he would say exactly the right thing to focus my mind.

Furthering my knowledge of the striking arts, I have to thank Steve Papp. He joined me at a very difficult time in my career and was a source of strength and enthusiasm when I couldn't muster any myself. I still enjoy working with Steve and his commitment to teaching, patience and humility and absolute love of the martial arts allows him to reach many people and be a positive influence in their lives.

Thanks to Eddie Bravo for many enjoyable and mind-opening sessions at 10th Planet Jiu Jitsu, and for encouraging creativity in martial arts practise. To my new team in Vegas, Shawn Yarborough and Ricky Lundell, thank you for your investment, and for having my back when I was coming off four losses and many people thought my career in the UFC was over. And to Jimmy Gifford, nothing but love and respect. One of the humblest, loving and most real people I know. Always good times, good laughs and good energy.

Along this journey I have trained with hundreds of great people and amazing fighters, of all disciplines, very few I would call brothers though. My second family, Team Rough House. My 'blood, sweat and tears' family. Paul Daley, Jimmy Wallhead, Dean Amasinger, Andre Winner, Ollie Richardson, Steve Tetley, Nick Osipczak, Paul Barton, Lee Livingstone and Tamai Harding, I'm grateful for every one of you and thank you for the arse-kickings over the years. My American team mates, Mac Danzig, Frank Mir and Alder Hampel, thank you for your guidance and friend-ship. Ricardo Samms, for evolving my way of thinking when I was in much need of an upgrade. My approach to professional competition and preparation for it was greatly influenced Ricardo, and I became a better athlete from the many soul-destroying runs that he would take me on!

Thank you to the UFC for providing me with a platform to challenge myself and allow me to do what I truly love. To Dana White, Frank and Lorenzo Fertitta for investing in and helping establish the sport of Mixed Martial Arts, and creating an industry for martial artists like myself to thrive. To the old guard, Joe Silva, Burt Watson, Stitch Duran, Huitzi, Bruce Buffer, Goldie and Joe Rogan, for the roles they played in my UFC career. Picking my opponents, looking after me during fight week, protecting my hands during battle, growing my mind and hear and, to the last three gentlemen, for providing the soundtrack to the best years of my fighting career. Thank you all.

And for a final few key individuals, Ian Dean for playing a pivotal role in my early career. Matchmaker for Cagewarriors, part of my management team, and valued friend. There is not a more selfless and giving individual in the sport of mixed martial arts and the European scene in particular is what it is today because of his investment and commitment. My trusted friend, Wad Alameddine, thank you for looking out for me, fighting my corner, running my errands and generally being the kind of support network that every fighter would be blessed to have in a manager. My brother, Beto, for accompanying me on a very important journey, sharing his beautiful photography with me in this book, and being the quiet wisdom and positivity of which the world needs more.

Thank you to John Gooden for being my partner in crime and for his commitment to the sport. You will be hard-pressed to find a more upstanding and conscious individual in all aspects of life. My amazing wife Lacey, for the love, support and guidance at challenging times, and for the patience and understanding when I haven't been the best version of myself (which is more often than I'd like to admit!). My favourite teacher, my best friend and my beautiful love.

And to the people that made this book possible. Richard Roper for assuring me that people may enjoy reading my story and setting the wheels in motion, and Paul Gibson for helping me pull this mess together. His patience while listening to me ramble on, and shoot off on weird and, at times, pointless tangents. It would have been impossible for me to put this into words and hand it over for printing without great reluctance if it weren't for his help. Over the last few months of working on the manuscript, he has served as a therapist and friend as well as writer, and I am very grateful for his efforts in helping me pass on my story so far.

And, finally, a huge thanks to you for taking an interest in my life. I truly hope that you have enjoyed the read, and I wish you peace, love and good health.

Caput Gerat Lupinum – Let His be the Heart of a Wolf

My life to date has revolved around fighting, around my pursuit of striking a man's jaw with the optimum speed, power and timing to rotate his head, disturb the grid of nerves and blood vessels connecting his brain to his skull, and render him temporarily unconscious. My fights are my reference points. And I admit that sometimes I struggle with that fact because I know most people tend to bookmark their journey with more traditional, much less malevolent, landmarks. They recall the likes of birthdays or holidays when seeking to put a moment in time from the past into context. *Where were you living in 2004?* Well, let's see. I turned forty in 2004 so that means I . . . *What were you doing with yourself in 2012?* That was the year we spent a month travelling through Europe so . . . Ask me the same questions and I'm beating Hidetaka

Monma into a bloody submission in Tokyo or putting Duane Ludwig to sleep with a sharp left hook in Vegas. Choose another year and I could be the fighter rising gingerly from the canvas in a semi-fugue state or battling to keep the blood flowing from my head back to my heart as my jugular vein and carotid artery are closed by an arm attempting to choke the life from out of me. Beyond that brief, exhilarating existence inside a cage, my mind's eye won't wander too far. To the torture of the gym or more psychological and spiritual preparation elsewhere perhaps, but certainly no further. Fighting. For thirty-four years, my journey has been signposted by fighting.

THE ORIGINS
OF A FIGHTER

From a foetal ball, curled up on a blue gym mat, I rolled my head to one side and tried to focus on a figure in the sparse crowd watching on. Through the haze of a fuzzy version of consciousness I spied my mother, sobbing and dabbing at the tears building in her brown eyes and threatening to flow freely down her cheek. I was seven years old and I clearly remember thinking, *no, this is not for me*.

It all began a few years before that. Looking back, Michelangelo has a lot to answer for. Like every other young boy at school in the late 1980s, I became obsessed with the Teenage Mutant Ninja Turtles. When the bell sounded for break time, I sprinted onto the playground with an imaginary orange mask tied around my head, swinging make-believe *nunchaku* in the air with innocent, childish glee. I chose Michelangelo out of the four because he appeared to be everything I was not. He was the loud and funny one, the laid-back free spirit. In that always-too-brief window between lessons I longed to be that character, for I knew as soon as I was back in the classroom I'd revert to Dan, the quiet, insular, still-unsure-of-himself kid. Many years later it dawned on me that Raphael, the darker lone wolf of the quartet, was closer to the real me, but at five years old that Californian surfer-dude persona was the one I most aspired to.

Life had been a pretty comfortable bubble up until that point. I was basically not long out of the safe confines of playschool and, with no older brothers or sisters to lock horns with, home life had been largely strife-free too. The first three years were spent at my grandparents' house in Clifton, three miles south of Nottingham city centre in the Midlands of England. My mother and father were both only seventeen when I arrived and did not yet have the means to fend totally for themselves. Mum, the youngest sister of three, was terrified of telling Grandad she was pregnant but he took it in his stride.

'It doesn't matter,' he said after a brief pause to consider the life-changing news. 'We will love it and look after it.'

I remember going to my parents' wedding when I was three, sitting on the church pew eating Jelly Tots and playing with a toy car. Before long we'd moved into our own small home. We were still in Clifton at this stage, regarded as a relatively rough working-class area of Nottingham, but we never had any major problems. A few weeks before I was born, my dad, Mark, began an engineering apprenticeship and for many years he worked twelve-hour day or night shifts. When he was on nights I remember having to tip-toe about the house, fearful of waking the potentially angry, hibernating bear upstairs. Thirty-five years later he's still at the same company, albeit now in a management role and long past having to grind it out through the night. After a few years we moved to the slightly more affluent, lower-middle-class environs of Silverdale so I could go to a half-decent school in neighbouring West Bridgford. Mum was a part-time aerobics instructor and began volunteering at the pre-school I attended. She would eventually go to university to earn a Bachelor of Arts and Master of Arts in childcare and now runs the school.

In many ways we all grew up together, Mum and Dad maturing and learning to handle their own emotions while I looked on and absorbed everything. The little I understood about conflict or aggression I picked up from watching them going through the regular trials and tribulations of daily life that we all experience in our early twenties. Mum was a lioness, a generally relaxed character until she felt the need to protect one of her own. So it was from my dad that I would catch more frequent glimpses of the combative side to our family's nature. He was an only child but my grandma is a very tough woman and, along with her sisters, she ensured her son was anything but mollycoddled. I remember standing on the touchline on a Sunday morning while he tore about the football pitch for ninety minutes. Grandad Ian was often alongside me, doling out sweets from a secret stash in his coat pocket. Unlike his son in centre midfield, sliding forcefully into every tackle and wading determinedly into the centre of the melees that pepper the average pub league match, it seemed to me that Grandad always had such a calm demeanour. Later I'd sit in the corner of the pub after the game and watch Dad enthusiastically participate in the caustic banter between teammates that British sporting environments are renowned for. I knew he was the same at work, nailing lunch-boxes to benches and verbally torturing any poor soul who had the misfortune of committing the most minor of mistakes. My sister Gemma was born when I was four and the following summer we went on a budget holiday to Mallorca, staying in a hotel that struggled desperately to justify the three stars on its gable wall. One day we returned from the beach to find that Gemma's cot had been removed from the room. When Dad went downstairs to ask for it back I was there to witness him lunge across the reception desk at an ignorant manager who dismissively suggested we drag a mattress off another bed and let the newborn lie on that. Even at four years old, I understood my dad's anger. I didn't know what he was angry about exactly, but I knew that he was arguing in defence of my little sister. I always took the responsibility of being a big brother very seriously and I remember immediately feeling very protective of her as soon as she was born. Gemma has been one of my biggest supporters from day one and a huge source of inspiration for me. I've never known anyone so musically talented and able to learn new things so quickly. After receiving a saxophone as a Christmas gift one year around the age of ten, she barely put it down to eat dinner and was playing like Lisa Simpson by the end of the day. She attended a lot of my UFC fights and I could always pick her voice out of the crowd above all others. Even with thousands of people cheering, my ears seemed to be tuned in to her particular tone. It may be because I'm so familiar with it, or perhaps it is down to us having basically the same DNA, but either way it gave me a much-needed boost at the right time in many of my fights.

Dad's short fuse when antagonised naturally shaped my own inter-actions with others and back in school it soon became clear that I had my own combustible side. The reserved, timid even, pupil during class had a temper that went from zero to sixty in a heartbeat. Inspired by the Turtles and the ninja moves with which they defeated all their foes, it wasn't long before I spent every spare minute charging around, aiming flying kicks and strikes at whoever happened to be in my way. It was never anything malicious, but it became wild and dangerous behaviour which the school felt obliged to bring to my parents' attention. Then a new boy joined our class and, presumably inwardly anxious about stepping into a foreign environment, decided he'd settle in and make his name through force. Bullying is a strong term among kids that young, but certainly he targeted me in particular, seemingly intent on boosting his own social status in the schoolyard hierarchy off the back of my downfall. But he had miscalculated and while antagonising me one afternoon when the teacher had left the class, I Sparta-kicked him in the chest and sent him careering backwards over desks to land on the floor in a frightened daze. I had ensured he would never bother me again, but my reaction was to run to the toilets and lock myself in a cubicle. Looking back now, I can see that I simply didn't have the tools to deal sensibly with such a conflict, either mentally or physically. My parents were again informed, of course, and it was clear to everyone that I needed both an outlet and a control for the aggressive energy that burned ever brighter within me.

I am sure my dad would have loved me to follow him down the football path, and I did play for a few teams. The fact that I am naturally left-footed, coupled with English football's infamous dearth of left-footed talent, normally ensured I could get a game on the wing. But I was never particularly good and, more importantly, I was never passionate about being one of twenty-one other kids kicking a ball around a muddy grass field. I liked being outside in nature, and enjoyed the Beavers and Cub Scouts for that reason, but I also spent quite a bit of time alone in my bedroom where it was all about pirates, Lego and, of course, the Ninja Turtles. For no other reason than my infatuation with those four sewer-dwelling reptiles, it was decided that a martial art might be the key to settling my volatile temperament.

I was immediately delighted with the suggestion and imagined myself soon pulling off the acrobatic ninja moves with which Michelangelo and his cohorts settled their differences. No one in our family had any real understanding of the different disciplines within martial arts, so taekwondo was chosen purely because there was a school just around the corner from our house. Again, I couldn't have been happier. Two of my friends, Ryan Middleton and Luke Rowlett, were among the coolest kids in the area and they both practised taekwondo. I had always associated their popularity and apparent total lack of a care in the world with that fact and now I was going to learn their secret.

I was giddy with excitement on the first night I strode into Eagle & Hawk Taekwondo School. The classes took place in the same local community centre hall in which I had attended playschool, Beavers and Cubs, so I was totally at ease in the surroundings and couldn't wait to get started. We were all standing at one side and I remember just looking up and down the line with a big grin on my face, almost dancing on the spot such was my positive nervous energy. From the top of the hall, a large man in a white uniform with a black belt around his considerable waist marched down the line and stopped abruptly right in front of me. He was middle-aged, somewhere in his forties, had a big gut, thinning hair and an ugly, greasy complexion. Without warning he suddenly tilted forward and yelled in my face at the top of his voice.

'What are you doing here?' he screamed. 'I don't want the likes of you in my class. Get out of here!'

I turned and fled, the tears streaming down my face before I'd reached the door. I sprinted home and straight upstairs to the sanctuary of my bedroom. That hall had always been a fun and safe place for me and I had walked around smiling ever since Dad told me I'd be learning taekwondo there. Within seconds, this guy had managed to shatter all that. Mum, the lioness, wasn't happy. I was reluctant to return but when she found out what had happened she marched in to the following class with me in tow and ferociously demanded an explanation. It turned out that the previous instructor was a one-off, just filling in for that night. The two regular instructors, Mick Rowley and Paul Allsopp, apologised profusely, put Mum's mind at ease, and I tentatively agreed to give it another shot.

It would be disingenuous to suggest I took to taekwondo like the proverbial duck to water, however. Mick and Paul were tough men who fostered a harsh and at times intimidating environment. Eagle & Hawk was a World Taekwondo Federation school, meaning the martial art was taught with full-contact strikes. Right from day one, punches to the body and kicks to the body and head were not just permitted, but expected. A commercial club, the type that hands belts out just for turning up every Tuesday and Thursday and devalues and delegitimises the entire grading process, it most certainly was not. Eagle & Hawk was the real thing, a place to learn both discipline and how to fight via a martial art. 'You'll know when you deserve a new belt,' Mick would often say when he learnt of someone pining for an upgrade.

But at the outset I was under the command of Paul, who took all the younger kids. Both men could come across as tough and unforgiving at times, but I always felt that Paul was sometimes mean just for the sake of it. Exercise and drills were fierce, often to the point of exhaustion, and the likelihood of consequences if the exercises weren't completed was enough of a deterrent to ensure I pushed past the point of pain. From his perspective I'm sure it was just an attempt to strengthen our minds, but it made my first few years of training a very unpleasant experience, full of silly, unnecessary physical tests that were dangerous for our young, undeveloped bodies. I remember doing leg raises as a six-year-old until my muscles seized up and there were plenty of nights like that. He pushed us very hard considering our age, and I normally rose a little gingerly the morning after class. When Mum noticed this, her maternal instinct kicked in and she began challenging Paul. As an aerobics instructor she was a stickler for doing physical exercise and movements the correct way. Because of her aerobics background, she believed that exercise shouldn't hurt, that you shouldn't wake the next day battered and bruised with muscles aching: certainly not when you're six years old anyway. Her interventions naturally rubbed Paul's macho ego up the wrong way and did me few favours during class. It seemed to me that I received his patented hawk-talon pinch on the chest more often than my peers. There were many moments in which I would have walked away if there was an easy escape route, but I could see how proud my parents were and didn't want to disappoint them. I think this was the first time I realised how stubborn I could be. I had been chased away from martial arts by intimidation on my first night, but I wasn't going to let it happen again.

Within a year I was deemed ready for my first tournament. I remember the creeping terror overwhelming me as early as the drive to Harvey Hadden Sports Centre. I sat in the backseat of my dad's beige Ford Fiesta, looking out the window and wondering what the hell I was doing travelling to an organised physical confrontation. We arrived and I stood on a scale and somebody scribbled down a note and I was told what category I was in and ushered off to the side. I felt a little abandoned then, as I sat waiting and waiting for my fight. I seemed to sit there for hours, the dreadful sense of anticipation in the pit of my hollow stomach growing all the while. Finally, I was called onto the mats. I had advanced two grades up from my original white belt and was now a yellow belt. Across from me stood a kid, two years older and substantially taller, with a blue belt around his waist. It is highly probable he was from a school with a much more generous approach to grading than Eagle & Hawk, but even so, two tags and a green belt come before blue so, if nothing else, my opponent clearly had far more experience than me.

More important than my foe's abilities, however, was the clear fact that I was just not ready for this environment, that I was totally under-qualified to deal with it either physically or emotionally. I had never before been in a situation in which someone with whom I had no previous argument was going to attempt to kick me in the head with genuinely bad intentions. It was all totally surreal. I felt more like a passenger, like I was at the side watching myself standing in a fighting stance. As soon as the bout began, I wished it to end. I was a rabbit caught in the headlights. I went through the motions, spinning and kicking, but I was removed from the confrontation. I kicked out, but with no real intention of landing. Suddenly, I got my wish and I found myself lying on the ground with the contest apparently over. The next thing I remember is seeing my mum crying. I later found out that my opponent had kicked me on the temple and briefly knocked me out. That was the end of my first ever competitive martial arts tournament and, sitting in the back seat of the car as we drove home, I was determined it would be my last. *Why on earth did I volunteer for that?* I thought to myself. *No chance I'm ever going back there.*

And for the next two years I didn't fight competitively. More than that, I immediately wanted to walk away from taekwondo altogether. But when Mum got over the initial shock of seeing her only boy curled up on the mat after being kicked in the head, I could see that the pride in her eyes shone even brighter than before. I wanted to quit, but I couldn't let her or Dad down. And so the following Tuesday I was back in the Eagle & Hawk School, going through my drills, with Mick and Paul's stern, watchful eyes looking on.

● ● ●

Two years after the trauma of my debut, I was back at Harvey Hadden Sports Centre for my second tournament. This time I knew what to expect but that made my nerves even worse than they had been as a trembling six-year-old stepping into the unknown. I was up against a kid of a higher grade again in my first fight, but we were evenly matched physically and I was now much more comfortable in my body. I remember my opponent had a red head-guard and red spots on his body armour and I just told myself, *aim for red*. And unlike two years before, I was now fully accustomed to landing kicks and strikes on a foe. I beat him on points, and then won my semi-final in a similar fashion to advance to the final, where a teammate was waiting. He actually suffered an asthma attack and the final was abandoned midway through the second round. As he was ahead on points at the time they awarded him the trophy, but I didn't really care about that. I was just elated to have felt so at ease within a fighting arena and to have walked away from the day with only positive memories.

I was never as nervous before a fight again, but it wasn't until the age of ten or eleven that I could honestly say I enjoyed taekwondo. By this stage the Eagle & Hawk had fractured and I went with Mick. He was still a hard taskmaster, at times backing me into a corner during sparring, provoking tears and other emotional outbursts. But when Mick pushed me to my limits, there was always a reason behind it, even if I couldn't immediately see what it was when I felt beaten up and humiliated. He also knew that I, as his most committed and consistent student, was the one who could be tested in such a severe way. On one occasion I stormed out, hurling the most vicious insults I could think of as I left, and Mick later said he was sure that it was the last he would see of me. But I now respected him unconditionally and trusted him implicitly. Mick had a much wider understanding of martial arts and what they represent than anyone else I knew. We were now training in a local school hall and on evenings when pedagogical rank was pulled and we were forced to vacate the space for a school play or parents' evening, Mick secured the use of a video room and arrived bouncing like a kid on Christmas morning with his bag of VHS tapes. He would have spent hours the previous night lining up precise moments within certain fight scenes.

'Now, lads,' he'd say, 'I want you to watch here how Benny "the Jet" Urquidez uses a jumping spinning kick to end this contest.' Then he'd eject that tape and plunge in another, excitedly warning us to pay close attention to Cynthia Rothrock's hand fighting in close. He introduced me to all the big names in martial arts: to Jean-Claude Van Damme, to Jackie Chan, to Sammo Hung and, of course, to The Master, Bruce Lee. I watched them all, particularly Lee, open-mouthed. In my eyes he was the truest martial artist on the planet. The likes of Van Damme with his balletic moves and Chan or Hung with their background in the acrobatic Chinese circus appeared to be entertainers and movie stars first and martial artists second. But Lee was totally immersed in martial arts. And what he did on that grainy video footage, on that 19-inch television screen that we all crowded around, seemed magical to me, totally unreal. They were unattainable skills but I liked to lie in bed at night and imagine doing what he did. Everything in life would be forever okay if I could fight like Bruce Lee.

I watched Lee's movies religiously and even at that young age I saw him for the martial arts revolutionary he was. In the opening scene of *Enter the Dragon* he defeats Hung by submission at a time when nobody in martial arts was talking about needing a ground game. In *Game of Death*, unfinished due to Lee's sudden and untimely death in 1973, the film climaxes with Lee fighting his way through a pagoda to reach the main bad guy, played by Kareem Abdul-Jabbar. He encounters a variety of opponent, including karate black belts and eskrima and hapkido masters, and adapts his style to defeat them all. This was the literal mixing of martial arts long before anyone coined the name Mixed Martial Arts. In that first fight in *Enter the Dragon*, Lee and Hung even fought one another donning Bong Sau gloves not at all dissimilar to what is used in the UFC today.

Even more important than Lee's somewhat stylised moves for the silver screen, however, were his words. Throughout his movies he shared his philosophy of martial arts and proved he had a perspective miles ahead of his peers. In *Enter the Dragon* he talks of being like water, of having no particular style, of being prepared for whatever might be thrown at him. This had a massive and profound influence on me. I could see I was developing the skills necessary for conflict in certain situations, but there was still so much I had to learn. I hated any feelings of vulnerability and was determined to learn enough to be comfortable in whatever scenario the old head on my young shoulders could envisage. *What if my opponent has a weapon? What if we are in an enclosed space? What if there are several attackers?* Before I was fuelled by my parents' pride, but now Bruce Lee drove me to train and better myself.

In the meantime, I had begun to perform consistently well in competitions in towns and cities all over the Midlands. Having been a relatively slim and slight youngster, around the age of thirteen I suddenly filled out. Unfortunately, this filling out was largely centred around my waist and consisted of a layer of unwelcome fat. It was useful bulk for the rugby pitch, and I was selected as a prop forward for the school team, but it did me no favours in the taekwondo dojang. Not only did the extra and unflattering heft make me an easy target for barbed jibes, but it also hurt me on the scales at tournaments where I would be forced to battle older, much stronger boys. Sometimes, if I was close to a lower weight-class, Mick would hastily pull me to one side and suggest a trip to the bathroom and ten laps of the sports hall before I officially registered. I was still too young to appreciate the importance of weight classes but I can now see the distinct disadvantage I was at and for a couple of years I lost fights because of it. It wasn't until a girlfriend of Mick started talking to me about nutrition and drew up a special diet to follow that I began reaching my potential. It was as if I progressed from unable to able within a year as the weight fell off. It was like removing a 10kg weight vest that had been dragging me down and sapping my energy. I now felt like I had an extra engine and this boost coincided with a testosterone increase that was a function of both the weight loss and simply entering my mid-teens. Suddenly, I was blessed with explosive power. Leg muscles that had been strengthening while they laboured under the excess weight suddenly propelled my lighter torso as fast as anyone else on the football or rugby field. Suddenly, I was launching a shot put metres beyond my schoolmates' efforts. And suddenly, I started winning almost every taekwondo competition I entered.

My grandad, my mum's dad, was by now a massive part of my martial arts world and taekwondo had become *our* thing. He had been driving me to and from class for a few years when one day in conversation with Mick he mentioned that he would love to be able do some of the moves he saw us execute.

'Well, why don't you, Derek?' Mick replied bluntly. 'You'd be more than welcome here and I don't see what there is to stop you.'

So the following week, at the age of sixty, my grandad had his first taekwondo lesson alongside his thirteen-year-old grandson. He kept going for five years and, despite health problems, gave it his absolute all in every class. I remember one evening when Mick had us all hang from a bar in a line to see who could hold on the longest. One by one, younger, lighter, fitter and stronger guys dropped, but Grandad held firm. He had closed his eyes as if in meditation and, by the time everyone else had fallen from the bar, he was still off in his own world. He hung from that bar so long without the slightest movement that Mick finally approached and gave him a gentle prod just to make sure it wasn't rigor mortis keeping him in position.

After Mum and Dad's pride and Bruce Lee's genius, my relationship with Grandad now became the anchor preventing me drifting away from martial arts. There were plenty of days when my mind wandered, normally warm summer days when all my mates were arranging to meet up in the park or organising a game of football. A part of me longed to ditch taekwondo for the night and go with them, but I knew that

Grandad would be waiting outside the house at 5.30pm in his white Austin Metro, thrilled to see me as always. Not that he would have outwardly expressed any disappointment had I told him I wasn't going that night. He never did that, never forced any expectations onto me. I was perfect in Grandad's eyes; whatever I chose to do was fine by him. But I would have sensed the pang of disappointment he kept buried within. I would have felt his regret that it would be a few hours he couldn't have with his grandson. I knew how much he looked forward to it, and so did I. As we grow up we naturally spend less time with individual members of our own family so I treasured this time that was set in stone each week. He must have listened to some nonsense spout from my mouth over the years during those drives to taekwondo and back. For a while I became obsessed with UFOs and anything supernatural. I'd talk him through episodes of *The X Files* and he'd turn up with newspaper clippings he came across that had anything to do with aliens or crop circles or any phenomena potentially difficult to explain. I look back on my moody-teenager days and wish I could have those evenings back. The times when I slumped into the passenger seat, stuffed in two earphones and listened in sullen silence to Megadeth for the entire journey. But even that was okay with Grandad too. He was never judgemental, never critical. All he ever did was love and support me. Whatever I needed, Grandad would have it within a week. If Mick mentioned a particular book worth having, Grandad tracked it down for me. When he saw we were starting to use the focus mitts more often, he bought me a pair. And he was brilliant with his hands as well, capable of making almost anything out of wood. When I wanted a heavy bag to practise my striking and kicking at home, Grandad went into the garden and built a frame upon which I could hang it. Nothing was too big of an ask for him, he'd always come through for me.

With that support I kicked on hard and fast with the taekwondo. After winning a load of tournaments in a row, I began going to competitions to try and judge how effective my taekwondo skills would be in an actual fight rather than focusing on winning the trophy. Taekwondo is largely a kicking art, with jumping, spinning and head-height kicks all emphasised. Some say it developed that way in order to fight an opponent on horseback from the ground. Lower-body strength is key and my quick, strong legs made me the perfect build for it. But from quite early on, I wanted more. I watched a teammate, Mahmood, closely when he fought. Smaller and more nimble than me, Mahmood was incredibly fast and skilful and invariably left with the competitor of the tournament trophy. He learnt Taekwondo in Iran before moving to the UK and, while my emphasis was always on fighting, Mahmood was always primed to leave with silverware. I knew I was a different and more aggressive beast, but I sought to integrate Mahmood's speed and technique and flamboyance into my own repertoire too.

I began entering tournaments in other martial arts disciplines as well, just to see how my fighting technique stacked up. In particular, I sought out competition in Japanese ju-jutsu – not to be confused with its Brazilian descendent jiu-jitsu. My mentality was to try and keep the fight within the range in which I could work and do my best. If I got beaten by a different skill-set, I'd go home and research it for weeks, building my own private library of information. I took something away from every loss: *win or learn*, as Conor McGregor's coach, John Kavanagh, says. I'd find books and videos and pore over the technique and how I could counter it, how I could add to my game and improve and inch closer to being a complete fighter. I had such a thirst for knowledge of every aspect of martial arts I hadn't yet explored. It was as if I had unlocked a door, walked into a new world, and life was a pick 'n' mix for me to dip in and out of whatever interested me. Then I'd go to Mick and work on how to put the new ideas into practice, on what was my next step to becoming a better martial artist.

And Mick was a kindred spirit in that regard. He too was a lateral thinker when it came to martial arts, always keen to think outside the box. In truth, I see now he was preparing me for a career in MMA from the first day I walked into Eagle & Hawk Taekwondo. In comparison to what my peers were doing in their karate or judo schools and gyms, Mick was already light-years ahead in terms of the variety of our training. The focus was on taekwondo, of course, but an extremely rough and ready brand of that martial art. The sport was edging towards Olympic recognition at this time and mutating into what you see on your screens now every four years: taller, slighter athletes flitting in and out of range on fast, light feet, aiming to score, but hardly damage. Mick remained old-school, however, and we were encouraged to march aggressively into range, throwing kicks and punches to the body in order to lower the head and target it with more kicks and punches. That suited me down to the ground.

But beyond taekwondo specifics, Mick always tried to spice training up and keep it as interesting as possible. He knew as well as I did that expertise of just a single discipline limited you greatly in an open fight. Unlike any other taekwondo school I knew of at that time, we were going through boxing drills, throwing mats on the floor and grappling, stick and sword fighting and spending hours working with focus mitts. I remember one class in which Mick came up with a novel way to use the mitts and started hurling them towards me at various heights and speeds. My goal was to jump and spin-kick each one before it got past me. I caught one particular mitt clean and it went rocketing towards the ceiling and smashed through a skylight window. Mick had me out in the pitch-black night, scrabbling about in the rain looking for his prized piece of kit. The term MMA was not yet well established but looking back that is exactly what I was already preparing for. We just happened to call it Mick's, rather than Mixed, Martial Arts.

● ● ●

By now I was sixteen and not what was termed a normal teen for the late 1990s in Nottingham. Basically, I was still struggling to find my niche in the world. I grew my hair out long, wore coloured and totally unnecessary contact lenses and sometimes painted my nails black just to sit in class and scratch it off with a penknife. Soon I was getting involved in music and ended up fronting a Rage Against the Machine cover band. I had completed my GCSEs and decided to stay on to study art and graphic design, but I never felt that school and I clicked. I hung about within a motley crew of about twenty misfits, mostly kids with behavioural problems or from broken homes. Every day we'd divide into teams at the first break time to ostensibly play a football match. The reality was we were going through the motions in order to facilitate a physical clash that would guarantee a fight. Scraps broke out, and from them a more organised confrontation was arranged between two of us for the second break. It was a strange and violent cycle that kept us occupied until we graduated.

I also had an innate aversion to the authority figures within school, especially when I didn't believe they deserved their position or my respect. And I hated being told I was wrong or couldn't do something I wanted to do. I gravitated towards art because success or failure couldn't be measured in such a black-and-white manner and I spent most of my days in the art block, where I could throw paint on the walls, build huge sculptures, take random photographs, or mould clay into whatever I wanted and be left in peace. Graphic design was more rigid and more structured and I found myself in continual conflict with teachers who were intent on telling me to colour in-between the lines.

Around this time, opportunities to practise my fighting skills on the street began to present themselves with alarming frequency. I don't believe I ever set out to deliberately look for trouble, but it invariably found me nevertheless. Having said that, I guess I did put myself in certain situations in which a violent outcome was predictable. I was very into Metal and Hardcore, musical genres inextricably linked to anger and aggression. My dad had introduced me to Punk music years before, but he was into the Sex Pistols and The Clash, whereas I was drawn to a much more extreme sound and culture. The music created a pretty aggressive ambience and that united us Hardcore and Metal fans. In the midst of it we felt like we were at war. I broke two ribs at a Biohazard concert in Bradford and that was just from being punched and shoved around in the mosh pit. I met some crazy friends in that scene, and fights in bars and outside on the street, occasionally organised but more often than not a function of alcohol and testosterone, became a weekly occurrence. Even within my group of tough young men, I soon became known as the go-to guy when it all kicked off, the first to wade in at any hint of aggro and the quickest to let his hands go when tempers frayed.

It was not a good way to be, but it did feed positively into my martial arts development. In the brutal setting of a drunken street fight, it soon becomes clear what techniques are and are not effective. I realised I was not as comfortable as I would have liked when someone got their hands on me, that I felt smothered at close range. There were close-range movements needed to pass grades in taekwondo but I didn't find them particularly applicable in the real world. Looking elsewhere, I soon discovered the Chinese martial art Wing Chun, which specialises in close-range combat. The up-close parries, deflections, and counter-striking that characterise the discipline immediately made me more at ease in the hustle and bustle of a bar brawl and were further strings to my fighting bow.

For a couple of years, I expected at least one serious fight per week. After training on a Thursday night I went out to either Rock City or the Old Angel Inn and drank, sometimes through to when the pubs closed on a Sunday evening. We frequently got into scraps with local bike gangs and firms, but failing that, any random arsehole mouthing off in the club would do. Alcohol was without a doubt the determining factor when it came to whether a confrontation would be defused or escalated, that liquid poison that seeps into the reptilian part of our brains and guarantees bad decision-making. I remember jumping in when three guys had isolated a member of my group in a club. I dropped one with a punch and then threw another onto the ground. I sat on his chest, grabbed him by the hair and began smashing his head into the floor, totally consumed by rage. At that moment I wasn't in control, there was something else driving me to really hurt this guy. I can see now that I was on a very dangerous path, one that has led old friends to prison or early graves, but one violent incident when I was seventeen saved me from a potentially similar fate.

It was a Thursday night and I was in Rock City celebrating a friend's birthday. I went to the club directly from taekwondo training, where I had spent two hours in a self-defence session, repeating a defensive block and throat strike move until it was practically hard-wired into my muscle-memory. After a couple of hours drinking, an inevitable situation arose between a few of my friends and another group. I strode into the thick of it as they were starting to square up and somebody threw a punch. Without thinking, I instinctively blocked it and struck his throat. It was a Bruce Lee moment: 'when there is an opportunity, I do not hit; it [raising his fist] hits all by itself'. He dropped where he stood, holding his throat with both hands and making an alarming wheezing noise as if he was struggling to breathe. In an instant I was sober. It was the first time such stark and jarring evidence of what I could do, and what the consequences of those actions could be, was held before my eyes. For a couple of minutes I was genuinely terrified that I had killed a man. I was fortunate that the lesson came without cost as the guy soon recovered and there were no serious repercussions, but I went home from the club a different person that night. I had been attacked first so I didn't feel guilty or ashamed, but I saw I needed to be in full control of my reactions or, if it was down to my subconscious, that I could rely on it to make the right decision. That was the last time I ever drank alcohol. The decision cost me some friends, as without the common bond of drinking to excess we naturally drifted apart, but I know I made a very wise decision. I still have a lot of love for that old crowd, but some of the more aggressive are already gone and others are in prison and I know there is every chance I would have made similarly reckless and destructive life-decisions.

In place of drinking and street-fighting half my week away, I recommitted to martial arts. I entered every tournament I could and was more focused than ever before on my goal of becoming a complete and well-rounded martial artist. I continued testing myself against other disciplines to see how my developing skill-set stacked up against judo's grips and throwing techniques, or jiu-jitsu's takedowns and submissions. I watched boxing too and loved the likes of Great Britain's super middleweight kings Chris Eubank and Nigel Benn, but I remained convinced that Bruce Lee would have dealt with both with ease in an open rules fight. Professional boxing just looked like a restricted form of fighting to me, hard-headed and inflexible. Boxers relied on their gloves to take most of their opponent's shots whereas martial arts demanded a higher level of skill and carried an air of mystique that set it apart.

Another reason I was looking beyond the confines of taekwondo was that I had outgrown the competition within my school and area. Other than Mick himself, there was no one who could push or test me. It is true that Mick always managed to get the better of me in some way or another, but I like to think a part of that was down to the innate human aversion to usurping a hero-figure. I remember reading an apt poem, 'The Follower' by the Nobel Prize-winning Irish poet Seamus Heaney, in school around that time and making the connection. The verse depicts a farmer's son idolising his father before growing up, taking his role, and becoming frustrated with the stumbling old man now following him around. I also thought about the battles between Mick and me years later when I read Robert Greene's *The 48 Laws of Power*. According to Greene, the first law is never outshine your master. He elaborates to say that you should always make those above you feel comfortably superior, that if you display too much of your talent in a desire to please you may just inspire fear and insecurity. 'Make your masters appear more brilliant than they are and you will attain the heights of power,' Greene concludes. To this day, Mick is far from being a stumbling old man, and my successes have caused him to feel neither fear nor insecurity, but I'm sticking to this explanation for why he was always the master and me the pupil!

Not long after I gave up the beer-fuelled late nights, Mick decided I was ready for my black belt. His final test was a brutal sparring session in which he and a policeman-friend of his, Nick Carroll, attacked me repeatedly and simultaneously for what felt like hours. It was fierce, as ferocious an experience as anything I had ever been in on the street.

They effectively beat me up as the rest of the class looked on and it was right on the limit of what should be allowed in a taekwondo dojang. I trusted Mick to know where the line was and not to cross it, but they broke me again and I stormed off effing and blinding with the threat of tears burning my eyes.

The six-hour-long grading process was then almost as intense. It began with running through a series of twelve forms. They begin with basic moves involving low blocks, straight punches, and short and long stances, then progress onto more advanced and complex catching and throwing patterns while turning in different directions to face multiple opponents. There were twenty-two separate moves in the first form and forty-eight in the twelfth and each one was graded in terms of skill, execution and balance. After that I had to spar six consecutive black belts, including two-on-one attacks. Finally I had to break bricks and wooden slats with a range of hand and kicking techniques. It was an important achievement for me because I felt I needed and deserved some tangible reward for all the effort I had put in over eleven tough years. But by this stage I already realised that it was all such a tiny part of the martial arts world, a very limited skill-set. I can't even remember those forms now because none of them are applicable in a real fight. They were more a means to build neuromuscular pathways and increase physical strength and endurance. They were varied in order to test every range and prove as good a way as any to provide a uniform test within a universal grading system. But I never saw the point in continuing on to do my second dan and beyond. That was never going to help me get to where I wanted to go. The first dan grading was like the end of my taekwondo journey, but that is not to say I wasn't extremely proud to strap on that black belt. I was proud because, as Mick always said I would, I knew that it belonged around my waist. The profligate manner in which belts are awarded in martial arts today has rid holders of the respect they may or may not deserve. Brazilian jiu-jitsu aside, I take every proclamation of 'I'm a black belt in such and such' with a pinch of salt and withhold admiration until I know what school they are from and where they did their grading. As far as I'm concerned, a black belt is someone who stands on the front line of a pitched battle and is ready to go at any time. Suffice it to say, not many of the so-called black belts walking the street today meet that estimation.

● ● ●

It was time to leave school now but with martial arts being my only true passion, I felt the options on the table in front of me were extremely limited. The only other vague interest I had was art and so I enrolled in Clarendon College, an art school in the centre of Nottingham. Almost immediately, I found myself back in conflict with tutors who insisted I spend more time reading books about who may have influenced my work rather than just creating something fresh myself. I was sure that my inspiration came from within or the environment I existed in, not long-dead artists, stuffy galleries or dusty tomes in the art history section of the library. But I went through the motions when I had to so I could escape as soon as possible to head to the gym.

Around the same time, I was walking through Nottingham city centre one day and decided to call into Virgin Megastore to see what martial arts videos they had. Among the various subsections, the letters UFC grabbed my attention. There were only two videos in the section, *UFC 2* and *UFC 3*. As I only had enough cash for one, I opted for the earlier instalment and rushed back to college to find a video player and check it out. I put the tape in, watched it in stunned silence, then immediately watched it again. This was the time of the Gracie dominance and Royce tore through the competition to win four fights, using three different submissions along the way, and claim the Ultimate Fighting Championship trophy. I was somewhat in awe and somewhat terrified. The Gracie family created modern Brazilian jiu-jitsu and later introduced Vale Tudo, a violent and largely underground fight scene which translates literally as 'anything goes', to the US. Royce was raised in this environment and so I hunted down some shadowy footage of the brutal fights in which it appeared everything other than biting and eye-gouging was encouraged. It was slightly unsettling to watch, but fear was a big part of the attraction. The UFC video was rated 18 and *Two Men Enter, One Man Leaves* screamed out from the cover. This was the ultimate of martial arts, I thought. This is what I had to aspire to. This is where I needed to go to prove myself a truly effective fighter.

I was now competing more than ever, and trying out different skills and techniques whenever I could. Where before I'd looked to martial arts to help me deal with the trouble that came my way, it now actually gave me space from conflict and fighting, a way to temper my rage. I became fascinated by kung fu and the animal styles of fighting that discipline adopts. The legend says that Shaolin monks, dislocated from the outside world in their Henan province temple, developed stylised versions of fighting by watching animals engage with one another beyond the temple walls. I fell in love with the romanticism of it all and began studying the fighting styles of the tiger, monkey, crane and praying mantis as I imagined the monks did in their isolation. Shaolin kung fu became like the final stronghold of the magical side of martial arts for me. Something inside told me I needed to go and see it and experience it for myself. I'd been to the shows and watched videos of the training. I'd seen the breaking of iron bars over shaven heads, the balancing on top of spears. I'd marvelled at the flexibility and gymnastic ability of these monks in their orange robes. But I yearned to go there, to travel to China and do nothing but focus on training and fighting. I wanted to spend years matching their dedication and learning everything I could from these mystical martial artists. And when I saw a Discovery Channel documentary about a Chinese businessman and a young Chinese boy spending three years in a Shaolin temple, I swore I would do the same.

From that moment on, whenever a tutor got on my case and criticised my lack of academic effort or warned me about an approaching deadline, my response was always the same. 'I don't care about any of this,' I would snap back. 'I'm going to China to learn kung fu.' Naturally enough, everyone laughed. 'Wise up and stop messing around with your life,' they invariably said as they walked away shaking their head. But I knew what I felt inside. This was my next step in martial arts. I had to go and see the monks.

2

I had it all worked out. To save money, I lived with my parents throughout the first year of a Contemporary Arts degree at Nottingham Trent University and then applied for the maximum amount allowed as a student loan for my second year. From the outside it looked like I was simply continuing with my studies, but all I was really waiting for was the £3,500 credit to hit my bank account and I'd be on the next flight to the Far East.

Internet and email communication was by now pretty standard, if very slow, but the language difference ensured that three years in a Shaolin temple was not so easy to arrange. I was disappointed to learn that I could not go to the Monastery in Dengfeng County, Henan, the main temple of the Shaolin school of Buddhism. It was the temple I had seen in the documentary but it was explained to me that non-Chinese were not allowed to stay and study within its walls, and so the monks there recommended another option, the Northern China Shaolin Martial Arts Academy near Si Ping City. Only having a few grainy photographs of this new destination from a basic website was rather unsettling, and for the first time some sense of caution made its voice heard in my head. I decided I would head out on a two-month scouting mission to make sure the place was legitimate and met my expectations. If everything was okay, I would then fly back to England, pack my things, tie up a few loose ends and then return to China for the full three-year stay.

I was nervous setting out that morning from Heathrow airport in London. I felt like a man but I was in reality still a teenager and I had never even taken a flight on my own before. But something about the chaos of Heathrow settled me and by the time the plane took off I was looking forward to my adventure. The journey was fine as well, pit-stops in the clean, modern airports of Vienna and Beijing helping put my mind further at ease. But this air of contentment evaporated the instant my third flight of the day touched down in Changchun Dafangshen Airport. The region has a new airport now, opened a couple of years after my visit, but the terminal I landed in felt condemned. Built by the Japanese during the Second World War, Changchun Dafangshen was a grim place for a jet-lagged teenage kid to find himself, 5,000 miles from home. There were no doors on the terminal building and as many goats and chickens as people wandering around. I had been the only Westerner on the flight from Beijing and as I tried to figure out where to wait for my bags, all the other passengers dispersed in various directions and never returned. I found a luggage carousel, but it never moved. Instead, a couple of guys simply wheeled in my bag and dumped it on the stationary conveyer belt. I slung it over my shoulder and walked towards what looked like a main exit. Outside was just dusty waste ground and a large crowd of people standing and staring. In my naivety I had expected to emerge into a luscious, pine forest setting and have a trio of orange-robed Buddhist monks meet me with a solemn bow at the door. Instead, a crazy-looking man at the rear of the crowd, well over six foot tall with a wild shock of hair and a half-smoked cigarette hanging limp from his unsmiling mouth, gestured for me to follow him and then walked away. I fought my way through the crowd barely in time to see him climb into the passenger seat of a battered Nissan car. Running, I just about managed to clamber into the backseat as the motor rattled into life and propelled us forward uncertainly. For the next five hours I sat in exhausted silence as my greeter and the driver, another unkempt chain-smoker, talked uninterrupted without once acknowledging my presence. I couldn't even fall asleep as there was a hole in the floor at my feet through which I could see the asphalt we were racing over. I had visions of nodding off, letting my foot slip through the gap, and being dragged to my grisly death in a burning mess of skin and bone. I was also pretty preoccupied with the fact I had just climbed into a car with complete unknowns, who had not once identified themselves, apart from the jutting motion of the tall one's chin. But as the drive continued, I began to relax, particularly when the scenery turned green and misty and I suspected we must be on the right path. We gained altitude fast as the forest thickened and then I saw it on a hill, the picturesque castle-like temple in which I was going to learn Shaolin kung fu.

We drove through the massive gates and I had barely stepped out of the car when I heard someone repeatedly shouting my name with a distinct Mandarin inflection. A monk approached and in very good English told me I had a phone call waiting upstairs. It was my dad, somehow timing the call to perfection. 'Son, is that you?' he said, but the conversation ended there. As soon as he heard my voice he passed the phone to Mum and I could hear him crying in the background. It made for an emotional start to the stay.

The first week in the temple was without doubt the most difficult of my life to date. It was the closest I had ever been to being broken, both physically and mentally, by training sessions. There was a group of about fifteen of us, all Westerners and all with different backgrounds and varying aptitude for the exercises we were being put through. But as in any group of fifteen young, fit men, competitiveness inevitably kicked in and we drove each other on, everyone desperately seeking validation from the monks who oversaw everything. We woke each morning at 5am and lined up for roll call outside the training hall. Anyone missing was soon roused from their slumber with a stinging whip on the back of the legs with a bamboo cane. We then set off on a forty-five-minute run out the temple's main gates, down the hill to the lake to complete a lap of the water, and then back into the temple grounds via the 360 stone steps that led to a side entrance. Two or three times per week, our *shifu*, or master, was waiting at the gate and keen to prolong the agony. Sometimes he'd simply send us back down and tell us to run up again. Sometimes we were told to ascend the steps two or three at a time or to scamper down hands-first like fleeing chimps. I can think of more pleasant ways to start the day.

We then completed a series of *chi gong* breathing exercises, involving drawing in energy from the air around us with deep, expansive breaths and storing it in our *dan tien*, an area three inches below the navel in the pit of the stomach. After that we practised the first two tai chi forms. My chi gong shifu was Master Long, a former personal bodyguard of Chairman Mao in the sixties and early seventies. He was an intense character to say the least, always the first up every morning despite the pile of empty beer bottles that amassed outside his bedroom door. He had a small, select group of three or four students that he trained in a clearing within the forest that the rest of us could never clearly see, but we knew his focus was the more mystical internal martial arts. His expertise was in building Chi, the life-force inside each of us, and then using that as a protective shield or in strikes during combat. You needed to be there for years to be accepted into his inner circle and the one guy I spoke to who was part of it, a Londoner named Darren, who had spent over three years with Master Long, was always evasive about what he learnt.

It is not a term I like to use very often, but Master Long had some supernatural qualities about him. I remember one day I was practising several forms inside the training hall because a storm had whipped up the sands of the Mongolian Desert and outside was just a haze of stinging dust. I was training with a couple of guys from Hawaii inside this rustic space, just a box with concrete floors really. In the middle of the hall sat a homemade weight-lifting bench, crudely welded together from chunks of extremely heavy metal with a strip of old carpet nailed on where the padding should be. It was rather in our way, obstructing our movements if the three of us were to practise the forms together, and so we all grabbed the metal beast and attempted to move it to the side. After a couple of minutes of blood-vessel-bursting effort, I think we'd shifted it about four inches and decided it wasn't worth it, that we'd work around it. About fifteen minutes later, Master Long strolled in, five foot seven and about sixty-five years old. He looked at us like we were idiotic children for training with this metal monstrosity impeding us and then slipped one hand under the bench, effortlessly slid it to the side wall, turned and laughed his distinctive wheezing laugh in our direction, and walked out. To this day, it gives me the shivers to think about it. I can't explain it. And if it weren't for the fact there were two other witnesses beside me to see it, I wouldn't even repeat the story for fear of ridicule.

After tai chi, we were served breakfast around 7:30. The three meals per day were basically identical. We sat at large, round, wooden tables with a massive bowl of rice in the centre surrounded by five smaller bowls containing various vegetables and scrambled egg. There was very occasionally meat and we knew we were getting it by the screeching sound of the chicken or pig being slaughtered somewhere within the castle walls. Powdered milk was on offer as a beverage. It was all basic sustenance and nothing more.

When breakfast had been devoured, morning training began with light warm-ups which consisted of jogging and a range of standard kicks and stances. After that it was time for an hour of absolutely brutal stretching. I remember frequently being certain I would snap every one of my muscle fibres. It was a case of finding the point of agony, and then pushing us past it. One involving standing with my back to a tree while a partner raised my straight leg and forced it back until my toes touched the trunk above my head was particularly harrowing. My nervous habit of laughing when in extreme pain did me no favours whatsoever. Then there were the prolonged periods in stressed positions. *Ma Bu down!* became a feared cry from a monk, as it was used as a punishment for any perceived misdemeanour or disappointment. Known as the horse-riding stance, it involves crouching with parallel feet, knees bent at 90 degrees, the base of the spine curved, and hands in the prayer position. Poles were wedged between thigh and stomach and on arms in the crook of the elbow to ensure the stance was being executed correctly and to allow the monks to quickly spot any movements we made.

There were kids stretching alongside us as well, local strays brought in from the surrounding villages. It made a bit more sense for them because their bodies were still developing and if they could tolerate the pain their limbs would adapt and lock in that flexibility for later life. We adults on the other hand were simply snapping or damaging muscles. But the kids would be crying in pain and it was hard to watch. Buddhist monks may have a gentle reputation but there is a lot less tolerance towards complaining in that culture compared to the Western world. Just like us, the children received neither sympathy nor help when they broke down and began sobbing.

The afternoon training following lunch was the most advanced and challenging in a technical sense and was by far my favourite part of the day. We began practising the spectacular moves, the jumping, spinning and flying techniques. Then there were sessions of *sansao*, a much more realistic, combative form of kung fu. With its hand-strikes, kick-catching, throws, trips and sweeps, I saw similarities with Muay Thai and immediately embraced it as a transferable skill I could utilise in a genuine fight. There was also weapons training, something I was fascinated by and wanted to absorb as much knowledge on as possible. For me, weapons forms were synonymous with the Shaolin monks and I was determined to learn how to use their range of swords and the staff during my time there. All beginners start with the bo staff and students that are only booked in for a short stay tend to go no further than wielding that long rattan pole. But all over the castle grounds you could find old bits and pieces of weapons that had been broken in training and in the first few of days I managed to collect enough fragments of a straight sword to fashion my own. I would then stand to the side and watch a group of straight-sword students being put through their paces before trying to replicate what they were taught in my own time. My enthusiasm and dedication was soon noticed and I was invited to join the group. Before it was time for me to leave, I also managed to learn a broadsword form and purchased a variety of weapons to bring home and continue my education.

We finished up at around 19:00 for a rice and vegetable dinner, and then had a couple of hours free to do as we pleased. Groups organically formed according to particular interests. Some practised tai chi and chi gong, others continued their weapons training. I fell into a gang of like-minded souls interested in striking and we would spar in the training hall and hit rudimentary punchbags filled with sand. By 21:30, we all fell exhausted into our beds and prayed our bodies would recover sufficiently to do it all over again at the crack of the following dawn.

A lot of guys broke and left, unable to keep up with the constant physical and psychological pressure. I remember one of the group, a rich kid from London living in Dubai, who must have thought he was booked into a Shaolin-themed holiday camp. He was clearly just there to have a cool story to tell his mates back home and, after a few days sitting around smoking or barricading himself in his room by pushing his bunk against the door, he packed his bags and trudged out of the gate, never to be seen again. I still remember him fondly and, although our love for the martial arts was on vastly different levels, he brought some much-needed comic relief when he did emerge from his quarters.

There were various points in this first week when I was sure my body was going to fail me too. I wasn't going to allow myself to be broken mentally and quit, but I could feel my muscles and joints slowly bowing under the onslaught. After two days, I couldn't move properly and struggled to drag myself out of bed each morning. After seven days I had already lost 4kg and would eventually lose another six to return home weighing in at just 63kg. But on that seventh day I woke up and realised, I'm still here and I'm still going strong. It was a realisation that my body could take this torture after all. It was a psychological breakthrough, a release from perceived limitations, and I embraced and enjoyed the remainder of my stay as much as I had toiled and laboured through the initial stage.

Some of that weight I shed also came off the top of my head. Having let it grow for almost six years, my straight, black locks reached half-way down my back. In many ways that hair had defined me through my teenage years after I emerged from my pudgy, early-adolescent self. I was ready to shear it, to leave that part of my life behind and stride forward, but I couldn't just go to my local barber's in Nottingham and ask for a short back and sides. I wanted a grander gesture befitting the importance I attached to the moment, I wanted something ceremonial. I actually expected the monks to insist my head was shaven before they began instructing me, but they seemed unmoved by the ponytail on the first day of training. Instead, I was informed by a few of my new, shaven-headed training partners that I would be getting the 'monk treatment' later that evening. I sat in front of a group of eight or so and they all cheered as big chunks of hair were shorn. In minutes, six years of me was on the floor.

All in all, I left China pretty content with how the two months had gone. Back home in the village hall, Mick and the others gathered round, anxious to see the results of my expedition. There was a sense of, *you've been to the source, what did you bring back?* Everyone was eager to see what I had learnt and so in an hour I went through all the forms the monks had taught me. In total, there were three kung fu forms, two tai chi, one bagua, one straight sword, one broadsword and one bow staff form. Everyone was suitably impressed when I concluded the demonstration and it felt good to show off new skills.

I stuck with my Shaolin lifestyle for a while. For months I woke at 5am and was doing chi gong and tai chi on the fields near my house at six before the sun had even risen. But gradually, the urge faded away as the mornings got colder and darker in the winter months. My experience with the monks in China was incredibly rich, but I found the nuts and bolts of what I learnt quickly lost value for me. I realised that the Shaolin culture is frozen in time and was not actually what I was searching for or needed. At my core I have always held the belief that the essence of martial arts is to be effective in combat. As soon as it became clear in my head that the Shaolin style of kung fu was not going to help me achieve perfection in real combat, I knew I would just waste three years of my journey if I returned to the temple. I decided not to go back to China, but I will forever treasure the two months I spent there with the monks. I maintain so much respect for the Shaolin way of life, as testing as it was on me. Perhaps the greatest value in that trip was the psychological breakthrough I made when after days of being totally and utterly convinced that I couldn't do something, I suddenly woke up and realised I was doing it. It is a lesson I have carried close to me for the rest of my career.

● ● ●

Back in Nottingham, there was nothing else for it but to continue training and return to my second year of university at Nottingham Trent. By now I had pretty much finished with taekwondo and had begun to focus on Muay Thai and kickboxing, training hard every day and taking amateur fights or entering local tournaments when opportunities arose. They are two tough sports but Muay Thai was always particularly brutal. In addition to striking with the fists and feet, knees and elbows were allowed, as was clinching, grappling and targeting anywhere below the waist bar the groin. Sparring and competing was so much more to-the-point than anything I had previously experienced in martial arts and I came out of each session or round feeling a little beaten up, even when I won. But I was convinced that this emphasis on striking was exactly what I needed to evolve as a fighter.

I was fortunate to train under Master Lec around this time. Master Lec began fighting before he had even reached his teens, hiking through the Thai jungle from village to village in search of an opponent as a means of making some money for his family. By the time he made it over to England, he already had over 400 fights under his belt so he was both legitimate and highly respected in martial arts circles. The first night I went to one of his classes, I ran the three miles from my house to the leisure centre and arrived sweating and ready to go. I think Master Lec saw me as someone serious about martial arts and he took to me straight away. He teaches a very traditional form of Muay Thai and it is real old-school, hard-nosed training, basically exactly the type of thing he had put himself through in the Thai jungle. With Master Lec, you march forward, blocking kicks with shins that have been conditioned by rolling bottles against the tibia until it is a solid calcified mass of bone. Rapping my knuckles on my shin to make a sound like knocking upon a mahogany door is still one of my favourite party tricks. Once in range, you elbow your opponent in the face then get your hands around his head and knee him as many times as you can. And if the referee does not explicitly warn you at the face-off, Lec encouraged us to land one good groin strike. There is nothing fancy or sophisticated about Master Lec's fighting style, but that perfectly reflects the raw and brutal nature of a true Muay Thai battle and I immediately fell in love with it all.

I also loved the ceremonial aspect of Muay Thai. Before a fight, Master Lec applied a Thai oil to my body, a liniment that made my skin freeze and burn at the same time and really switched on my senses and ignited something deep inside. I walked to the ring with a Mongkhon around my head for luck and to protect against harmful spirits. Then, unlike some other schools, Master Lec would insist his pupils adhere to the full Wai Khru Ram Muay ritual before each bout, so I performed the ceremonial dance to seal the ring, offer thanks and respect, and throw down the gauntlet to my opponent. The traditional Sarama music, a wailing clarinet and beating drum ensemble, helped dictate the pace of the fight. My first competitive outing with Master Lec was in a night-club in Manchester and after years of scraps in pubs and clubs I felt at home in the surroundings. It didn't last long and following a few wild and imprecise exchanges of punches, I viciously kicked my way to the first of many stoppage victories.

But I was always eager to expand my knowledge of the martial arts and one day I heard about a jiu-jitsu class taking place at the campus sports hall and decided to go along and check it out. The instructor was a man named Paul Lloyd Davies and when he saw my striking ability and how seriously I took each session, he knew he could do something with me. After a couple of classes he pulled me to one side and told me not to waste my time in the university group but to come to his gym and train properly. Well known in British sports circles, Davies worked with all sorts of athletes, including elite rugby players, Olympic weightlifters and professional golfers. He was also the head of Sports Science at the university and he immediately made big changes to what nutrients I put into my body. Up until that point I'd been surviving on pasta, beans and toast, and attempting to stomach a few portions of broccoli each week. Now I was taking Creatine, ZMA, whey protein, fish oils, selenium, vitamin C and plenty else. It was a whole new world to me and the beginning of my appreciation of the lengths to which a dedicated athlete must go outside the gym if they are to succeed.

Fighting was all I wanted to do now. Confrontations on the street had all but disappeared since I gave up alcohol, so I had a lot of pent-up aggression that needed an outlet. Davies saw this in me, but in the beginning I wasn't too sure exactly what he wanted from me. There was always a handful of other guys in his gym, each from a different martial arts background, but none appeared to have the desire to actually fight and they tended to come and go, or drift away completely. It was only after a few months that I realised Davies was intent on putting some sort of team together. He spoke continuously of someone who was going to come down from Manchester one day and become the leader of our competitive group. This guy was supposedly a natural-born fighter with skills and gameness to boot. His name was Michael Bisping.

When Bisping did eventually arrive, finally there was someone else in the gym who was clearly determined to fight. He strolled in like a big mean bully, staring hard at whoever caught his gaze until they backed down first. He was six foot one, about 115kg and looked ferocious in each training session, putting everything he had into every exercise. Soon the group thinned out to just Davies plus four of us. As well as myself and Bisping, we had a specialist Thai boxer named Mark Ferron and a mad farmer named Andy Harby. Andy was a big hairy beast with that freakish farm strength that comes from manhandling livestock like they are cuddly toys every day. He drove a Jaguar, always carried a huge wad of cash in his pocket, and invariably gave off a distinct odour of the countryside. I learned a lot from Andy, but mainly about life in general rather than the martial arts. He was a fascinating man and had done so many unusual jobs that I found his life-experience intriguing. Many hours were spent sitting in the passenger seat of his car on the way to training or competition, listening to his stories. The one that always stands out is his tale of the motorcycle accident that broke both of his femurs and shattered his kneecaps. He was forced to drag himself out of the bushes on a dark country lane and back into the road so someone would stop and help. I found his determination to continue training inspiring, especially as his physical limitations must have become even more apparent while training with a bunch of much younger, fitter men.

Bisping would drive down from Manchester each Monday morning and pick me up in an old blue Volvo which was christened the Batmobile. He'd often be munching on pasties or sausage rolls ahead of seeing Davies, who had him on a strict diet to bring his weight down. We then drove to our training hut, a unit on an industrial estate with mats and a punchbag, which inevitably became known as the Batcave.

There, each day, we trained to fight. Davies's martial arts background was in traditional Japanese ju-jitsu, and he put on regular Knockdown Sport Budo tournaments in which we could participate. KSBO was yet another of the modern-MMA precursors and was essentially a full-contact form of jiu-jitsu in which kicks, punches, knees and elbows were permitted and no protective clothing was worn. Bisping was taking part in these largely no-holds-barred fights against grown men when he was just fifteen years of age, and he had a game, based around Yawara Ryu Jiu-Jitsu, perfectly tailored for the job. But the style of fighting was new to me and for the first half-dozen contests I invariably found myself taken down, smothered and beaten on the ground. Back in the Batcave I proved to be a fast learner, however, and my fortunes quickly changed as soon as I had mastered a little basic takedown defence.

I was winning and I was enjoying it, but something just didn't feel right. The penny finally dropped on a training trip to Wales. When we got there, we found that Davies had invited a friend along who had a bit of spare cash and was interested in investing it in an MMA fighter. It was a very strange weekend, more like an assessment centre than a training camp, and over the course of it I realised that the only beneficiary of any investment was going to be Michael. Looking back now I see that all the time I thought I was training with Davies for a fight, the focus had been on Bisping. The rest of us were only there to get him ready for his professional debut and at the end of the weekend contracts appeared which would have tied me to such an arrangement.

I returned home a little disillusioned, thought the situation over, and then phoned Davies to tell him I was leaving the team. I said that

I was a legitimate fighter in my own right, that I was more than ready to start my MMA career, and that he didn't seem to be actively doing anything to move me along. I told him I had some Muay Thai and kickboxing matches lined up and I was going to go away and focus on them. Davies took the news calmly and much better than I had expected. *No worries*, he said and wished me all the best. It was only when I started calling sparring partners to try and arrange sessions to prepare for my upcoming fights that the full impact of leaving Paul's set-up hit me. One by one, guys I was close to and had trained with many times before made lame excuses for not being able to help me out. Finally one let it slip that he had been warned off working with me. Word had somehow spread throughout the local martial arts fraternity that I wasn't to be helped. And as Davies was a very influential figure in the fledgling British MMA scene, it was a difficult bridge for aspiring fighters to potentially burn and I understood their position. But it didn't help me, the persona non grata of MMA in the East Midlands. That unwanted social status is why my fighting moniker became the Outlaw. It made sense on another level because I was born and raised in Nottingham, just down the road from Robin Hood's Sherwood Forest hideout, but it was really all down to my days as a post-Paul Davies outcast. I first used it when I needed a nickname to log on to the new Cage Warriors Forum and it has stuck with me ever since.

For a while I was struggling. The only place I could get sparring or training was in the Leicester Shootfighters gym but that was over thirty miles away and I had neither a car nor a driving licence. I was restricted to bussing it everywhere, making each effort to reach training as long and arduous as the work I put in once inside. Then, with a couple of strokes of fate, my luck changed. I had dropped out of university by now in order to focus all of my energies on fighting, but I needed income from somewhere. So I took on two jobs, one in the stockroom of a shoe shop and the other in the gym of Portland Leisure Centre. The latter role was great in terms of getting time off to train and fight and they even turned a blind eye when I spent an hour of my shift working out. On one of those occasions I found myself training alongside an impressive-looking boxer named Ricardo Samms and his coach Owen Comrie. Owen was actually a Muay Thai fighter and when he saw me kicking rather than punching the heavy bag, he came over for a chat. We immediately clicked, and I agreed to go along to one of his classes in another gym the following Saturday. One thing led to another, and Owen would go on to be my chief trainer and cornerman for the next six years.

A second pivotal moment in my career soon followed when, climbing the stairs on my way to the Formula One strength and conditioning gym on Nottingham's Victoria Street one evening, I spied two guys training in a second-floor studio. I paused to watch and recognised them as Paul Daley and Matt Howell. I knew both fighters from the local martial arts scene and, in fact, I had always wanted to fight Matt at the KSBO tournaments as his bleached-blond hair reminded me of Tito Ortiz. I knocked on the door, introduced myself and they told me they were training for Paul's upcoming MMA bout. It was just what I was looking for and I was delighted to join in. This was the genesis of Team Rough House, an MMA team that would eventually boast six UFC fighters among its alumni. The name was coined when an uninitiated member of the public inadvertently walked in on one of the sparring sessions and was moved to ask, 'What is all this roughhousing going on in here?' The original T-shirts were printed with *Rough House Domination* on the front and *Anytime Fucker* on the back but, partly due to concern over what our mothers might think, they were toned down for the second batch.

Matt soon drifted away as his university studies demanded more and more of his time, so it was left to Paul and I to keep Rough House growing. We basically set about recruiting anyone we came across that appeared dedicated and capable of improving our own games. We were forming a team but there was no charity involved; if someone lacking the skills Paul and I wanted to work on entered the gym, they would struggle to get an invite to join Rough House. Hundreds have come and gone over the years, the majority lasting little more than a session or two, but a handful did match our expectations, beginning with 'Psycho' Steve Tetley. Steve worked with Owen and was just a naturally tough man with mean intentions. I sparred with him on his first day with us and after he elbowed me in the nose out of frustration during a wrestling session I immediately christened him Psycho, a moniker which has stuck fast ever since. But he was a very talented fighter in his own right, the type of guy you only needed to show something once and he would be able to immediately run with it. I remember sitting in the dressing room with him one night before a fight and just before he went out I gave him one piece of advice. 'Everyone knows you as a Thai boxer,' I said, 'and that's what your opponent will be expecting. So look at his leg in the opening seconds so he presumes you're about to shoot a takedown, then level change to sell it to him and surprise him with a left hook.' Psycho marched straight out, followed my recommendation to the letter, and knocked his man out inside the opening thirty seconds. He fought four times as a pro, retiring after losing to future UFC fighter Ross Pearson at the end of 2007. But more than that, Steve was a unique character, the father of a full first-team of eleven boys and the artist who inked my first three tattoos. Rough House was lucky to have him.

Another important member of the team who joined later was my best mate in MMA, 'Judo' Jimmy Wallhead. Jimmy is from just down the road from me in Loughborough and a similar age so we always seemed to be fighting on the same cards as we came up through the ranks. He was a crazy man in his youth, all shaved head, tattoos and hyped-up rage seeping out of every pore. I saw him debut at heavyweight, face-barring an overweight chef from a local military base into submission in the first round. I remember then sharing a warm-up space with him at one show and looking on a little bemused as his team physically slapped him into a rabid fury before unleashing him in the cage. 'You're a bad man, Jimmy,' they yelled, 'a bad fucking man!' 'Yeah,' Jim screamed back, 'I'm a bad fucking man!' He then charged a talented French fighter who simply weathered the early frantic storm before calmly submitting him. The truth was his team didn't really know what they were doing, their qualifications being little more than watching the UFC every night. It was Jimmy's father-in-law who took him to one side after a defeat and told him he needed to drop that lot and join Rough House if he wanted to get anywhere in mixed martial arts. Thankfully Jim heeded those wise words and in 2016 made his long-overdue entrance into a UFC Octagon in Hamburg.

There were three or four other long-term and key fighters in the Rough House family. We found Andre Winner in the Leicester Shootfighters gym and with his all-round athletic ability and naturally fast hands, he was an excellent man to practise striking with. Tamai Harding and Dean Amasinger also proved to be invaluable additions while they were with us, as did Lee Livingstone, a Brazilian jiu-jitsu black belt from Nottingham. Lee actually opened his own gym called Bushido MMA in the city and that became the unofficial Team Rough House headquarters for the sessions in which we all came together to train and share skills. The rest of the time we were scattered about the Midlands doing our own thing in various combat sports establishments. I worked out in a local leisure centre and also spent a lot of time with Daley in a spit-and-sawdust boxing gym on Prospect Place named Majestik. It was also used by bodybuilders and the steroid-fuelled atmosphere was thuggish and attracted a good portion of the local criminal underworld to its doors. It was in the Majestik that I first started working with Ricardo Samms, the incredibly talented super middleweight I saw the first night I met Owen. Ricardo would eventually go 4 and 0 as a pro before growing disillusioned with the sport and returning to university. At that time he was in the British Olympic squad, although he would miss out on a place at the Games after being robbed in a final qualifier in Germany. Coming from such a background, Ricardo had a different mentality when it came to fight preparation, a much more advanced and scientific approach. He was already gearing everything towards one fight or tournament six months down the line, whereas Paul and I were still training to fight 365 days of the year. Looking back I see that Ricardo was miles ahead of us in terms of how to look after our bodies and peak at the right time, but it would be a few years before I could even dream of such an approach. Until then it was non-stop pushing myself to the limit to break into the professional MMA world.

● ● ●

By the spring of 2004, I felt ready to fight professionally for the first time. Having forged a strong bond with Paul Daley, he asked me to work his corner as he took his first few professional MMA fights. While I was still competing in local Muay Thai and kickboxing events, Paul was winning two and losing two in MMA events held under a variety of promotional banners. At that time in the UK, Cage Warriors and Cage Rage were probably the two biggest promotions but there were promoters putting on shows in the likes of Bracknell, Coventry, Sheffield, Liverpool, Sunderland and London every other weekend. It was a bit of a free-for-all trying to get a slot on a card, but that wasn't really surprising when you considered the stage of the sport's evolution and the characters that were running the business side of things. This wasn't too long after Senator John McCain had described the sport as human cockfighting while the future presidential candidate was leading the drive to ban MMA from American TV screens. In the UK, press and public alike continued to refer to MMA as cage fighting, thus fostering a sinister image of bloody, underground violence. And in truth, plenty of practitioners, keen to be seen as hard and dangerous men, were more than happy with the negative connotations. It was no surprise then that the criminal underbelly of Britain's large cities were drawn to the sport and it tended to be figures from these shadows that ran the events. But I didn't really care whether they were drug dealers laundering money or not. All I wanted to do was fight and earn some cash so I could train for the next one.

The Cage Warriors forum was then the centre of the UK MMA world. It was the social and business hub that fighters needed to be connected to if they were going to be anyone in the sport. I was on there as the Outlaw and logged in throughout the day to check what was happening as frequently as I might access my emails or Twitter account today. But it was actually Paul who made my first fight for me. He had debuted on an Extreme Brawl promotion and he knew the seventh event of that show was taking place in Bracknell in June. He also knew that Lee Doski, a fighter he had just beaten, was on the card and in need of an opponent. Doski was an awkward southpaw with boxing experience and some crafty submission skills. With six fights and three wins under his belt he was more experienced than me, but he was exactly the type of name I needed to get my career off to a flying start. I had no intention of simply dipping my toe into this to test the water, I had an eye on the British rankings and was planning to rip my way through the domestic scene as quickly as possible. I had watched from the corner as Daley dropped Doski with a left hook and finished him with punches inside the opening minute of their bout and, having sparred hundreds of hours with Paul, I was certain I would destroy him too.

My purse for the night was only £150 but that was totally irrelevant to me. I just couldn't wait to get in there and compete with no amateurish restrictions and against a game opponent primed to hurt me if I made a mistake. But in the weeks and days and hours building up to the fight, the anticipation turned to impatience which soon developed into a frustrated anger. It was the opposite of the anxiety that had consumed the six-year-old me in advance of my first taekwondo bout and led to me freezing in the limelight, but my state of mind now was just as dangerous. Backstage, Paul was busy getting me riled up. He needs that before a fight and, as I was in some ways following in his footsteps, I presumed I did too. Many fighters do thrive when they are whipped into a Berserker-like frenzy, the Brazilian Wanderlei Silva, known as the Axe Murderer, being an obvious example, but I would later learn that rage didn't work for me. I didn't know any better on my debut, however, and so when 'Drag the Waters' by Pantera blasted out over the loudspeaker, I literally sprinted to the cage and ripped my T-shirt off like a madman.

After so long without a street fight, this was going to be my release. With zero thought process, I launched myself into an attack and threw everything I had at him. From the very first punch, I was looking for and expecting the knockout. There was little technique, and zero tactical sophistication, as I swung from the hip for the entirety of the five-minute first round before sitting down in front of Owen and Paul. Owen is generally a very laid-back, Caribbean dude. But when he is in the mood, he can be a wild man and I had the two of them screaming me into another fury before marching out to continue my all-out assault for the second.

Only the fact that I was in decent shape allowed me to keep up this aggressive offensive for as long as I did. But I had expended so much energy even before the first bell that it was no real surprise when midway through the second round I started to feel the foolish pace I had set. I also saw that Doski, having covered up well and weathered my uncouth storm, was still in relatively good shape and I would need to try something different. Taking a step back, I inhaled a couple of deep breaths and decided I would take him down and beat him up on the canvas. In my head, it was just that simple. But I had been doing a lot of kickboxing and that proved to be inadequate preparation because there was less to think about in comparison to the MMA arena. Inside any type of boxing ring there are much more limited points of attack to defend against and that can lead to complacency that has no place in a cage. Seeing my chance, I shot for a double-leg takedown landing in his guard, but Doski sat up, secured a *kimura* grip and instantly hip-bumped me over onto my back to take a mounted position. I saw him twitch to begin striking my head, so I bridged to escape, but, experienced enough to see the opportunity, he lifted his body weight and allowed me to spin beneath him and expose my back. Doski gleefully took it and secured a rear-naked choke before I had time to resist. I fought it for a few seconds, but he had it locked in tight and, with just one second remaining of the second round of my professional MMA debut, I was forced to tap out.

I was devastated. Having genuinely expected to blow through everyone in the UK and Europe, here I was at zero and one after facing what I considered to be a very beatable domestic opponent. The fact that I had tapped out, accepted I was beaten in the most visible way, made the pill all the more bitter to swallow. One of the lessons I learnt was that if you can tap, you can strike. Don't give the fight up, fight until it is taken from you. Added to the realisation that I had won every minute of the fight up to that point on aggression alone, I was not a nice person to be around in the immediate aftermath. I remember going through all the factors that led to the loss. The over-excitement which turned into rage with the addition of Pantera. My lack of respect for my opponent's skills in comparison to my own, and a lack of acknowledgment of his willingness to go to war. I also felt frustrated with my corner that no one was on the timer letting me know that the final seconds were ticking away. It was a rude reminder of why I don't like team sports. But I soon calmed down and accepted that I had no right attempting to pass the blame to anyone other than myself. This was fighting to me, genuine fighting. And in a real fight there are no breathers and no being saved by the bell. If a fighter is ever saved by the bell, that means he actually lost the fight. I probably would have recovered in the break between rounds and been able to go on and get a W on my record, but in the back of my mind I would have always known that Lee Doski really beat me as he would have choked me unconscious given a few more seconds. The fact was, I lost that fight fair and square. I made a mistake and paid for it. All I could do now was move forward and use it as motivation.

It was a massive wake-up call. As early as the next day, I could see clearly all the mistakes I had made, both during the contest and in the days and hours of the build-up. I was nowhere near as efficient as I needed to be. I was still too much rage and not enough technique. I needed to be cold and clinical in combat but was still getting dragged back to brutality and getting lost in a feeling of being on the battlefield ready to die. But at the same time, I acknowledged that it was very much a case of having to learn on the job. In an ideal world, I would have flushed all those schoolboy errors out of my system during a few years on an amateur circuit, but no such thing existed then. I knew I should have done more Muay Thai, more jiu-jitsu, more grappling and wrestling, but such training or sparring was not so easy to set up back then. I would have loved to have organised hours of proper MMA sparring as well, but who was there to do it with me when we were all making it up as we went along? The Doski fight was the first time I had ever faced someone under full unified MMA rules, sparring included! I had just watched Chuck Liddell beat Tito Ortiz at UFC 47 in Las Vegas, but the UK scene was still so far removed from that world and there was no point complaining that it should be any other way. I had to focus on myself and what I could do, and my only concern was getting back into the cage as quickly as possible to improve and win and banish the losing record that haunted me every time I thought about it. And as I had already signed the contract for my second fight before I had even fought my first, I didn't have to wait long.

THE OUTLAW GROWS

3

A couple of weeks before the Doski fight, I was chatting to Grant Waterman, promoter and matchmaker of Full Contact Fight Night, when he let it be known that Paul Jenkins was still without an opponent for the main event at an upcoming show in Portsmouth. Paul 'Hands of Stone' Jenkins had been competing on the British MMA circuit from the very beginning, appearing at the original incarnations of the likes of Cage Warriors, Cage Rage and Pride & Glory. He was popular and relatively successful and by the summer of 2004 he had compiled a record of 25 wins, 16 losses and 3 draws. Certainly no mug, he had already fought most of the fighters on the European circuit and had picked up a lot of useful journeyman skills along the way. He was crafty, well-rounded, calm to the point where he would be cracking jokes and fooling around mid-fight, and adept at surviving when he was outmatched. FCFN were reluctant to put a debutant in against Jenkins as a bill-topping fight, but I foolhardily assured them I would already be 1 and 0 by then. When I then showed a willingness to accept a paltry £100 purse for my efforts, they agreed to give me the gig.

The venue was a dingy pub at the end of Portsmouth pier. Paul Daley fought a kickboxing match first and then it was my turn to wade through the second-hand tobacco smoke and find the boxing ring. I remember jumping on the spot in my corner as I waited for Jenkins to arrive and my head went past a low-hanging light fitting. The ring seemed small, and the boozed-up punters so close at ringside that I felt slightly claustrophobic as I listened to the referee's final instructions. Then the fight began and, sadly, lived up to the inadequate setting in which it took place. Jenkins was smart enough to realise that he couldn't give me any space whatsoever to work and, in such a cramped arena, it wasn't difficult to deny me that luxury. For a good portion of the fight, he pinned me to the corner buckle and stomped on my bare foot until it swelled up like a balloon, but that was the grand total of the damage I suffered over the course of the fifteen minutes. It was my hand that was raised as a majority decision winner at the end, but I took no real pleasure from the victory and drove home disappointed with both the fight and my performance, unable to even get my shoe on over my swollen foot.

Within a month, our paths crossed again, this time at a Cage Warriors show in Sheffield that had been christened 'Brutal Force'. I was on the card for a K1 kickboxing contest and Jenkins was to fight Andy Melia under MMA rules. Daley was scheduled as the main event but on the evening of the show his opponent withdrew and Jenkins got bumped up the bill as a replacement. This left Melia without a dance partner and me spying an opportunity to get another win on my record by offering my services. So after winning my K1 fight in the second stanza, I quickly swapped Thai shorts and 10oz gloves for Vale Tudo shorts and 4oz gloves, stretched and practised a couple of double-leg takedowns, and marched out to face Melia in an MMA contest. My shins were marked up where bone had been striking bone under K1 rules half an hour earlier, but that pain was soon forgotten as I set about dismantling Melia's comparatively limited game. I bullied him in the first to earn the round on points, but nothing much of note took place. Early in the second I dropped him with a head-kick but he did well to ward off my attempts to finish him. A minute later his luck ran out, however, as I took him down against the cage and he tapped out under a barrage of punches. Paul and Owen burst into the cage to hoist me aloft and I screamed some guttural, atavistic cry of delight for my first submission victory. Within an hour we were all back in the cage celebrating Paul's win over Jenkins in the main event: it was a strong showing from the Rough House.

My hunger to learn and improve was all-consuming at this time. I watched every MMA event I could get my hands on and studied the evolution of the sport and the development of individual fighters. Thanks to the Gracie family, Brazilian jiu-jitsu was the dominant force in the early years and we all scrambled to learn some of the techniques which Royce utilised to comfortably deal with men twice his size.

Martial artists often feel like something is missing from their game, that they must continue searching for the missing piece – hence my pilgrimage to China, for example. Yet Royce was apparently so at ease against bigger, stronger, more intimidating opponents. For a while we all believed that Brazilian jiu-jitsu must be the answer, the final piece of the puzzle. But then powerful and athletic wrestlers like Team Hammer House's Mark Coleman and Kevin Randleman, and later Tito Ortiz and Randy Couture, came along with their ground-and-pound style and started taking these Brazilian masters down, smothering them, and beating them up on the canvas floor. It shouldn't have been a surprise given the very earliest form of mixed martial arts was the ancient Greeks' Pankration, which in turn spawned Greco-Roman wrestling, but I always thought of wrestling as a sport and MMA as a fight, so I did not originally hold it in sufficient regard. In my eyes, it was also a much more brutish and animalistic style of winning fights, lacking the finesse of a jiu-jitsu sweep or a spinning hook-kick to the temple, and I saw a martial artist as being able to subdue and defeat a strong athlete that was trained in physically controlling other humans. But the effectiveness of ground-and-pound was changing my perspective of what I required from my skill-set if I were to compete on any worthwhile stage. I had gone from taekwondo to Thai boxing to Vale Tudo, but now I was looking up wrestling techniques in books and on the internet. I remember watching Ortiz versus Vitor Belfort at UFC 51 in awe. *Now this is the future*, I thought. It was a tough wrestler with good boxing skills against a Brazilian jiu-jitsu black belt with incredible speed, power and striking ability. They were two well-rounded fighters, proficient in everything, in perfect shape and at the ideal weight and size for the division. The transitions from striking to grappling to submissions were so seamless and I saw wrestling as the glue that held their whole game together.

But the evolution of MMA never ends; there are always questions being asked and answered, and by the time Chuck Liddell was on the scene and utilising his wrestling experience defensively, sprawl-and-brawl was the new approach to be mastered.

The importance of being able to dictate where the fight takes place, controlling your opponent and taking away his offensive, became paramount and there was a shift towards a more all-encompassing approach to training. Phrases such as 'ground-and-pound' or 'sprawl-and-brawl' became specified training sessions. And drills like boxing with takedowns, or grappling with strikes, isolated parts of the game where seams were present. Fighters initially trained in the different disciplines separately, but when the lines between striking, wrestling and jiu-jitsu were blurred, the holes in their games became exposed. By training the transitional phases in isolation, it forced those wanting to stay standing to integrate takedown defence into their game, and for those wanting to fight on the mat to take into consideration the striking range which had to be negated to close the distance. The same deal applied on the ground. You couldn't focus on chasing submissions without paying attention to striking, and if you wanted to work your ground-striking, a comprehensive understanding of the submission attack was a necessity. Where before strikers might wade forward without regard and get slammed to the mat, or jiu-jitsu guys would leave themselves vulnerable for ground-

and-pound, fighters became more savvy, more well-rounded, more like true mixed martial artists.

I needed to be learning and practising all these different styles and approaches every day if I wanted to keep progressing, but the skills simply weren't yet in the UK. I tried to go along and work with the Team GB Olympic wrestling team, but their governing body didn't want to have anything to do with an MMA fighter. I had Owen as my Thai boxing coach and Nathan Leverton and, later, Victor Estima training me for all ranges of grappling. Victor is a world class Jiu Jitsu player, and very much focused on the grappling arts with little concern for the danger of ground and pound. Training with him was a great opportunity to see what standard of grappling I could ultimately face at the top level of competition. Nathan cornered me for several of my fights, both before and after I signed my UFC contract. His method of teaching was the most up-to-date I found in the UK. He was excellent at watching videos of an opponent, deconstructing their grappling game and creating training plans to prepare us for what we were likely to encounter. I felt that with those sessions, my Thai boxing with Owen, and our Rough House sparring sessions, I was covering all parts of my game, but there was still no sense of having an overall, complete MMA training session. We did our best to use our specialities to round each other out in Rough House, and with Wallhead and his judo, Winner and his boxing and Daley and his kickboxing and ninjitsu, we didn't do a bad job. But it wasn't enough and I knew I needed to travel and seek out the best in the business if I was ever going to fulfil my full potential.

So in the autumn of 2004, Paul and I scraped together enough money to finance a month-long expedition to the US. Our destination was the American Top Team headquarters in Coconut Creek, Florida and the baptism of fire that awaited us. ATT was founded in 2001 by Ricardo Liborio when he left Brazilian Top Team and it has gone on to become one of the most influential MMA academies in the world. The likes of Amanda Nunes, Robbie Lawler, Brad Pickett and Dustin Poirier are all products of Liborio's school and his focus on Brazilian jiu-jitsu and boxing. We arrived as young, unknown, English outsiders, and were clearly regarded as cannon fodder for the Tuesday and Thursday full-contact sparring sessions. It was hard graft but as I kept holding my own, they kept pushing. I learnt a lot, although in the immediate aftermath I felt more beaten up than educated. But I was determined to prove myself, come what may. So when I forgot my running shoes on cardio day, I decided to run laps of the building barefoot on scorching hot asphalt and destroyed the soles of my feet. The same hard-headedness ensured that when one of their fighters was forced to withdraw from a bout at the last minute and I was asked to take his place, I didn't hesitate.

There are so many reasons why I should never have taken that fight with Pat Healy, but the most important revealed itself in a sparring session during my first week with ATT. I was in against Jorge Santiago while head coach Liborio looked on. Santiago and Liborio are both Brazilian and at one point, with Jorge several metres from me, Ricardo yelled something in Portuguese and, not hearing what had been said over the sound of forty fighters brutalising one another, I stupidly turned to see if he was instructing me or my opponent. It all happened in less than a second, but as I turned back to face Santiago, he had leapt towards me, detonated a right hand on my chin and knocked me out cold. It was a sucker punch, but at the same time I shouldn't have allowed myself to be distracted. As The Master says to Lau in *Enter the Dragon*, 'Never take your eyes off your opponent.' By the time I came to, I wasn't sure who or where I was. I stood up manfully, but then had to furtively ask Paul where the changing rooms were, for I couldn't remember. In fact, I couldn't remember anything beyond sitting in my parents' house in Nottingham, discussing going to the airport. I had basically lost a week of my life. It was the worst concussion I have ever had and I had no business fighting just a couple of weeks after it.

The second major issue arose at a pre-fight medical on the day of the weigh in. The doctor checking me out claimed to detect something strange with my heartbeat and refused to sign me off unless I went for an electrocardiogram (ECG) test. For some reason, that proved to be more difficult to set up than you might think on a Saturday afternoon in Fort Lauderdale. I spent the entire day in the passenger seat of the local promoter's car as he ostensibly tried to arrange the ECG, but in reality just drove around sorting out tickets, putting up posters, dropping off T-shirts and generally doing his promoting business. I had no food or water aside from a brief stop at a Wendy's fast food restaurant where I ordered a baked potato that came out microwaved and soggy. Finally, I was hooked up to an ECG, passed to fight, and given about twenty minutes in my hotel room to get ready before boarding the fighters' bus to the arena. I was in a terrible frame of mind, feeling I had done them a big favour and was not being looked after accordingly.

My mood hardly improved when Healy entered the ring. I hadn't cut much weight, although possibly became the first professional fighter to actually lose weight between weigh-in and bout after my day in the promoter's car, whereas Healy had clearly cut hard and had now rehy-drated to a formidable size. I also discovered I had been lied to about his pedigree and rather than a losing-record journeyman making up the numbers on the local circuit as I was led to believe, Healy was an experienced contender who had already faced the likes of Chris Leben, Denis Kang and Dave Strasser, and would later make it to the UFC. When the referee instructed us to fight, I felt there was nothing for it but to go at him. We exchanged strikes in the opening minute and I caught him clean and broke his nose. But soon after he slammed me to the ground and was able to control me from there. At one stage he had my back and rained illegal blows down on the back of my head, causing the ref to penalise him a point. But not long after he secured a guillotine and forced me to submit.

I was naturally disappointed with the loss, but I didn't, and still don't, regret taking the fight. Aside from the macho aspect of never backing down from a challenge, it was great experience and exposure to be part of an American event and it all fed into the educational rationale of the trip. It was also a huge honour to have had Ricardo Liborio and the Olympic boxing gold medallist Howard Davis Jr. in my corner, even if just for one fight. What I picked up in ATT in terms of jiu-jitsu and striking techniques was great, but what I learnt outside of sparring ses-sions was perhaps even more valuable. It was a real eye-opener to see first-hand how professional fight preparation was in terms of nutrition, diet, strength and conditioning, warming up and cooling down, cutting weight, psychological training, visualisation techniques and much more. These were professional athletes in the truest sense of the word. It got me thinking about the ebb and flow of my own condition and fitness. I hadn't really changed from my years of training and fighting continuously all year round in taekwondo, but now I was considering how I could manage my schedule to peak at precisely the right times. It was also very interesting to see how ATT planned a fighter's camp to fit the different fighting disciplines together inside one week of training. So rather than stewing over the defeat to Healy, I flew back to the UK inspired and eager to share the new knowledge with the other Rough House guys. And, feeling like my game had taken a giant leap forward, I was also dying to get into a cage or ring, put my new skills to the test, and get back on the winning trail.

That opportunity presented itself in December with a slot on Cage Warriors' seasonally named Xtreme Xmas. My opponent was Aaron Barrow, a short, squat, hairy, caveman-like fighter. He was known to be heavy-handed and was on a decent run of form, so I was warned not to take him lightly. The week before I had been in the gym with Owen, drilling a switch head-kick for hours on end. It is a pre-set move that I am particularly adept at given the happy coincidence that, although I fight from an orthodox stance, my left leg is actually my strongest. I sometimes wondered about the value of such sessions but the Barrow fight ended any doubt over their worth. Looking across the cage, I saw him poised and growling with a pair of boxing gloves tattooed on his neck while he repeatedly shook out his left arm. If he's a poker player he must lose every night because I knew exactly what was coming. He charged across to my side of the cage and I switch-kicked him under the jaw with the full force of my shin rising skywards. His eyes were already vacant before he completed his descent and I immediately looked to the referee to stop it. But upon getting no signal from the official, I got down and battered Barrow for a few seconds more until I was finally dragged off him, just thirteen seconds into the bout. That hesitation from the ref cost me a £150 knockout bonus, but I wasn't thinking about that as I sprinted a victory lap and then clambered up the cage wall like a deranged chimp to gesture triumphantly and aggressively towards the crowd. Though I didn't quite know it at the time, for thirty seconds I was in full-reptile mode. Watching the footage again now, I don't even recognise myself, but that is what a win means in the cage. It was the perfect end to my first year as a professional mixed martial artist, and an ideal platform from which to attack my second.

● ● ●

I fought nine pro MMA bouts in 2005, which proved to be my break-through year. It culminated with a world title challenge, but the opener was just as important to me: a chance for revenge over Lee Doski. The fight formed part of a card put together by a shortlived promotion named Fight Club UK and the purses on offer were as derisory as ever. But I had dreamt of getting even with Doski from the moment he submitted me in my debut and would have happily paid to get back in the cage with him. A couple of days before the fight, however, a phone call put everything into perspective. It was about 3am and I was sitting downstairs with insomnia watching old fights at my parents' house. When the phone rings at that time of night, you suspect bad news and instinctively know what it is likely to be. Grandad had been rushed to hospital and the doctors were not convinced he would live much longer. Complications had arisen from a metal heart valve he'd had inserted a few years before and the medics were struggling to regulate the thickness of his blood. We all immediately jumped in Dad's car and sped to the Queen's Medical Centre. It was hard to concentrate on the fight with Grandad lying there. I needed to weigh in and then assume my fighting psyche, but all I could think about was losing him. I still wasn't where I needed to be mentally on the drive to Sheffield, but as soon as I saw the arena, I switched on. I'm usually pretty jovial in the dressing room during the build-up, but this time I was all business. I didn't want to speak to anyone: just fight, win and get back to Grandad. Long before it was my time, I was pacing back and forth menacingly in front of the cage door so that Doski had to walk around me to enter. I had a dangerous rage inside me and it showed in a wild first round that wouldn't have been out of place in a saloon full of drunken cowboys. But in the second I settled down and started utilising my kicking game. I backed him up against the cage and executed a body-kick that he blocked with his arm. I knew I had caught him hard, right on the bone, and seconds later he threw a limp jab, winced in pain, and then motioned to the referee. I looked over from the neutral corner and saw the abnormal dip in his forearm where the fractured ulna pressed against his flesh. I had my revenge but I cut the celebrations short as all I wanted was to get back to Grandad's bedside.

But he was a tough old guy, my grandad, and he survived that scare and lived to fight another day. I got back to the gym and back to work and waited for my next fight. It soon arrived in predictably haphazard fashion when I took a call at the leisure centre at 8.30pm on a Friday evening. I was just about to knock off an hour early and make use of the facilities when the voice at the other end of the line told me an opponent was needed for the main event of a Cage Warriors show in Sheffield the following night. I was keen, of course, but when the caller told me it was against a guy named Andy Walker I turned it down. Firstly, a win over Andy was of no use to me. He was just a local jiu-jitsu player who enjoyed competing but had no big aspirations in MMA. He wasn't in my path, wasn't a rival, and there was little benefit to be had from defeating him. But more importantly, I trained with Andy and we always got on really well.

'Well, he says he wants to fight you,' came the reply from the Cage Warriors' matchmaker.

That changed everything. That was me hearing that Walker believes he is better than me, that he thinks he can beat me. Why would he agree to the fight if not? So now I'm angry. *How dare he even dream of beating me?* I took the fight and the next night in the cage I needed no extra motivation. But just in case, Walker provided it when he drove a clumsy knee into my groin and left me gasping for air with that horrible nauseous feeling in the pit of the stomach. The ref warned him, gave me a minute to recover, and then I decided to make it a short night. He took me down and attempted an armlock, but I easily resisted then manoeuvred him onto his back and began dropping bombs. I saw his eyes go vacant after one thumping left hand and, a series of hammer fists later, the ref was hauling me off him and calling the paramedics in to make sure he was okay. He was, and minutes later we both embraced with big smiles on our faces. I later asked him about how the match-up came about and he had had an almost identical conversation with the Cage Warriors matchmaker in which he expressed little interest in the bout until told I was eager to beat him up. The matchmaker had played us off against one another, but no great harm was done in the end.

A month later I was back competing under the Cage Warriors banner, this time in a UK versus France tournament. I spent my training camp preparing for Makhtar Gueye, a tough but reckless striker with similar experience to myself, but at the last minute I was told I was facing an unbeaten judo specialist by the name of David Baron. Baron, who would spend every second hunting a submission, was a totally different proposition to what I had been training for. He was also a huge step up in class, a guy good enough to go on and fight in both PRIDE Bushido in Japan and the UFC, and it turned out to be a hugely frustrating experience for me in which I spent the duration just trying to make a fight happen. He was like a spider monkey, all over me on the ground as the last thing he wanted to do was engage on our feet. He was hitting me with these tippy-tappy punches that were far more irritating than damaging. He was never going to hurt me with strikes and if I could have just kept the fight in the range I wanted it, I wouldn't have had a problem. But I couldn't. Even as the fight was progressing, I was making mental notes of the skills I still lacked and what I needed to work on. He totally nullified me and towards the end of the second he managed to get a secure triangle choke in place and I could feel my consciousness slipping away. It was my third loss in my first eight fights, but I was more philosophical about this one. I accepted it as part of the process, as an indication of the weaknesses in my game and exactly what I needed to improve.

And I was always keen to highlight and focus on my flaws. In fact, I viewed such introspection as a vital and necessary evil of being a mixed martial artist. Plenty of fighters shy away from such an approach and are content to keep working on their own speciality or what they know they are good at, but my logic was that if I improved on my weaknesses I would remove doubt or worry from my mind and be able to focus on my strengths during a fight. The Baron defeat reaffirmed what I already knew. Striking and kicking was no problem. I had Daley and Andre Winner to spar with at Rough House. With my Muay Thai experience, and the additional flamboyance of my taekwondo pedigree, I moved into range throwing head-kicks and launching knees whereas many others came in jabbing due to their boxing backgrounds. I was long, quick and enthusiastic, but at close quarters I soon developed a strong clinch, allowing powerful knees and elbows. Basically, I was confident I could hold my own on my feet in any MMA gym I entered and what I really needed to work on was an enhanced takedown defence and ground game. Or, in other words, I needed top-level Brazilian jiu-jitsu and wrestling coaching from someone with an understanding of how to apply it to professional MMA. With all the best trainers in the world based in the US, that meant more trips across the Atlantic, which in turn meant more shifts in the leisure centre and shoe shop to pay for flights and expenses out there. But that was fine for I always knew I was investing in myself. In those early years I was living to train and fight, rather than the other way around.

● ● ●

I flew out to American Top Team again, this time on my own, and the two weeks were a bit of a nightmare. I had sourced the cheapest possible accommodation within a ten-mile radius of the ATT academy, but the dive turned out to be a good three-mile walk from the nearest bus stop. Doing that every day in 100 per cent humidity, under an unforgiving Floridian sun, with all my gear slung over my shoulder, left me sweating and knackered before I even arrived at the gym. They knew me now inside, but the outsider treatment barely let up. On the first sparring day I was put in with a lightweight, a welterweight, a middleweight and then a light-heavyweight, and given little time to catch my breath in-between shifts. But it was another valuable two weeks in the bank, particularly being able to focus on Brazilian jiu-jitsu under the expert eye of Ricardo Liborio.

Another man that I met briefly that fortnight, but who had a big impact on me, was the MMA pioneer Marcus 'Conan' Silveira. Although his official record only has ten fights on it, he was active before anyone was keeping track and the true number is thought to be in the multiple hundreds. I remember watching grainy footage of him competing in rough, underground events, dominating guys with a strong Brazilian jiu-jitsu game and vicious striking. He has contributed to the development of many great fighters and when you watch him interacting with his athletes you can see why he is so successful. His commanding presence is juxtaposed with a calm, fatherly energy, and you can feel his genuine love for every fighter under his care. It is clear how seriously he takes the responsibility of guiding them through the trials and tribulations of a career in professional combat and I'll always admire the way he cultivates a close family-like bond within his team.

From there I took a five-and-a-half hour flight across the country to Portland, Oregon and the Team Quest headquarters. This time I had no problems with the daily commute as I stayed in a low-budget EconoLodge across the road from the gym. But the accommodation was less than salubrious and I spent the fortnight washing my clothes in the bath and surviving on peanut butter, the occasional tin of tuna, a loaf of bread and a bag of apples. Once a week, as a major treat, I ordered either waffles or pancakes in the diner next door. But it was all worth it to spend time with one of the world's premier MMA teams in which the vast majority of fighters came from a wrestling background. Quest was known for being a wrestling powerhouse, with some of the greatest fighters in the sport preparing there. Guys like Randy Couture, Matt Lindland and Dan Henderson would all be on the mat at the same time during team sessions, but as I spent most of the day there I got to know some of the younger members of the team a little better. Ed Herman, Chris Wilson, Ryan Schultz and Matt Horwich were all great training partners during that four-week stay. Pretty much everyone involved with TQ was doing well on one circuit or another while I was there, and they all built their success off a solid base of either freestyle or Greco-Roman wrestling. The former is more about attacking the legs and ankles for takedowns, while the latter, forbidding holds below the waist, relies more on throws and upper body control. It was all gold to me and I absorbed the knowledge like a sponge before filtering out what would be best for me to introduce into my own repertoire.

Back in the UK, I had three fights and three wins in less than a month. The run began with a trip to the Aston Villa leisure centre for a bout with Stuart Barrs. The Scotsman was coming off two submission victories, but he had lost to both Doski and Paul Jenkins earlier in his career and I was extremely confident. I saw him sitting with his family when I walked into the sports hall to check the ring out and gave him a look to let him know I was here to fight. His energy appeared to be more like a Sunday morning football match whereas mine was, *I'm coming for blood*. The fight itself was relatively straightforward. He attempted a few takedowns and we scrambled about a bit in the first, but fresh from sparring with the elite of Team Quest, I was always in complete control. Barrs seemed like he didn't really want to fight and as soon as I landed cleanly a couple of times he didn't like it. I beat him up and won by technical knockout midway through the second round of a fight that contained little excitement.

The following weekend I fought in Sheffield on a huge show put together by King of the Cage. KOTC was an American promotion and, along with Gladiator Challenge, sat behind only the UFC and PRIDE in terms of size and prestige. I watched a lot of their shows and followed the careers of the likes of Joe Stevenson and Mac Danzig as they appeared regularly on KOTC promotions across the US. I could see how those guys were progressing and improving with every fight and I knew they were destined for the UFC. So when someone in the UK acquired the rights to put on a KOTC event in the UK and invited me to fight on the card, I saw another massive opportunity to advance my career.

It took place in iceSheffield, a newly-built £15m, 1,500 capacity arena and there were some big names competing, including future UFC star Martin Kampmann from Denmark and future PRIDE fighter Joey Villaseñor from the US. It should have been a massive night for British MMA, but unfortunately those in charge badly mismanaged the event. By blowing most of their budget on the venue, the quality of the line-up, and simply acquiring the franchise rights in the first place, they had little left for marketing or promotion. As a result, barely 300 tickets were sold and, in such a vast space as iceSheffield, the cries of those in attendance echoed eerily around the ice hockey stadium. It was disappointing from a legacy point of view, but it had zero impact on me as I readied for battle. Once more, I had to take a late and drastic change of opponent in my stride. I had been preparing for Henrique Santana, a Brazilian who had recently defeated Paul Jenkins and the highly regarded Matt Thorpe. He was a strong and wily grappler with legitimate submission skills and always had a sizeable group of his jiu-jitsu school with him for support. When he withdrew at the last minute, his jiu-jitsu instructor, Alexandre Izidro, agreed to step in for a two-round contest. Izidro was a totally different kind of problem, a really slick and crafty operator with great submission skills. We had a good tussle for the full ten minutes, spent mostly on the floor as he threw submission after submission at me. I stayed sharp, using the defensive skills I'd been honing for six weeks in the US to escape dangerous positions and land strikes. I wasn't able to hit him cleanly with anything damaging, but at one point in the first he locked in a loose triangle and I saw my Rampage-Jackson opportunity. I rose to my feet with Izidro clinging on with his triangle partially locked in, walked him across the cage with my hands aloft, and then jumped as high as I could before slamming him onto the mat right in front of my corner. Izidro had a style that turned out to be a real spoiler for my refined striking skills, but the fact that I could deal with constant attack from someone with his black-belt pedigree settled some of my concerns about where my submission defence was at. I felt comfortable throughout and my hand was deservedly raised at the end. It could have easily turned into another fight like the one I had with Baron, but was instead the clearest sign yet that the trips Stateside to train with top jiu-jitsu fighters were paying dividends.

Next up was an appearance at the Skydome Arena in Coventry for a Cage Warriors event and a match-up with Lautoro Arborelo from Spain. Arborelo was another submission wrestler looking to ground-and-pound me. He was a short, thick-set guy, very strong and with a low centre of gravity. In the first two rounds he did have some success with his stubborn grappling and surprise takedowns, but once on the ground he simply held on defensively. Having encountered much more advanced wrestlers in my US training camps, I was always comfortable and never close to real danger. By the time the third round began, his tank was already empty and I was able to use the extra space between us to land at will with head-kicks, knees and strikes with my fists. I had him bloodied and bruised before an overhand right buckled his knees and he almost collapsed against the cage wall. As he leant on the fence, covering his head with his eyes closed, I teed off with upper-cuts, skip-kicks and more knees until the ref stepped in to save the brave and durable Spaniard from himself.

Keen to maintain the momentum from those three victories, I was back out again in September against Sami 'The Hun' Berik. Berik was a bit of a strange phenomenon on the British MMA scene in those days. He would post weird training videos on the internet which tended to feature soft-focus tai chi sessions in a forest to a background of poor-quality kung fu movie soundtrack music. He was a regular voice on the Cage Warriors forum and many believed his ultimate goal was to become a kung fu movie star. Perhaps with that dream in mind, he moved into MMA to test his skills and, if he could prove himself effective in a real fighting environment, catch the attention of the entertainment world.

Not long before we faced off, Berik attended a seminar with Royce Gracie and managed to get his blue belt in Brazilian jiu-jitsu. He was rightly proud of this achievement and his confidence was suddenly through the roof. He began chasing submissions and had some success, but he was fighting mediocre fighters at best, or certainly nobody trained to defend against Brazilian jiu-jitsu. He let these victories go to his head and when our fight was announced he was straight onto the Cage Warriors forum, mouthing off about how he was going to knock me out. I had never encountered such confident trash-talk before and this was the first time someone had come at me with total self-belief. I wondered where it was coming from but my response was pretty simple: come what may, I was going to give Berik the full fifteen minutes to make good on his promise to knock me out. The anticipation in the Octagon Centre in Sheffield was electric as the fans in attendance had clearly been following the online quarrel and were eagerly anticipating this score-settling bout. It was the first time I could see with my own eyes the power of the trash-talking and hype that the superstars of combat sport seem to devote a lot of their energy towards. I even changed up my musical choice to accompany my arrival and, rather than the usual Hardcore, Metal, or UK Grime offering, I picked 'Nowhere to Run' by Martha and the Vandellas. I had loved the verbal back and forth between Berik and me and wanted to keep trying to get inside his head until the final moments before we traded on the canvas.

As I had promised, I gave Berik his fifteen minutes. It wasn't particularly competitive, other than for the first third of the contest when my complacence in front of this apparent lack of challenge was met by Berik's gameness and will to win. But after that I began managing the range, landing more shots, wearing him down, and generally beating him up quite badly. Midway through the second, his gumshield was already hanging out of his mouth, half from exhaustion, half in surrender. At one point I aimed a punishing kick to his liver and he dropped, but I just waited for him to get up and continue. I kept hurting his body, but I was landing on his face and head at will. By the third, he was bleeding from his nose and cuts on his brow, while swollen pockets of flesh around his eyes were obscuring his faltering vision. I could have finished him, but I had an agenda: I was going to let this go the full fifteen minutes and hurt and embarrass him for every second of it. Looking back now, it was actually quite a sadistic game-plan, but it was good that I was disciplined enough to stick to it. I guess I had a touch of blood lust inside the cage as the animalistic side of my psyche sought to dominate. That's why I never went looking for submissions. I knew I had to dedicate a massive portion of my time to practising submissions, but that was always simply to improve my ability to defend against them. If I could execute a perfect *kimura*, it follows that I would also be able to better avoid getting caught in one. If someone was lax enough to present me with an opportunity to use one, I'd certainly capitalise, but I took no great satisfaction from submitting a rival. What I took pleasure from was inflicting damage on an opponent, on drawing his blood and leaving the canvas stained with it. But the pleasure was always part of a bigger picture for me. If I split someone's skull open, not only would it represent immediate success, it was a statement to future opponents. I was looking to strike fear into potential rivals looking on from cageside. I wanted everyone to be under no illusions that fifteen minutes with me was their worst nightmare. And if some of them then chose to duck me and allowed me to leap up the rankings, so much the better. I wanted to be seen as dominant in a very violent, as well as technical, way. That is why I would always keep beating the face of the man lying underneath me until the referee physically dragged me off. And if I could, I'd land a couple of final blows as I felt the official's arms on me. In my opinion, that is how an MMA fighter should be. When you are facing a man like Wanderlei Silva, the question within yourself as to whether you really want this is asked long before the bout starts. That's a powerful position for any athlete to hold, but particularly in combat sports. This is a game

Above: Grandad and I at my Christening, outside Holy Trinity Church in Clifton on 24/10/82.

Left: With my dad at the top of Thorpe Cloud in Derbyshire, about three years old.

Below: Keeping a close eye on my new little sister, Gemma, while my grandad holds her for the first time.

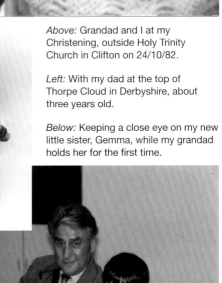

Right: After my first Taekwondo grading, receiving a double pass to yellow belt.

Below: Mick Rowley cornering me at my first Taekwondo tournament as a black belt. I was fortunate enough to have a great martial artist, teacher, cornerman and friend to guide me through my early years as a fighter.

Above: Master Long (left) and Master Wei (right) on my last day of training in China. On the training ground where most of our practice was spent...

Below: ...unless the weather was bad, then we would all crowd into the training hall. The heavy weight bench that Master Long lifted is bottom left.

Right: Paul Daley and I backstage at Extreme Brawl 7, in Bracknell, UK. This was my debut fight and I was so impatient I couldn't hold still. It was good to have Paul there to share the experience with me and he always gave me strength, even if sometimes he'd get me too riled up!

Below: Owen Comrie at Majestik in Nottingham, after a training session for one of my early professional fights. He was in my corner for the majority of my Muay Thai, Kickboxing and MMA fights, and his knowledge lead to many of my victories.

Above: My grandparents Ian and Barbara, after my revenge fight against Diego Gonzalez, at Cagewarriors in Coventry.

Below: The core of Rough House for many years. We shared sweat, blood, tears and a lot of laughs, and I consider every one of them family.
From left to right: Jimmy Wallhead, Dean Amasinger, Ollie Richardson and Andre Winner.

My Dad invading the Cagewarriors cage in Nottingham, after my TKO victory over Alex Izidro. The first time my parents came to one of my professional fights, and hid in the back so I didn't know they where there. Probably my favourite fight photo.

Team Rough House after a successful night of scrapping. Left to right, top then bottom: Paul Barton, Nathan Leverton, Tamai Harding, Dean Amasinger, Owen Comrie, Kristoff Swinoga, Mahmood Besharate, Steve Tetley and Jimmy Wallhead.

Backstage at Harvey Haddon Sport Stadium in Nottingham, after my win over Manuel Garcia, with Mum, Dad and Gemma.

That unanimous decision loss to Forrest Petz…

…and the shock on my face when they gave my Cagewarriors title to the guy with the broken face.

One of two light-welterweight bouts I fought at 73kgs (160lbs) which was the PRIDE lightweight limit. A lead left hook against Izidro. I remember feeling very fast at this weight.

The final ceremony at the end of my first trip to Peru. Don Ignacio blowing Mapacho smoke over me for cleansing and protection. He is a powerful teacher and I was fortunate enough to have my great friend Beto with me to translate his words. Credit also goes to Beto for capturing this moment for me to share with you.

of psychological as well as physical dominance. Some may find it hard to imagine that an otherwise warm and friendly character can behave so brutally, but I always felt my profession demanded I be this way. I wasn't trying to earn victories, I was taking them from opponents with violent force. And it was from such means of victory that I drew my confidence and was able to re-enter a cage and do it all over again.

Sami raised my hand up in victory before we even heard from the judges. It was as unanimous as a unanimous decision could ever be. But when interviewed immediately after, I gave Berik great credit for not looking for an easy escape route as I battered him and then encouraged him to drop to lightweight where he could be a force. I also had to thank him for his role in the manufactured antagonism between us that guaranteed our bout was the most talked about of the night before we'd even thrown a punch or kick.

Three weeks later, I was on another Cage Warriors show, this time Strike Force 3 in Coventry. My old pal Izidro was there, submitting the very useful Swede Jani Lax inside three minutes, and Bisping and my Rough House teammate Jimmy Wallhead both impressed with first-round stoppages. My opponent was a Swedish grappler, deceptively named Diego Gonzalez. He was another submissions specialist and was in the middle of a run that would see him lose just once, to me, in fourteen bouts. He was also streetwise, as I discovered to my cost at the beginning of our fight. Up until that point, my routine had been to walk to the centre of the canvas and respectfully touch gloves with my foe once the referee had ordered us to fight. Only after that ceremonial formality took place did I consider the fight to be on. But Gonzalez was sly. As I walked forward to meet him, he held his left hand out at length as if to reciprocate my goodwill gesture. Then, six inches away from the ritual fist-bump, he threw an overhand right that cracked the side of my head and shot for a takedown that sent me crashing into the side of the cage. He had attacked me in that split second before I'm mentally, and thus physically, ready for war. It was like being fast asleep and suddenly tipped into a pool of iced water. I started scrambling, trying to get back on my feet, but he felt strong and heavy on top of me as I struggled to turn. I managed to get halfway round, but as I did so he dropped a series of elbows and fists onto my skull at the base of my neck and behind my ear. And that is the last thing I remember about that fight. It continued for another six minutes, but I have no recollection of anything that happened up to and including the moment he submitted me with a rear-naked choke.

I was still in a daze in the dressing room after the fight, but my team were raging. The sucker punch at the outset wasn't an issue to anyone, however. It was sneaky and certainly not particularly sportsmanlike, but nothing in the rulebook forbids it and I should have been alert to the possibility. The big problem was the elbows to the back of the head. It doesn't take much for violent blows to that region of the human head to damage the spinal cord, or even detach a brain from its stem and thus end life, and for that reason they are understandably outlawed in MMA. One side of my face was numb for about two months after that night. I would be chewing my food and suddenly become aware that everything bore the unmistakably metallic taste of my own blood after I had bitten a chunk out of the inside of my cheek without even realising. In time, I made a full recovery but it was a scary sensation while it lasted.

The referee should have picked up on the illegal attacks at the time, but he was officiating his first professional bout and was perhaps too nervous to make such a dramatic intervention so early in his own career. So my team immediately took our complaint to Cage Warriors and they agreed to sit down and watch the fight again and make a decision on the validity of the result. They also brought in top ref Marc Goddard to get his input into how the incident should have been handled. What they saw was Gonzalez landing several times in the vulnerable zone, suggesting it was not merely a one-off accidental strike as we twisted and turned on the canvas in the heat of battle. The verdict was unanimous: Gonzalez had clearly benefited from a severe breach of the rules and the bout was declared a no contest. I guess I was pleased and relieved by Cage Warriors' decision to overturn an unjust defeat, but all I can remember thinking at that time was, *Let me get back in the cage with that bastard*. Yet that revenge mission would have to wait as I had already been informed that I had earned a shot at the vacant Cage Warriors welterweight title. And as an added incentive, Cage Warriors told me I could make my first defence against Gonzalez if I managed to win the belt.

Standing between me and a first major title was a submission wrestler from Bolton by the name of Matt Thorpe. Thorpe was part of the Northern Cartel, an affiliation of different teams from the north of England. He did a lot of his training in a gym in Huddersfield alongside quality guys like Ian Butlin and one-time UFC veteran Leigh Remedios, who fought on the first UFC event in the UK back in 2002. We were very familiar with the Northern Cartel and knew they were no joke. They were also up to date with how the elite in the US were preparing for fights and were particularly adept at cutting weight. They were absolutely convinced of the importance of being the bigger man in the cage and there were even rumours that they had a fighter once donate blood in order to make weight. There was a big rivalry between Rough House and the Northern Cartel, and we made sure to play up to that on the internet in order to hype fights, but in reality there was always a healthy respect between us as teams and individuals.

What made Thorpe such a tricky proposition was his size. At six foot four inches tall he was an absolute giant in the welterweight division and those long limbs gave him two major advantages. First, he was always going to have a longer reach and greater leverage in his punches than everyone he fought, and secondly, the lanky limbs ensured he had great submission skills off his back, particularly triangles. So for the first time in my career, I sat down and analysed an opponent in order to devise a sound game-plan. It did genuinely feel like I was making a step up in my career now, a little like moving from GCSEs to A Levels and immediately realising that, despite how it felt at the time, GCSEs weren't shit. The prize of being a world champion was huge and I decided I should prepare accordingly. I watched all the footage of Thorpe I could find, and then put myself in his shoes and watched my own fights. I knew that he and his team would be developing a specific approach to defeat me and I wanted to try and second-guess them. To be honest, it wasn't difficult. Nobody in British MMA, outside my own team, rated my ground game and so everyone presumed I would always rely on my stand-up striking ability. I was Rough House after all, the sprawl-and-brawl, kill-or-be-killed guys that don't stop throwing kicks and punches until the victory is secured. So while Matt Thorpe was in his training camp, working on trading on his feet, I was in my own with a trick up my sleeve: I was going to take him down, hold top position and, while defending the inevitable submission attempts from the bottom, rain down punishing punches and elbows.

The only problem I could see was that we had no one in or around our team of the physical stature of Thorpe with whom I could spar and perfect the tactic. Long, rangy, six-foot-four welterweight mixed martial artists don't exactly grow on trees in England or anywhere else for that matter. Then, as if sent from above by someone looking out for me, Tamai Harding strolled casually into the gym one afternoon. Big T, as he was soon known, was a six-foot-four kickboxer and Snoop Dogg lookalike. He was also hoping to get into MMA. It couldn't have been any better and for the next eight weeks he became my Matt Thorpe impersonator. And he did a fantastic job. Sparring with him was like kicking a bag of wrenches: everything was sharp and angular on him. I hurt my hands and feet every time I connected with his knees, elbows or hips. Even hitting him in the ribs hurt sometimes. But it was perfect preparation for the biggest night of my career to date.

It was my first five-rounder, but my cardiovascular conditioning was always good and I had no concerns about going the distance. Thorpe on the other hand had never been beyond one round in his MMA career and I sensed a slight desperation in his work in the opening stanza as he chased submission after submission. It was a competitive start and, although I was never in any danger, I can see how the judges may have been swayed by his constant, if futile, attempts to finish. But from the second onwards, it was my fight. Every chance I had, I took him down, climbed on top, and tried to crash fists or elbows into face. He struggled gamely to get up or even just keep me in his guard, but he rarely managed to do that and thus had to resort to merely tying up my arms to limit the clean strikes with which I marked up his face. There was just one close call in the third round when he almost locked in a nasty armbar, but I twisted and squirmed like a barracuda on the end of a sport fisherman's hook and freed myself within a few seconds of struggle. Almost the entirety of rounds four and five were spent with me in a top position, striving to create enough space to batter him, and Thorpe struggling to stay offensive beneath me as I worked from a controlling position. I blackened his right eye, marked up the bridge of his nose, and generally did enough damage to catch the judges' attention. One particularly sharp elbow opened a sizeable gash on his brow. When the end arrived, I was exhausted but confident I had won the belt. The almost commiserative shakes of the hand from his team, while my Rough House boys leapt about the other side of the cage in jubilation, said it all. One judge saw it differently, meaning I won by a split decision, but I didn't care in the least. I had eight hundred plus two hundred more for winning in my account, my teammates gathered in celebration and, most importantly, a nice gold-plated belt was around my waist to signify that I was the Cage Warriors welterweight champion of the world.

THE PROMISED LAND

4

I was extremely proud of that Cage Warriors belt, but life did not change in the slightest after becoming a recognised world champion within my sport. To be honest, there was still a lot of doubt about making the leap from small European shows to the UFC, or even earning decent money from being a full-time, professional mixed martial artist. I was simply living to train and training to fight. Fighting was the be all and end all to me. If money came along off the back of it, great, I'd reinvest it in another training camp. But the financial rewards were still something of a novelty or a bonus at that time and I would have stepped into the cage for free just for the sheer pleasure of it. I never discussed money or tried to renegotiate purses like other fighters did after they had a little success. I just accepted what was on offer. Having a management team trying to squeeze a little extra cash out of promoters may have been useful, but when most purses were still three figures it was hardly worth playing hardball in negotiations and there was little incentive for a legitimate management company to get involved. Instead, most fighters were managed by a friend or relative or, as in my case, the promoter on whose show they fought the most. I had little concern as long as I was getting matched up regularly, and was able to pay for my coaches and training camp. I've never been much of a money-chaser, it was always about the competition. That may seem naive of me, and maybe it was in some respects, but I know that while such an approach may have cost me a few quid in the short term, in the long term it opened up doors and provided opportunities that may have otherwise gone to the guys on the circuit willing to accept hard fights for less money. But, as I say, dreams of achieving fame and fortune through fighting in MMA were still the furthest thing from my mind.

A big part of the reason for that was down to the British public perception of the sport and the lack of positive support or recognition it received from mainstream media. To the average punter on the street, it was still just cage fighting, violent thugs punching each other bloody and senseless for a baying mob. To them it was human cockfighting. The very presence of the cage, a simple matter of athlete safety, even seemed to offend our hyper-sensitive critics. That it is in place for the perfectly logical reason of preventing fighters from falling through the ropes of a boxing ring and injuring themselves, a scenario not uncommon in training when cages are hard to come by, rarely entered the discussion. But I must confess that, due to the negative connotations, I always hated the term cage fighting and avoided using it as much as possible. When asked what I did for a living I would answer that I'm an athlete. If pushed for more information, I'd specify that I'm a mixed martial artist. 'Oh, like karate and shit,' was then a common response. When I tried to elaborate and educate, even the mention of a caged arena would engender visions of some basement or warehouse straight out of the *Fight Club* movie. Most fighters were working to move opinion forward, but there were also plenty of wannabe tough guys latching on to the sport, calling themselves cage fighters, and continuing to sensationalise the violent element. The involvement of criminals looking to clean money and earn street cred helped perpetuate the sinister, underground image. This association with morally corrupt, ego-driven or shameless self-promoters left a bad taste in a lot of people's mouths upon their initial introduction to what was a relatively new and polarising sport. It also turned most mainstream media outlets off. Even the likes of Alex Reid and his escapades on reality TV cast a negative light on what should be respected as a high-level sporting endeavour. This all left British MMA struggling to gain the widespread acceptance and recognition that its American or Japanese counterparts were beginning to enjoy.

But I certainly didn't blame the average member of the public for the perception they held because the truth is that the sport of MMA had done little to help itself in the early days. Original UFC marketing had *no holds barred* plastered all over it and sensationalist slogans like *two men enter, one man leaves* screaming out from menacing posters. It was all very short-term and narrow-minded thinking. But it revelled in its dark reputation for years and it wasn't until Zuffa took over that MMA was truly successful in moving away from the violent, quasi-legal freak show image.

Zuffa LLC, the name taken from an Italian word meaning fight or clash, was the company the Fertitta brothers, Lorenzo and Frank, and Dana White formed when they paid Semaphore Entertainment Group $2m for the struggling UFC business in 2001. Lorenzo later admitted they basically paid the money for the three letters alone and Zuffa immediately set about polishing up the UFC's bad name and mainstreaming the sport of MMA across the globe. Within three months, standardised regulations were drawn up, accepted by the New Jersey Athletic Control Board, and adopted as the Unified Rules of Mixed Martial Arts. They covered everything necessary to govern MMA as a modern sport, with the list of fouls gaining particular attention as it expanded from the original three – no biting, gouging or groin attacks – to over thirty. The next target was to secure sanctioning from the Nevada State Athletic Commission, the gold standard in combat sports' regulatory bodies. This goal was achieved six months later, just in time for UFC 33.

Zuffa kicked on and grew the brand worldwide by debuting the UFC in England and later introducing it to another fifteen countries in four continents including Canada, Mexico, Ireland, Germany, Australia, New Zealand, China and the United Arab Emirates. They lost money hand over fist for the first four years, but when a final roll of the dice launched the hugely successful Ultimate Fighter reality television series, the organisation turned a corner and has never looked back, ultimately signing a seven-year, $700m television deal with Fox in 2011. Fighter safety has improved beyond recognition from the early days and in 2015 the UFC contracted the US Anti-Doping Agency to implement one of the most stringent drug-testing regimens in all professional sport. One by one, states across America saw the light and agreed to legalise and sanction MMA events, with New York the last of the fifty to do so in 2016. The road to universal acceptance is probably never-ending, but in the space of fifteen years the UFC has carried mixed martial arts a lot further along the journey than it was before Zuffa arrived on the scene.

Throughout this evolution, however, the UK was always playing catch-up. A huge swathe of so-called mixed martial artists were indeed little more than thugs who had done a bit of boxing and drunken street fighting and now wanted the reputation of being a no-holds-barred cage fighter. I was loath to be lumped in with that subsection and for that reason I never fought on a Cage Rage event. They had great fighters on their cards, with the likes of Anderson Silva, Cyborg Santos, Jorge Rivera and my mate Paul Daley all appearing regularly, but the whole promotion was packaged in such a thuggish manner that it never appealed to me. I was never interested in gaining a tough-guy image. All I wanted was to test myself in a fair fight, in an arena, in a sporting environment.

So around the time I was a Cage Warriors champion, MMA in Britain still had a distinct underworld feel about it. Many of the characters you encountered who had the spare capital to risk were shady to say the least, but they were integral to the sport so there was no way they could be avoided if you wanted to fight. Many of them were involved in the shows that, along with the Cage Warriors forum, were the only things keeping MMA alive in this country. I always presumed the guys putting the money in and taking the money out were criminals involved in the drugs trade who invested in MMA purely for the money laundering and extra street-cred opportunities, but I never let any of that concern me. By and large, I was treated well and fairly by whoever was my nominal manager or promoter at any given time. Even the one from the darker shadows of society who was so paranoid I could only speak to him through his wife! There were only a couple who ever gave me serious cause for concern. The first was Dougie Truman, the founder of Cage Warriors. He was clearly dodgy, almost comically so, like a Del Boy character from *Only Fools and Horses*. He would wear a shirt only half-buttoned up with too much jewellery on show and drive a Bentley with the registration CAGE. I later heard he was involved in an attempt to retrieve drugs from a family member's car in a police compound but was predictably caught and sentenced to a substantial stay at Her Majesty's pleasure. He had to take a step away from the sport during that stretch and I haven't seen him since.

The second miscreant in charge of my affairs that I could throw further than I could trust was Tony McDonagh. He was always running scams and trying to squeeze out some extra money for himself. He'd organise coaches to bring my fans to shows and then charge through the nose, or sell cheap T-shirts under the auspices of growing the support, but really just so he could further line his pockets. I also know that on more than one occasion he failed to pass on the full amount I was due from the meagre sponsorship deals I managed to secure. But they weren't all bad, and Andy Lillis springs to mind as one of the good guys. He was the only one I saw to be truly invested in the sport of

MMA and who genuinely hoped it could become a success. He cared about my career too, making every effort to be cageside for my bouts and looking just as gutted as I was after a defeat. He had a good heart and always treated me well, yet even Andy got involved in something he shouldn't and ended up serving time inside. Such was the world of MMA in the UK back then that even the angels sinned.

So within that environment, even though I was now a recognised world champion, it was difficult to envisage professional MMA fighting becoming a secure and lucrative long-term career any time soon. In the meantime, my focus was fully on exacting revenge over Diego Gonzalez. Some fighters would have been fine using the no-contest ruling as a means to justify and then totally forget about what happened in my first encounter with the Swede, but I was still burning up inside over it. At the end of the day, I felt like I had lost a fight. While it is true that I only lost due to a sucker punch and then illegal strikes, it is equally true that Gonzalez was only able to land those blows because I stupidly left myself vulnerable to such attacks. He may have bent or broken the rules which governed our battle, but he submitted me and won by doing so and I took no comfort from hiding behind excuses or complaints or Cage Warriors overruling the original result. It all comes down to the conflict I always have in my heart and soul as to the balance between MMA being a fight or a sport. It is a conflict I have never quite reconciled, but as a fighter first and foremost, I raged inside for the six months I had to wait to get my hands back on Diego Gonzalez.

The night finally arrived on 25 March 2006. I set the tone inside the opening minute when, after he had taken me down, I easily rolled him over and then smashed forearms and elbows into his face. Every blow was venomous. I wanted to really do some damage to this guy. I sought to punish him, not just for being a dirty fighter and for what had gone on in our first meeting, but for the arrogance with which he approached this rematch. I had seen him swaggering about the hotel acting the big man and I knew he had come over with a large posse who sat at the cageside tables liked they owned the place. He was so cocky, so sure he was going to win, and I just thought to myself, *You're going to get something, motherfucker, but it's not my belt.*

He was already blowing hard at the end of the first and looked tired in his corner as he struggled for breath. I opened the second round with some sharp strikes and then we grappled against the side of the cage. I could feel his tiredness and it gave me more strength. Once again I turned him, mounted him, rolled my wrists out of his controlling grip and unloaded with punches and elbows and hammer fists in an attempt to shatter his nose and open up cuts around his eyes. If he was tired at the end of the opening round, he was completely exhausted now. Marc Goddard was thankfully in charge of proceedings this time and he had to practically manhandle Gonzalez's lingering corner team out of the cage to begin the third. I looked across and saw that as a reluctance on his part to recommence war, saw it as a man close to the end. I was buzzing, knowing exactly what was coming next. I marched forward and landed a spiteful jab to his jaw before immediately following up with a low kick to the outside of his thigh and a high kick with my stronger left leg that connected my shin to the side of his head. He backed off in a semi-fugue state and then wearily shot for my legs in a desperate takedown attempt. I sprawled, flattening him out before he turned to pull guard and I postured up and was ready to end the bastard when Goddard intervened. He called in the doctor to look at the damage my high kick had caused and within seconds the medic had seen enough to know Gonzalez now belonged in a hospital rather than in a cage with me. I later learned that he did go straight from the arena to University Hospital, Coventry, where it took nearly sixty stitches, inside and outside of the wound, to close the gash over his right eye.

I had the swagger now as I strolled about the cage, yelling out, *Who's the champ!* A photographer appeared and took a picture of my first ever tattoo, freshly inked just a few weeks before. It was a skull and crossbones on the inside of my lower lip, the only part of my body which would heal quickly enough to let me fight almost immediately after, and the photo of me revealing it made the front cover of *Fighters Only* magazine the following month. The one and only Ian 'The Machine' Freeman, the first Brit to fight in the UFC and conqueror of Frank Mir in the Royal Albert Hall at UFC 38, then entered to do the post-fight interviews. I was in China when Ian stopped Mir but the photograph of him astride the cage wall absorbing the adulation from the crowd is iconic and was a big inspiration to me. When he asked me what it was like to get my revenge, I went off on one. 'Fucking sweet,' I began before ripping into Gonzalez. 'There's one thing in the world I hate more than anything and that's losing. The second thing is unsportsmanlike fighting. Fucking touch gloves, it doesn't take much. We're fucking athletes, not thugs, we touch fucking gloves.'

Not done there, I then decided to challenge anyone who might have felt like I didn't deserve to wear the championship belt. 'Don't anyone say I'm not the fucking champ,' I yelled. 'Because if there is anyone out there who thinks I'm not the champ, I'll rip your fucking head off. All right!?'

The combination of sweet revenge and adrenalin is a terrible cocktail for post-fight interviews, but it was all good: part theatre, part self-pro-motion, and part a need to get some genuine feelings off my chest. All in all, it was a very productive night. I'd cemented my status as the best welterweight this side of the Atlantic and gained a lot of exposure and new fans along the way. I was on top of my own little world, feeling invincible, and when I got a call a couple of days later offering me a fight in the US against Forrest Petz for the vacant Fightfest welterweight belt, I didn't hesitate to start packing my suitcase.

● ● ●

Forrest Petz was a solid fighter with an impressive 15 and 4 record. He was a heavy hitter with decent wrestling skills, and good enough to go on and make seven appearances at the UFC, but I knew I'd beat him. It was also just a great career move for me. I'd gain more experience seeing how another major US show operates and, as it was for an American belt, I'd be guaranteed an invitation back across the pond to defend it. My prized title would also be on the line, but thoughts of losing that strap didn't even enter into my head.

I flew into Akron-Canton airport with Owen on the Tuesday before the fight in order to have enough time to acclimatise to Ohio. There was a gym near our hotel where I could work out and a sauna inside the Pro Football Hall of Fame in which I could sweat off the excess weight. I cut 15 pounds pretty comfortably and felt great. I remember the weigh-in took place in the risqué surroundings of Christie's Cabaret Club and we got changed upstairs in a room used by the working girls before two strippers linked my arms and walked me down to the scales. I recognised the pair the following night as the ring girls holding up the round cards and it made me realise that cross-promotion Stateside wasn't a great deal classier than it was back home. The fight itself took place in a massive sports hall with a stage at one end to host a live heavy metal band that blasted out their hits at any interval in the action. Eric Esch, the multi-disciplined fighter more commonly known as Butterbean, was the co-main and turned out to be a really nice guy. I had a few meals with him during fight week and couldn't believe that, despite his 385-pound heft, I probably ate more than him and I was cutting weight!

The fight was competitive in a raucous and entirely partisan atmosphere, but I was always at ease and always on top. We both knocked each other down a couple of times, and took each other down a couple of times more, but once on the canvas I beat him up or threatened submissions whereas he offered very little as an offensive force. I broke his nose during a barrage of elbows in the first as the ref warned Petz he'd stop the fight if the American didn't get out from under my sustained attack. His only option to escape was to give me his back and allow me to lock in a body triangle, but the move allowed him to make it to the bell at the end of round one. I didn't let up for the rest of the fight, making a mess of his face throughout the full twenty-five minutes. Seeing he had zero defence against it, I also pounded his legs with low kicks at will. I was so comfortable that I spent the minute between rounds casually chatting with an old friend that used to live in Nottingham and had made it cageside to watch me perform. The major difference was my conditioning and after one last flurry of elbows from half-guard at the end of the fifth, I stood up and could easily have done five more. Petz on the other hand was shattered and covered in his own blood.

Herb Dean, now a top referee in the UFC, was officiating inside the cage and he told me he believed I had done enough. I was confident of victory, but as the seconds ticked away without a decision being announced, I started to get an empty feeling in my stomach. The promoter who had brought me over was now standing behind Petz with both the Cage Warriors and Fightfest belts in his hand and a massive grin on his face. It turned out that in addition to putting on the show, he was also Forrest's manager. After what seemed like an age, they declared a new champion by unanimous decision. I stood rooted to the spot, in shock at the verdict. I looked at Petz's battered face, the cutman still holding a compress to his wounds to stop the bleeding, and thought there must have been some sort of mistake. Back in the dressing room I flew into a violent rage. As Owen stood outside the door so nobody would walk in, be startled and raise an alarm, I trashed the place, destroying anything I could get my hands on. I'd been robbed in a title unification bout and the belt I had worked so hard for and was so proud to wear was gone too. Unable to accept the nightmare I found myself living, I stormed out to confront the three scoring judges. There they were at a table beside the cage, all grey hair and glasses, officiously shuffling some papers. Inside the cage, Petz was posing for photos with my belt, his blood still flowing and dripping onto the canvas while his mangled face contorted painfully into a victory smile.

'Look at him,' I shouted to the three old boys. 'How could you score that fight to him?'

I could see they were intimidated by this confrontation, but one attempted a mumbled response. 'Effective striking,' was all he could muster.

'Effective striking!?' I roared back. 'He's going straight to the hospital to get his face fixed and I don't have a mark on me!'

The crowd had thinned out fast, but plenty stopped to watch this bonus feature as I remonstrated with the three blind mice. At one point I actually jumped up on their table and asked the remaining fans who they thought won the fight. There were only Americans in the bleachers, but plenty shouted back that I had.

As our flight wasn't until Monday morning, I had all of Sunday to sulk about the hotel and simmer over the injustice of it all. Then on Monday, our car to the airport mysteriously never arrived and we missed our flight. I thought the thirteen-hour wait in the airport for the next plane out must have been the bitter cherry on top of this toxic sundae, but unfortunately that was still to arrive. I paid for fifteen minutes of internet on one of the computers near the departure gate and logged straight on to the Cage Warriors forum to see what was being said about my title loss. It was there that I read for the first time that, not only had I lost my belt, but I had also been suspended for six months for apparently refusing a drugs test. This seemed even more persecutory when I learnt another fighter on the card actually tested positive and only received a three-month suspension. My nightmare was complete.

It turned out that while I was rearranging the furniture and light fittings in my dressing room after the fight, the testers had arrived and Owen told them they'd need to come back in fifteen minutes when I'd calmed down. Instead, they simply packed their sample kits away and drove home. Naturally, we appealed and explained the course of events. We also questioned why, when they knew I was sat in a Canton hotel all day Sunday, they made no effort to track me down there either. Our appeal was successful and, apart from a token fourteen-day slap on the wrist, my name was cleared. Not that I really gave a shit. As Petz was awarded a UFC contract off the back of robbing me, I was feeling sorry for myself in Nottingham, eating junk food and hardly training. I can take an honest defeat on the chin, but this felt like being cheated.

I was still mired in my two-week sulk when the promoter Paul Hennessey called one Friday evening to say he needed a fighter for a Thai boxing match the following night. 'It will be more like a demon-stration-type affair against a local lad who has sold a few tickets,' he promised me. 'Call it a warm-up for your next MMA outing,' he said, and then offered me £300 if I'd get him out of a hole. *Fuck it*, I thought, *why not*.

When I arrived at the venue the next day, I found out that yet another promoter had been slightly economical with the truth. Rather than being an exhibition fight, I was the main event in a world title bout. I didn't get to see my opponent weigh in, but he was there to watch me step onto the scales and he was clearly a much bigger guy. I was out of shape at nearly 82kg as I'd just spent a fortnight eating whatever I wanted, lazing about the house, and generally not looking after myself. The fight, five three-minute rounds of full Thai boxing rules, was an all-out war. He had held the world title for a long time and was a very good fighter. I managed to knock him down twice, but he had me on the canvas three times and broke my nose. Given time to prepare I'm sure I could have won, but he earned the decision and kept his belt that night. Now, backstage having my deviated septum reset, I'm even angrier at life. But after icing my nose for a couple of days until the swelling went down, I headed back to the gym and began training. I was disappointed that my efforts were genuine and considerable, yet these promoters were not allowing for a fair playing field. Still, I enjoyed the rawness of the Thai boxing ring and, even though I was drastically unprepared and fighting on emotion alone, it reminded me why I loved competing. The blood, sweat and adrenalin were an addictive trio. A week later, my next match-up was confirmed.

It was yet another redemption mission. Having previously gained revenge over Doski and Gonzalez, I now had a chance to put things right with my old French foe David Baron in a four-man tournament in Holland. But even more important than personal vengeance, the winner of the tournament was guaranteed a place in the promised land of the PRIDE Fighting Championships in Japan. Although I loved the UFC, at this point in my career I probably felt more drawn to PRIDE. It just seemed to have better match-ups, more exciting fighters, and mercifully fewer wrestlers reducing proceedings to twenty minutes of attritional writhing on the canvas. The red- and yellow-card system, in which the referee could penalise fighters a portion of their purse for perceived lack of action, helped greatly in this respect. I also liked the structure of the bouts, with a long ten-minute opening round followed by two five-minute sessions, allowing twenty minutes in total. Later on, PRIDE Bushido arrived and simply pitched the best against the best without looking to protect an individual or build him up. I loved watching those events and knew my style would be perfect for it.

There was also the natural lure of Japan, and Asia in general, due to their historical appreciation of martial arts. The UFC was always more of a monster-truck ambience, a beer and nachos night with thousands of excitable fans chanting *knees!* and *punch him in the face!* But the traditional air of respect that is still prominent in Japanese life was present in PRIDE, with fans sitting and watching studiously, applauding appreciatively for good exchanges on the ground and recognising astute game-plans when they paid off. It always seemed to me like the Asian audience, more keenly aware of the beauty and intricacies of martial arts, held fighters in a higher regard.

The shows were all presented in a much more upmarket way as well. They had an opening ceremony with the beating of Japanese drums against the backdrop of sounds of swords being unsheathed and clashing, and blood splattering on a wall. Immense white curtains of cloth hung from the ceiling to divide the four quarters of the arena from one another with traditional images or Japanese calligraphy projected onto it. As many as 90,000 turned out to watch the limited number of events that took place each year and the fighters were presented like gladiators or demi-gods. It was a real martial arts fighting atmosphere. You felt like you could have been waiting for a contest at the Colosseum in ancient Rome. The UFC, with its American razzmatazz, was a place for sportsmen and entertainers, while PRIDE felt like the home of true warriors.

And over the years it boasted some of the best mixed martial artists on the planet. Guys like Wanderlei Silva, Rampage Jackson, Mirko Cro Cop and Fedor Emelianenko all graced PRIDE during their long and dominant reigns. Fedor in particular was special, for a long time the undisputed best heavyweight on the planet. Politics got in the way to ensure he never fought the elite of the UFC in his prime, but few doubted that the Russian would have beaten any man put in front of him. He was like a cyborg, his nondescript face never changing even as he unloaded full-power shots to finish a faltering opponent. The grainy training videos enhanced his myth, running bare-chested through forests in combat trousers and army boots. I remember watching Kevin 'The Monster' Randleman slam Fedor into the canvas head-first with a suplex that looked like it could have broken his neck. Seconds later, Randleman was tapping out. Emelianenko was that rarest combination, a naturally instinctive fighter and a supremely prepared mixed martial artist.

PRIDE had its home-grown superstars as well, with Kazushi Sakuraba perhaps the most famous of all. Sakuraba was an unassuming and not particularly athletic submission wrestler, but he was shrewd, confident and unpredictable and enjoyed great success as he racked up wins over MMA legends such as Vitor Belfort, Rampage Jackson, Kevin Randleman and Ken Shamrock. But it was his assault on the great Brazilian MMA dynasty, when Royler, Royce, Renzo and Ryan Gracie were all defeated in little over a year around the turn of the millennium, that Sakuraba cemented his status and earned the moniker The Gracie Hunter. The vast majority of the other Japanese fighters in PRIDE were nowhere near as successful as Sakuraba or the top foreign imports, but so long as they embodied the to-the-death spirit of a samurai warrior, they were guaranteed unlimited respect and admiration from the fans. It is something that resonates deeply within Japanese culture and I loved how even outmatched fighters received a lot of love if they fought with heart and determination until the end. It led to some brutal, but strangely beautiful, displays of combat.

In addition to the elite fights and fighters, PRIDE also had a freak-show element to it. Unlike the UFC, there was no upper limit in the heavyweight division and that opened the door to a host of weird and wonderful, freakishly large human beings. Emmanuel Yarbrough, a six-foot-eight, six hundred-pound, African-American sumo wrestler from New Jersey competed for a while. As did Giant Silva, the seven-foot-two ex-Brazilian basketball player. The ex-NFL player Bob Sapp was another fan favourite. When such monsters stepped into the ring it was more a comic-book battle than a genuine sporting contest. Japanese professional wrestlers arrived, a kind of extreme reincarnation of their WWE counterparts due to the notorious brutality and bullying of the Japanese wrestling schools they learnt their trade in. In one famous bout, Don Frye, a manlier version of Tom Selleck and a UFC hall-of-famer, and Yoshihiro Takayama beat each other's faces to tender pulp ice-hockey-fight-style in a show of almost comical, gung-ho brutality. PRIDE signed madmen as well, the type of fighter the UFC wasn't prepared to take a chance on. Charles 'Krazy Horse' Bennett was a good example. He could fight, but he couldn't be controlled or trusted. You might find him scaling the cage and sitting on top of the side midway through a contest. But the Japanese really got into characters like Krazy Horse. They could become obsessive in their following of a particular fighter and that ensured they created an unreal atmosphere to perform in. It was where I wanted to be.

In Holland I had to cut down to 160lbs to face Baron in a light-welterweight contest. The other two in the field were Cengiz 'The Mosquito' Dana and a local fighter named Joey van Wanrooij. Dana, still going strong today, was a 7–7 German lightweight and, although tough, he didn't really concern me. Van Wanrooij was a decent kickboxer but, having watched Paul Daley handle him well in a Cage Rage fight, I did not see him as a threat either. My thinking was, beat Baron and I'm going to Tokyo and, despite my still delicate septum, I was confident of doing just that.

The first sign that I was up against it came on weigh-in day when I was given faulty, or tampered-with, scales in the hotel to check my weight. I was bang on target in my room, and yet a taxi-ride later I was magically 2kg over. Cue running around for an hour in too many clothes to frantically sweat off the excess. As the away fighter, I got to the point where I would expect tricks like this. And I can deal with it. When I'm in fight mode it is no longer a sporting environment as far as I am concerned. We're in a fight, and a real fight is never truly fair. I give no quarter and sure as hell don't ask for one either. But it soon became clear that the local promoters had just one goal from this tournament and that was to send Joey van Wanrooij to PRIDE. As soon as I arrived at the venue I was told I was on in ten minutes. So much for chilling out in the dressing room and then getting a decent warm-up under my belt. I then started my ringwalk and 'Crazy' by Gnarls Barkley blasted out. I'm always precious about my entrance music and, coming from a hardcore, punk and metal background, the cheerful soul pop was never going to suit my mood in that moment. On top of that, there was absolutely zero atmosphere in the place, despite the best efforts of the cheesiest MC ever to grab hold of a mic. It was as if they'd dragged in a bunch of bewildered Dutch families off the street and told them they'd get a free dinner if they sat down and didn't leave until the action was over. Maybe as a result of all of the above, the fight never really got going. Baron probably won the first round, and I probably won the second. With it only being a two-round affair, they flipped a metaphorical coin and gave it to the Frenchman. It was all very anti-climactic and deeply unsatisfying. I watched then as Van Wanrooij had his nose broken by Dana but was gifted a decision. Baron then won the final so clearly that even the local scorers couldn't manufacture another Dutch win. The Frenchman went to PRIDE, where he fought once and was outclassed by Takanori Gomi.

It was frustrating for PRIDE to have sailed so close and then disappeared over the horizon. And there was always a fear that it might be a long time before they once again paid attention to what is going on in Europe. I worried that my one chance had passed me by. The fact that I was convinced I was superior to David Baron made it all even harder to accept. I knew I would have been a better fighter in PRIDE than he was and that a decision had been made based on the debatable credentials Baron had from winning a joke of a tournament in Holland, rather than on watching us all perform over the previous twelve months. But at the same time, this knowledge that I was a better mixed martial artist than a man who had just been given a spot in the second biggest MMA promotion on the planet reassured me. My frustration was a precursor to determination. I was very close. And when I got there, I'd be even more ready. I still spent a restless summer lost in thoughts of what might have been, but come September I was back in the cage.

This time it was a revenge mission of sorts for the other guy as I was matched with Matt Thorpe's coach, Danny Rushton. He was supposed to be a real veteran of no-rules combat, with stories of him bare-knuckle boxing in Russia always doing the rounds online. Enjoying a four-fight unbeaten streak, including impressive victories over Paul Jenkins and Lee Doski, Rushton was very confident. His team also did their best to spice things up and make it about vengeance for his student's loss in the Cage Warriors title fight. Rushton was regarded as being a massive welterweight and so my plan was to get as big as possible and then cut hard. I ate and ate and a few days out from the fight I was 18lbs over. On the day of the weigh-in alone, I cut 12lbs but I felt fine. I knew all high-level fighters were cutting, and as a member of the Northern Cartel Rushton certainly would have been, so I was comfortable doing the same.

In the end, Rushton only lasted a round of what was a pretty spiteful fight. Right from the off I caught him with hard strikes and solid inside and outside low kicks. One left hand cut him deep and forced referee

Goddard to call the doctor in to take a look inside the first thirty seconds. Allowed to continue, Rushton shot in and I grabbed a guillotine. He managed to pick me up and slam me onto the floor where we scrambled about until the ref again intervened when Rushton landed an illegal knee to my head on the ground. Back on our feet, I continued the punishment, targeting his blood-covered face. In the dying embers of the round I stalked him into a corner, dropped him with a jab, and landed a few more hard blows as I stood over him. I saw in his eyes he was struggling and wasn't surprised when he didn't come out for the second.

My next outing was a five-rounder, back down at 160lbs again. I knew PRIDE were keeping an eye on Europe for fresh talent and so I wanted to keep fighting known and respected guys. The Brazilian jiu-jitsu black belt Alexandre Izidro, whom I beat previously over ten minutes, fitted that bill. He was mistakenly convinced that he had done enough with his submission attempts to deserve the nod in our first tilt, so I was happy to defeat him again and end any lingering arguments. At this point he was the Cage Warriors lightweight champion, so meeting me at a weight class five pounds heavier was no problem. Representing Brazilian Top Team, I'm sure Izidro also had eyes on fighting in PRIDE alongside many of his teammates. I cut the weight professionally and relatively comfortably, despite the best efforts of my good friend Judo Jimmy Wallhead. After sitting and suffering in a sauna together, he left to weigh in and told me he'd soon be back for moral support until I hit the 160lb limit. *That's nice of him*, I thought, knowing that all a fighter wants to do after such a period of abstinence is get food and fluids into his system as quickly as possible. True to his word, Jim was soon back and sat down outside the glass door, right beside me as I lay wilting in the humid heat of a 90-degree sauna. I looked over to nod my thanks and there the bastard was with a huge bag of cookies and a cold drink in his hand. It was typical Jimmy and typical Rough House banter. There was never a bad time to mess with each other, and often during the week of a fight the psychological attacks would keep us sharp and offer some comic relief at the expense of a teammate. But the sight of someone enjoying those luxuries made the torture of losing the final few ounces a hundred times worse!

Hardy versus Izidro 2 was put on as the headline act of the first ever Enter the Rough House show, an event dreamt up by Cage Warriors and held in Nottingham due to the growing strength in depth of the Rough House team. It took place in the Harvey Haddon Sports Centre in the same hall in which I had frozen in my first taekwondo tournament as a six-year-old, and I warmed up in the same room in which I took my yellow belt grading at the age of eight. I felt at home, and walked to the cage wearing my Nottingham Panthers ice hockey jersey to emphasise Izidro was encroaching on my turf. I have been a huge fan of the Panthers for many years. Living next door to the arena, I attended all their home games and occasionally travelled for an away day. That was the one break I allowed myself from MMA during training camp. I treated watching other fights as homework, so it was nice to go to an ice hockey game and enjoy the sporting environment without being truly invested in it. Of course, like everyone in the arena, I loved the fights that broke out when a team's enforcer decided to seek retribution. Supporting a team, we all become so passionate about each player, especially when they are trading punches with the opposition on the ice. Those hockey fights are very real. They are heat-of-the-moment conflicts, the realisation of very genuine human emotions. What goes on in a ring or cage or Octagon is all manufactured to a certain extent, but on the ice someone snaps, it kicks off, and everyone watching reacts with an equally visceral outpouring of emotion.

It was a tough fight this time around as Izidro threw every submission he had in his arsenal at me. I was by now known in Europe for my stubbornness in resisting submissions, but I needed all the knowledge and skills I had picked up at my training camps in the US to keep this jiu-jitsu master at bay. At one point in the opening round he caught me in a guillotine so tight that I actually passed out for a couple of seconds. Luckily, the ref didn't spot it and when he moved to tighten it again, it somehow snapped me back into the land of the living. But I controlled the stand-up range and often had him either backing away or trapped up against the fence. At times he would create a scramble and test my takedown defence, but when he had some success I would look to reverse and ground-and-pound from guard, knowing that he would rather work from his back than attempt to trade on his feet. It was an even contest as it moved into the third round and he went for a tight footlock. Sensing the danger, I forced all my weight onto Izidro to prevent him securing my heel in the crook of his elbow and isolating my knee. With my weight on top of him I was able to land heavy punches, causing him to release my foot and push away to escape more damage. I chased and held my top position, this time pinning him against the fence as I unloaded. Seeing the Brazilian incapable of intelligently defending himself, the referee stepped in to save him and declared me the winner by technical knockout.

It was a great win for me and I was elated. I walked to the centre of the ring and knelt down to soak it all in. Then, from nowhere, I was being hauled to my feet by my dad of all people. I had no idea that he or anyone else from my family were in the arena that night. To be honest, I had always insisted they not come along to my fights. It would have just been extra pressure on my shoulders knowing they were close by and watching. But with this one being in Nottingham, they had snuck in and watched the action from the bar area through a small window overlooking the cage. As soon as I won, Dad went tearing down the stairs, bustled his way into the cage and was jumping around like a madman trying to lift me up in jubilation. I always knew how proud he was of me but it was a beautiful moment to see it up close in his eyes.

● ● ●

I began 2007 with a few Thai boxing matches to keep me ticking over and then received news that the Japanese promotion Cage Force wanted me to take part in an eight-man tournament in Tokyo, with the winner allegedly guaranteed an Ultimate Fighting Championship contract. By now, the UFC had won the battle for supremacy over its Asian rivals and installed itself as the globe's pre-eminent mixed martial arts powerhouse. Ever since Dana White made his brash $250,000 bet that the UFC's Chuck Liddell would beat the PRIDE superstar Wanderlei Silva and ended any chance of genuine, lasting collaboration between America and Japan, the two promotions were set on a collision course that could end well for only one of them. When Zuffa, the UFC's parent company, bought PRIDE in March of that year, any doubts about who would become the dominant force were dispelled. My heart had been set on PRIDE, but now my sights were firmly fixed on reaching the Octagon.

The first fight of the Cage Force series was scheduled for May, so I thought I had better squeeze in an MMA fight to shake all the Muay Thai out of my system. Enter the Rough House 2 had already been announced for April and Cage Warriors were happy to put me on the bill against Willy Ni from the Netherlands. Ni had lost only three of his eighteen contests and was considered to be very proficient on the ground, but when I looked down his record I realised that, although he had compiled an impressive run of victories, he hadn't beaten anyone of note. The truth is, I didn't regard Ni as any sort of threat to me and treated the bout as a warm-up for the real deal in Japan. Willy reaffirmed this mind-set when he asked for a photo together at the arena on the afternoon of the fight. He was just happy to be there and wanted to enjoy the thrill of starring in a big British show. He had brought his brother over with him to act as cornerman and, more importantly it seemed, film as much of the experience as possible. It all fed into what was a lazy and poor performance from me. For the first and only time in my professional career, I took no pleasure in hurting my opponent. I took him down in the first round and was landing some heavy shots when over his shoulder I saw his brother pressed against the cage recording everything with his video camera. It was bizarrely unsettling and I subconsciously pulled back and allowed him to survive the opening five minutes. But during the sixty-second interval I resolved to go out and end it early in the second. I realised I was just going through the motions, a little like that first taekwondo bout all those years ago when I failed to engage and ended up defeated on the floor. The last thing I was going to do was miss out on the Japanese tournament due to a moment of carelessness against Willy Ni. As soon as the second began, he shot under my wild head-kick and tried to charge me across the cage, but I manged to wrap his neck in the rush and secure a guillotine. I then paused to consider my options. My preference for beating an opponent into unconsciousness or submission rather than twisting their limbs or restricting their airway has been well documented, but at this moment I was no longer invested in the fight. I didn't feel like I could get anything else out of it and I didn't have the rage in my heart to cause Ni serious damage. So, standing with his head secure under my arm, I decided to finish the contest the cleanest and simplest way possible. I jumped guard, holding tightly onto his neck. From there, I pushed with my legs to elongate his body while at the same time wrenching my forearm up and into his throat to cut off the oxygen supply to his brain. He started tapping just as he fell asleep and, to this day, Willy Ni remains the only submission victory on my record.

One month later, I was in the Far East as one of eight fighters vying for a single spot in the UFC. There were four Japanese fighters, Yoshiyuki Yoshida, Hidetaka Monma, Daizo Ishige and Akira Kikuchi, and four overseas opponents flown in to be sacrificial lambs. In the first round of fights, Yoshida was drawn to face Matt Cain of Australia, Monma got Janne Tulirinta of Finland, Kikuchi drew Jared Rollins from the US and I was left with the tournament favourite, Ishige. Ishige was a very strong judo guy, had a 20–2 record in MMA, and was the current welterweight king of Pancrase, a promotion second only to PRIDE for prestige in Asia. As expected, everything was weighted in the locals' favour and it was no surprise when Cain, Tulirinta and Rollins all lost their bouts. I got flown in late for my own fight, arriving at 4pm on the Thursday after a twelve-hour flight. I was to weigh in just twenty hours later and still had 10lbs to cut. I immediately sourced a nearby sauna, but was refused entry on account of my tattoos. Tattoos are associated with the underworld in Japan and the average sauna in the country doesn't want that particular class of clientele on their premises. So I bought a roll of black bin bags instead, wrapped myself up nice and cosy, and set off for a hot and sticky run through a humid downtown Tokyo. I just about sweated the extra pounds off in time, but the effort drained me and I was probably only operating at 60 per cent when ordered to fight at 7pm the following evening. Despite that, I started off strong, dropping Ishige twice in the first round and cutting him badly. But by midway through the second, I was basically exhausted. I kept landing cleanly on him with everything I had, but he wouldn't drop. I practically used his head as a punchbag for the full fifteen minutes, striking him far more than any fighter should ever be struck, but was unable to summon the strength to knock him out and finish the fight. It was exactly like a recurring nightmare I often have in which I'm given multiple free shots at a rival but can't knock him out. That feeling of futility in the cage is my ultimate fear. But the beating was so one-sided that, even allowing for home field advantage, a unanimous decision in my favour was the only possible outcome.

It was only the next day I learnt that my punches did in fact knock him out. Unfortunately it wasn't until he was back in his changing room that he collapsed, however. Unconscious, he was rushed to hospital where they found substantial bruising on his brain. With the obvious communication barriers, I wasn't sure what was going on as I boarded a flight back to the UK but I was relieved to later hear he made a full recovery. I chatted to him about six months later and he appeared to bear no lasting damage, but his career as a fighter of any description was over. It was a worrying episode, but I remember thinking the promotion had brought the tragedy on themselves by trying to screw me over on the weight cut. Had I been afforded adequate time and facilities to lose the ten additional pounds, I would have been in peak condition in the cage and I would have knocked him out cleanly in the first round. I blamed whoever booked me that late flight for the punishment Ishige was forced to endure. Certainly, I saw no moral implications for me to ponder; Ishige chose to enter that cage and he deserved to be there fighting me. It was an organised and fair fight, not an outmatched street brawl, so I had no problem whatsoever with my actions, regardless of their consequences. The potential for tragedy is present in many sports and we as athletes must deal with that. Knowing what I know now about fighter safety, I might find it difficult to support an MMA event that is not as prepared to handle injuries as it should be, but I have little time for moral objections to two athletes participating in their chosen, legal profession. From a purely selfish point of view, I also flew home feeling I had just taken a huge stride forward in my career. I had made a big statement by beating the tournament favourite so convincingly but, more than that, I had beaten a Japanese fighter in Japan. Before that night I had lost every time I had left England, so it felt like a monkey off my back, a major obstacle overcome. It also ensured I couldn't wait to return for the semi-final.

That was Hidetaka Monma in September, so I had the whole summer to prepare specifically for the challenge he would pose. Monma was a huge man, a middleweight really who cut ridiculously hard to get down to 170lbs. He was well known for his excellent guard game and the ability to work submissions off his back, and was particularly fond of the rubber guard technique developed and perfected by Eddie Bravo. Bravo is a one-of-a-kind jiu-jitsu instructor in California. He learnt his trade under Jean Jacques Machado, who was in turn nurtured by the Gracie family, so his pedigree is unquestioned. A strong proponent of the benefits of marijuana, Bravo attributes smoking the plant to a lot of his creativity, including the development of the rubber guard and twister system. He teaches both out of his 10th Planet school in Los Angeles, counting top fighters like Tony Ferguson and Ben Saunders and the UFC commentator Joe Rogan among his alumni. I knew that if there was one way to get inside Monma's head before we fought it was to fly out and spend a few weeks with Eddie.

And so that is what I did. I travelled to California and spent just over a month on the mat, attempting to tie training partners up with my arms and legs as if I were an octopus dragging its dinner to a watery grave. The idea is to develop the flexibility and dexterity in your hips and legs to make them an extra pair of arms and hands to choke and submit with. My priority was actually to practise reverse engineering it in case Monma tried it when we met, so every day I grappled with Bravo's top students until I felt comfortable that I had the knowledge to free myself from any submission attempt that Monma locked on.

It turned out to be time well spent, for Monma's Plan A, B and C was to submit me from his back. He entered the cage with the mind-set that he was either going to submit me or lose. And, despite everything suggesting it would be the latter, he persisted with his doomed strategy until his bitter end. In the opening twenty seconds I rocked him with a right cross, then dropped him with a jab and he basically didn't get up, save for the one-minute respite between rounds. The fight consisted of me in his guard, comfortably defending ever weakening submission attempts, and then punishing him with massive punches and elbows. He was extremely slow getting to his feet at the end of the second and I sensed he didn't have much left. Five seconds into the third, he was on his back again, sent there by a right-left, right-left combination in which every blow landed clean. I jumped on top of him and split his brow with a vicious elbow, draining the last ounce of fight from his body. Immediately, there was blood everywhere and the sight of it sent him into a panic. I could see it in his eyes and his corner obviously did as well, for the white towel came over the fence seconds later. Save for an awkward post-fight interview in the cage, conducted via a particularly attractive Japanese translator, my work in Tokyo was done for another three months.

Waiting for me when I returned for the final in December was Yoshi-yuki Yoshida. Yoshida was a fourth dan black belt in judo and known as a hard striker and early finisher. Six of his previous seven victories had come by way of first round KO or TKO and I anticipated him coming out hard against me and putting everything into getting another early stoppage. My aim, therefore, was to see through the first safely and then rely on my superior conditioning to beat him up in the second and third. And after five minutes of rather scrappy, uneventful action, everything was going to plan. He pushed as expected, but I easily absorbed what he had. It was a fifty-fifty round but, being Japan, I imagine he was given the benefit of the doubt. The important thing was I knew he was now tired while I was fresh as a daisy and ready for a ten-minute war. When the ref ordered us to commence the second round, Yoshida approached fast and I aimed a low kick to the inside of his leg. Unfortunately, at that exact same moment he level changed, causing my foot to land on his thigh and then rise into his groin. It was clearly accidental, and his thigh bore the brunt of the kick, but I knew he'd been caught in a tender area and so I held my hands up in apology and moved to a neutral corner while he recovered. I've received similar blows in the cage on countless occasions and while you certainly feel a little winded and perhaps sick for a minute, the 300 seconds you are afforded to fully recuperate are more than enough. But as those seconds ticked away, Yoshida remained lying on the canvas in apparent agony. There, he was surrounded by an ever-growing gaggle of stony-faced medics and observers who looked like they were contemplating calling in a priest to administer the last rites. At one point he rolled over and attempted to stand up, but after a barked order from his corner, he gave up and lay back down. By now I was sure he was milking this for all it was worth, perhaps hoping he'd win the sympathy of the judges in case it went the distance. It wasn't a direct hit, and we wear protective cups anyway, so I knew he couldn't have been in as much pain as his anguished expression and prostrate form suggested.

Not long after the aborted mission to rise, the referee made a motion with his arms to suggest the fight had been called off. I was still standing in the neutral corner, with no idea what was happening. Unbelievably, a stretcher then appeared and a tearful Yoshida was delicately lifted on and carted away, presumably to collect his Oscar for best dramatic performance in an MMA arena. With everything being conducted in Japanese I didn't have a chance of understanding what was being said around me, but I was thinking that the absolute worst-case scenario was that the bout was declared a no contest and a rematch organised for as soon as Yoshida's balls recovered from their glancing blow. It was only when I saw the Cage Force welterweight belt disappear down the aisle after him in the hands of his coach that the penny dropped. I'd been disqualified. He'd been announced the champion. And, most importantly, he was the one going to the UFC, where he'd eventually win two and lose three before being cut from the roster.

Now I felt like the one who should be crying. I was absolutely livid and called my manager from the hotel that night to tell him I was on my way home and wanted to fight as soon as possible. The fifth Cage Warriors' Enter the Rough House instalment was taking place in Nottingham the following weekend and I had been planning to go to support my teammates and show off my shiny new belt. But after that travesty I now wanted to be there hurting someone and expelling the rage building inside me. I was desperate. 'Anyone with a winning record,' I told him.

It was short notice, but he managed to find me a sacrificial lamb in the form of Manuel Garcia. The Spaniard had won twelve of his eighteen MMA bouts but I watched a couple of videos of him, saw him tap out from punches, and knew he had neither the heart nor the strength of mind to live with me for fifteen minutes. In the end it only lasted 120 seconds, but I punished him for the duration. At the first sign of pressure he looked to clinch but I kneed him in the face and then sprawled on a poor takedown effort before he lay back and allowed me to secure half-guard top. When I caught him with a clean shot, I noticed him turn away and, sensing he was looking to tap out, I unloaded until the ref had to trail me off him. He deserved those extra two or three strikes because I have no respect for a fighter who taps out from punches like that unless they are seriously injured. The victory hardly lightened my mood, however, and I was a nightmare to be around for a few months. The UFC had been so close, only for a stray foot and a pair of over-sensitive testicles to ruin everything. Just like after the Petz robbery, I felt like I was doing everything right but the universe was conspiring against me. But after a while I stopped feeling sorry for myself and started looking ahead with a more positive attitude. I *had* been extremely close to the UFC, so there was no reason in the world why I couldn't get back there. What I didn't expect was to be given another bite of the cherry so quickly.

● ● ●

Cage Warriors called to offer me a fight with Chad Reiner in Florida at the end of March and the American was exactly the type of opponent I needed to face at that moment in time. Not only was he a respectable name in the MMA world and a decent test for any welterweight at my level, but he had also just fought twice in the UFC. When I sat at home and built the case in my head for why I should be signed to the UFC, the lack of a victory over a fighter with Octagon experience was one of the holes I needed to fill. I believed that with a win over an established name they could over-look me no more. A couple of weeks out from the fight, my belief was proved accurate. It was all hush-hush and totally off the record, but my manager had been told by an insider that if I beat Reiner I could expect a call from the UFC. I was absolutely buzzing. I trained like a demon and then we flew to Kissimmee for Cage Warriors USA: Battle Royale. It was a big expansion move by the British-based Cage Warriors and I was installed as the main event, ably abetted by my Rough House teammates Andre Winner and Jimmy Wallhead. A fourth guy, Greg Loughran from Northern Ireland, was also on the bill and after surviving with us for the week in our rented accommodation, he became an honorary member of the team.

On fight night, I was primed and ready in the dressing room as the time approached midnight. Jimmy was out in the arena in the middle of his fight, then Andre was up, and then me. My hands were wrapped, my mouth guard was in, I'd built up a sweat and couldn't wait to get out there. Jimmy's fight went the distance and he lost a unanimous decision, and sitting in the dressing room we could hear the roars and the applause and then the crowd dying down to near silence. The com-missioner entered and Andre stood up, expecting to be told to make his way to the cage. Instead, the gentleman announced that the show was over and we may as well start packing away our things.

'Hold on a minute,' I immediately countered. 'The show isn't over. It can't be, there are still two fights to go.'

'I'm afraid not, sir,' the commissioner replied gravely. 'The promoter only paid for insurance for the day of the event, and that policy unfortunately expired when the clock struck twelve midnight. We all need to get out of here now.'

I couldn't believe it. While Andre, the most laid-back man in the world just shrugged his shoulders and started getting changed, I sat grinding my teeth. I was all-consumed by the energy to fight. I had begun the physical and psychological process that can only end with a violent confrontation. In my early years on the MMA scene I had fought with too much rage and not enough control and over time I had learnt to redress that balance. But I still flicked some switches inside my head that could not simply be ignored. I had engaged the part of myself I reserved for combat and it is difficult to put that monster to bed without satisfaction. The next day I went on a pre-planned trip to the Disney theme park Typhoon Lagoon with my fiancée at the time, but I was still seething inside. Mickey fucking Mouse and his pals were walking around with inane grins on their faces while all I wanted was to have had my fight and my closure. Somehow I kept it together, but as soon as I got back to the UK I was on the phone to Cage Warriors demanding a solution. To their credit, they were apologetic and, more importantly, promised to rectify the situation as soon as possible. 'We'll try and get Reiner over here to England in the next couple of months,' they said before adding that my purse may suffer due to the budgetary requirements of flying Reiner and his team in from the US. 'I couldn't give a fuck about my purse,' I told them. 'Get him over here so I can knock him out!'

True to their word, Cage Warriors brought Reiner over five weeks later and we met in Nottingham on another Enter the Rough House card. Given the importance of the fight for me, I was pleased when it was announced as a five-rounder for the vacant CW welterweight title, the one that Petz had vacated but never returned when he signed his UFC contract. Chad came into MMA via wrestling and he was a good, tough, ground-and-pound fighter. It was no surprise then that he spent the first ten minutes of the fight attempting to take me down. He had some success early on, and locked a relatively tight guillotine around my neck for about thirty seconds, but he was mistaken in underestimating my takedown defence. I sprawled well to defend the majority of his shots and when he was successful, I coped comfortably on the deck and was soon back on my feet and in the range in which I knew I would dominate. My effective takedown defence started to wear him out and, beginning with the very first exchange of the second round, I was soon landing good, hurtful shots with fist and elbow. At the very end of the round I dropped him with a thudding knee into his face and as I marched back to my corner with a spring in my step, I looked back and saw a rather forlorn Chad Reiner on his knees and breathing heavily. To emphasise the difference between our current physical conditions, I bounced hyperactively on the spot as we waited for Marc Goddard to clap us back into battle.

I knew Reiner was more or less done and all I needed was one clear opportunity to knock him senseless.

I never gamble because fighting provides all the adrenalin rushes I need without having to chase more by throwing my hard-earned cash away. My dad doesn't either, but once a year he puts a 50p bet on a horse in the Grand National for each of us in the family. My luck was in that April at Aintree and Dad's low-stakes punt won me a crisp five pound note. I decided to keep riding that luck and slipped it into my wraps as they were going around my wrists and hands in the dressing room. My signature punch was always the left hook and I originally thought I would put the fiver in the left wraps. But having spent part of training camp working on slipping the jab and landing a big overhand right counter, I concealed the note in my right hand and forgot about it. Forgot about it, that is, until I forced a faltering Reiner up against the side of the cage with a double jab midway through the third. From there he held out a lazy left and, bang, over the top of it I detonated a right on his jaw and he crumpled. It was over there and then but just to make sure I crouched and swung with both clenched fists until I felt the referee's intervention.

Elation. Just elation. I roared in delight and then Dad came barging into the cage, grabbed me in a bear hug and started bouncing. I'd done it. I had reached the Promised Land. I was in the UFC.

5

THE RISE

Joe Silva couldn't believe his ears. 'What the hell do you mean, you're fighting next week?' he shouted down the phone. 'I have your goddamn UFC contract sitting right here in front of me.'

'I'm sorry, Joe,' I told the UFC matchmaker supreme, 'but I made a promise to the promoter before the offer came through, and he's already announced that I'm fighting.'

'Well, if you lose this fight you realise the UFC contract is off the table, don't you?'

'I know, Joe. But listen, if I can't beat this guy, I don't deserve to be in the UFC.'

● ● ●

This guy was Daniel Weichel, a talented German fighter well known for his grappling prowess. The Ultimate Force promoter had asked me to appear on his show in Doncaster before the whispers from the UFC became a concrete agreement, and I said yes. And despite how much certain promoters and managers had messed me around in the past, I'm a man of my word, UFC career in the balance or not. I told him I would fight for him, but only if he could secure decent opposition. My days of going through the motions or taking bouts to keep the motor running were over. I needed a genuine challenge, someone I could get easily motivated for, in the opposite corner of the cage now. Weichel fit the bill as he was undoubtedly a test. But he was naturally smaller and lighter than me and I didn't consider him to be of UFC standard so I was comfortable and confident accepting the bout.

The Ultimate Force cage is different to most in that where the mat meets the fence, it has a triangular wedge of padding running along the joint. It was presumably to prevent a fighter ever getting a foot caught between mat and fence and twisting an ankle, but in a well-constructed MMA cage such additional precaution is largely unnecessary. It seems a small and insignificant detail in the wider scheme of the dangers present in an MMA fight, but as soon as I stepped into the cage on the Saturday night, it caught my eye. It was probably still preying subconsciously on my mind when at the instruction to fight, Weichel charged across the canvas, smashed me up against the side, and tried to drag me down to the only range in which he had a chance of causing an upset. Instinctively, I attempted to press my foot into the corner to fix the length of my leg tight against the fence and prevent him getting his arms around my thighs and meeting his hands together. Once those hands are joined it is very difficult to separate them and you are left with few options against the takedown. But with that extra padding, it proved impossible to close the gap between the fence and my leg, and Weichel exploited this unavoidable defect in my defence and took me down. For most of the remainder of the first round, Weichel was all over me, taking my back, squeezing my neck, and generally probing aggressively for any sniff of a submission. I managed not to give him any but the entire five minutes was spent in frantic defence, struggling to get to my feet to beat the fight out of him, and he clearly won the round.

Back in the corner a panic gripped me. That extra padding had caused me more problems than the majority of my previous opponents combined and I couldn't pull my mind away from it. Baron had denied me a PRIDE contract. The disqualification fiasco in Japan had cost me my first crack at the UFC. And now a few damn metres of Toblerone-shaped padding were threatening to slam the Octagon door closed again without me having had the chance to step inside. I hadn't seen it yet, but I knew that my UFC contract was sitting in a brown envelope on the table at cageside with my manager. He hadn't let it out of his sight since it arrived from the US but we decided not to sign it until Weichel was beaten. I knew my parents were seated at that table too, so proud that I'd finally done it. Standing in my corner, I had visions of the contract being ripped up in front of my face. And all because I took a fight that I didn't really need to take. *I shouldn't even be in this cage*, I started thinking, *and I'm going to screw this whole thing up again*.

Jimmy was cornering me that night and I'll never forget the look on his face as he peered through the fence to offer me water and instructions. He seemed almost stupefied by a combination of shock and bewilderment, but thankfully he found the exact words I needed to hear to snap out of the paralysis of dread that briefly gripped me. 'What the fuck are you doing!?' Jim roared. 'Fight him for fuck's sake!'

And fight him I did. I decided I wouldn't bother wasting any more energy trying to get up if he took me down for I was confident that I could match him in any range, including on the ground. And as the absolute last thing this guy was going to do was stand and trade with me, we found ourselves on the canvas early in the second with me in half-guard bottom and Weichel looking to attack my neck. I was able to control the ankle of his free leg and tie his other leg up with a lock-down, a position that I had worked extensively with Eddie Bravo and the 10th Planet crew in Hollywood. From here I was able to use a sweep known as Old School to roll him onto his back and take half-guard top. Now I could shift the momentum of the fight in my favour. Rolling his wrists, I dropped elbows like anchors and forced him to cover his head in fear. Any respite this move provided was short-lived, however, as I immediately slammed the point of my elbow into his solar plexus, knocking the air out of his lungs. His arms involuntarily dropped to hug his ribcage and left his head slightly exposed. Switching straight back to a head attack, I brought my elbow down between his hands and cracked him right on the side of the skull. He turned away and covered his face, clearly hurt, if not partially separated from his consciousness. Seeing the effect, and knowing the inevitable barrage of successive elbows that would follow, the referee stepped in and waved the fight off. Cue my manager striding into the cage with the contract in his hand and a grin as wide as the River Trent across his face. And cue me promising everyone I wouldn't lay another glove on anyone in anger until I was inside the famed UFC Octagon.

● ● ●

I knew I was ready for the Ultimate Fighting Championship. In fact, I believed I had been ready for at least eighteen months and had begun to get frustrated when I saw other guys around me were getting the nod before I did, guys I knew I was superior to. But now I can look back and see that perhaps the UFC had a bigger plan in mind for me. Rather than simply adding me to a bill due to the need for a sprinkle of British talent to assist with marketing and ticket sales, they allowed me to develop, made sure I was truly ready, and then gave me my chance. This had been my goal for the past couple of years, but, now I had actually made it, I immediately revised my target. Just reaching the UFC was never going to satisfy me. I didn't want to be one of those myriad fighters who get there, lose once or twice, and then disappear onto the minor circuits for the rest of their careers, never to be spoken of in UFC circles again. In my mind, that fate is even worse than being the guy who never got there but is always told he should have. So now my focus was set on becoming a contender at the top of my division.

My first assignment was a pretty tough one for a debutant. I got matched with the veteran Japanese campaigner Akihiro Gono in the opening contest of the main card at UFC 89 in Birmingham, England.

Bisping versus Chris Leben was the headliner and big names such as Keith Jardine, Chris Lytle and Marcus Davis also crossed the Atlantic to be a part of the seventh UFC event to take place in the UK. Gono was a veteran of almost fifty professional MMA bouts and, having watched plenty of him when he was competing in PRIDE, I was fully aware that he was an awkward and crafty opponent for any welterweight on the planet. Having only lost three of his previous thirty fights, he was also full of confidence and that showed in his typically extravagant entrance to the cage. Sporting wigs and comedy sunglasses, he and two of his team paused halfway to the Octagon to break into a well-rehearsed dance routine that even incorporated one of the burly minders who guarantee their safe passage. Gono clearly had no worries about fighting such a long way from home and was determined to bring with him the entertainment element of Japanese combat sports.

Waiting backstage, I surprisingly had no nerves either. In fact, I actually started to feel unnerved by my lack of nerves ahead of the biggest fight of my life. I knew Gono would be tough and tricky, but I felt at ease as I made my own entrance to the Octagon. This was the first fight in which I used 'England Belongs to Me' by Cock Sparrer as my music. It was a deliberate statement to all of the fighters coming over to my home country looking for a victory to add to their record, particularly those in or around my weight class. I wanted them to know that I was here now and all the pretenders to the throne need to quieten down. I felt that I had already established myself as the best welterweight in the country by a distance. There was always chat about who was number one and who was number two between Paul Daley and I, but I excluded Paul from my thinking because as a teammate and a brother, we would never fight one another. But as far as the rest of the domestic competition was concerned, England belonged to me now.

I started the fight well, aggressive and on the front foot. I caught him with a couple of solid hooks and a couple more stinging jabs. I kicked him in the chest and knocked him back-pedalling towards the fence. At one point he secured double underhooks, but I shook him off immediately. I felt bigger and stronger than him and wanted to bully him around the Octagon. He finally managed to take me down in the second, but I exploited his moment of rest in a front headlock position and was able to sit out, scrambling back to my feet within a few seconds. But he was as wily and inscrutable as promised and within his unorthodox attack he found the means to have some success. He began to land wild-looking left-hand leads, but never with the knuckles and force of his arm and shoulder behind him. Basically, he was bitch-slapping me every time my right sank low enough to allow it. With one such counter left he caught me with the seam of his glove and split my skin, the first and only time I've been cut in an MMA bout. The third was a messy affair in which I was ticked off for an inside kick reaching his nether regions, and Gono received a much more severe warning for landing two illegal knees to my head while I was on all fours. He got me down a couple more times but could do absolutely nothing with me while on the ground. On our feet I continued to boss the action and landed heavily throughout, drawing blood and swelling his right eye almost shut by the end. As we waited for Bruce Buffer to make the announcement, I was sure I had won but I felt more frustration than satisfaction. Gono was a big Roy Jones Jr. fan and he revelled in making an opponent miss with his loose style and elusive head movement. Unlike Jones Jr. in his prime, however, Gono often forgot that the real challenge was to make someone miss and then punish them as well. He was more a pure spoiler, literally running away from me at times. Part of my job was to pin him down, but for my UFC debut I would have much preferred someone who really wanted to fight. When Buffer announced me as the winner by split decision, I felt relieved more than anything. Relief that I had cleared the first hurdle and was now guaranteed at least two or three more shots to really show the world what I was capable of.

I expected a bit of acclaim from the MMA world for the victory, but the reaction from many fans outside the UK was sadly a little more cynical. This was in a large part down to the view that local fighters were always given the benefit of the doubt on British soil, an opinion many people formed after Bisping was awarded a controversial decision over Matt Hamill in their grudge match at UFC 75 in London. Similar to the reputation Germany has within boxing circles, it was joked that in the UK you needed to knock a Brit out just to secure a draw. I beat Gono fair and square, but it was easy for the ill-informed to dismiss it as just another home decision for an English fighter in England. Even if, just as was the case in Bisping versus Hamill, the one British judge on duty actually scored against the guy with a British passport.

It was a bit of a shame, but a chat with Marshall Zelaznik, who was then running the UFC's European office, let me know that the people who really understood, and really counted as far as my career was concerned, were suitably impressed. He shook my hand, thanked me for both the performance in the fight and all the effort I had put in to media duties beforehand, and slipped me an envelope with a cheque for more than my total fight purse had amounted to. I was on a sliding pay scale for my first four fights, so long as I kept winning. I was to receive $3,000 for the fight with Gono and another $3,000 for winning it. Then $5,000 plus $5,000, $7,000 plus $7,000, and $9,000 plus $9,000 before the deal was up for renegotiation. It wasn't life-changing money, particularly when you consider I had to cover all my own training expenses out of that, so any additional bonus cheques made a world of difference. It was at that moment that I realised I truly belonged in the UFC and that I could do very well here by just being myself. I saw that these were people I could work with. Right from the off, there was a feeling that I'd be looked after so long as I performed and deserved it. Excel at your job and reap the benefits: it is an approach to business that suits me down to the ground. I also realised that I was marketable, perhaps more so than the majority of non-Americans in the organisation. A lot of the other Brits that had made it were either naturally quiet characters, or communicated in a way that the US audience struggled to understand, often to the extent that they required subtitles in UFC programming! I sensed the UFC felt I had a little bit more to offer, and having thrown me in at the deep end against Gono and watched me chase the finish against a tough veteran, they knew that I had the potential to be a name in the sport and a useful person to help recruit new fans in Europe.

● ● ●

The next call I received from Joe Silva informed me I was to face Rory Markham at UFC 95 in London. Markham was exactly the type of opponent I wanted, the antithesis of the sneaky and cautious Gono. He was a big, powerful athlete with good striking skills, wrestling and takedown defence, but his greatest attributes were his size for the weight and his heavy hands. To give an idea of his true size, he weighed in 25lbs over the welterweight limit four days before the weigh-in for our bout, and fought Nick Diaz at a 177lb catchweight in his next outing. He was also durable, although he had never gone the distance. His record was 16–4 and he had a kill-or-be-killed attitude to the Octagon. I hadn't been shy in calling for an in-your-face brawler, and the UFC duly obliged. They also bumped us up to the co-main event, alongside Diego Sanchez versus Joe Stevenson. MMA lights as bright as Chael Sonnen, Paulo Thiago and Josh Koscheck were supporting. Being just my second UFC bout, this was another huge confidence-builder for me to know the organisation had such faith in my ability and marketability.

I had watched Markham fight Brodie Farber from cageside in Vegas the previous July and after ninety seconds I wasn't overly impressed. *This guy isn't as slick as I had imagined*, I was thinking, as Farber backed him up and landed clean time and time again. Then Rory suddenly landed a head-kick and turned away before Farber had hit the deck, already certain that he was unconscious. That definitely caught my attention. It shouldn't have been a surprise really for Markham's skills were honed in Pat Miletich's gym. Miletich was himself a former UFC champion and he managed to ingrain that winning mentality into his stable of fighters, eleven of whom became world champions themselves. Among their number sit the likes of Matt Hughes, Jens Pulver, Tim Sylvia and Robbie Lawler, so this was the environment Markham came from. He would be my first match-up with a top-level, well-rounded American fighter who was prepared for every range of MMA.

I knew Rory would be fragile at the weigh-in after his significant fight-week cut and that this was my opportunity to rattle his cage and whip up a bit more interest in our fight. Backstage in the West End theatre in which the weigh-in was taking place, I saw him with his head hanging in a delicate-looking state. *Perfect*, I thought. He weighed-in first and when it was my turn and he was standing by the side of the stage I stepped onto the scales without taking my eyes off him. I just kept staring and staring, while he looked anywhere else that meant he didn't have to make eye contact. As soon as I stepped off the scales, I marched right up to him and pushed my forehead against his. Immediately, I felt the alarm shoot through his body like an electric shock. He dug his heels in to prevent me bullying him backwards, but he was definitely struggling. The fans, unanimously behind me of course, loved it and went wild. Every one of them left the theatre knowing that ours would be the war they all hoped to see on Saturday night.

And it was, while it lasted. He stormed out looking to decapitate me. After that severe weight cut, he probably knew he didn't have three hard rounds in the tank and sought to end it early. I do enjoy a scrap, and I am sometimes the one to go looking for it, but what I really love more than anything is slick counter-punching. Catching someone cleanly as they move in to knock you out is the most beautiful thing you can do in an Octagon or ring as far as I am concerned. That is the point where fighting can meet art. So I moved in and out of range, utilising my superior footwork. I've always had good feet in a fight, cultivated from years of taekwondo and thousands of rounds with elite-level boxers combined with a natural spring in my step and heightened ply-ometric ability. It was easy for me to glide and bounce over the canvas, always a step or two ahead of someone heavy-footed like Markham, frustrating him into an ill-disciplined rage all the while. But when the chance presented itself, I pounced. I caught him flush on the nose and saw his leg stiffen. He was staggered and, as his nose dripped blood and bothered him, he chased towards me recklessly. Studying his fights during camp, I knew he tended to bowl his right hand over the top, putting all his weight onto his leading leg and committing his entire body to the strike. He did this because he was so confident in his own wrestling ability that he had little fear of his opponent countering by shooting for his legs and taking him down. So I decided to counter in a different way and threw my own right hand as he launched his. We both missed, but I had kept my balance and was set to follow up with my trademark left hook on his unguarded temple. It landed clean and he dropped like a dead, lead weight. He was effectively unconscious, but his head made an involuntary jump to get up so I was required to hit him again on the deck. At that precise moment, in the milliseconds it takes between thought and action, I remembered some words Ricardo Liborio once spoke to me when I was in camp with American Top Team. 'Take a breath,' he told me. 'When you've caught someone and hurt them, don't just go charging in for the kill wildly. Take a breath, focus on the exact point on his body you want to strike, and then finish it cleanly with one decisive blow.' I looked down at Markham, focused on his chin, and detonated a right hand on it as the referee began his swoop to save the American fighter from serious damage. Five minutes later, he was still confused as to where he was and what had happened. The roar from the English crowd was special. I beat my chest and then ran across the Octagon and scaled the side of the cage the better to take it all in. Almost 15,000 people were there to watch me fight. I looked across to the other side and found my family brandishing a Cross of St George flag with Dan 'The Outlaw' Hardy on it and generally going crazy with joy. I love it that the cameras picked them up too and that footage appears regularly in any promo or highlight reel of my career.

● ● ●

I was flying now and couldn't wait for my next fight. Life in the UFC was proving to be everything I had hoped for. After the years of grinding in the bush leagues, it was like I was now operating in a totally different dimension. I'd been trundling along in a second-hand Ford Escort and was suddenly upgraded to a top-of-the-range Mercedes Benz. The UFC is a polished machine and it is all the little touches that make it such a unique and special experience for a fighter on their roster. Backstage pre-fight there is a level of comfort and professionalism unheard of in the British domestic MMA scene. Officials are everywhere keeping an eye on things, where before I had been used to seeing guys doing a line of cocaine off the dressing room table before striding to the cage. The principal characters like Joe Rogan, Dana White, Burt Watson,

Bruce Buffer and Stitch Duran then add a sprinkle of stardust over proceedings.

I'd got to know Joe while training alongside him at the 10th Planet in California, but it was still slightly surreal to have him put his hand on my shoulder and conduct the post-fight interviews. Whenever I visualised my career in the UFC as I was coming through the ranks in Europe, Joe's distinctive voice was always the narrator. Like Rogan, Dana has become synonymous with the UFC during his long reign as president and figurehead of the organisation. I used to love the talks he gave after we had successfully weighed in, where he'd call just the fighters alone together into a room and sit us down for a five- or ten-minute motivational speech. The theme or focus of his words varied, but Dana knows how to talk to fighters. Whatever he said, he knew how to put it in a way that made you determined to deliver. Sometimes he'd say that a lot of people are talking shit about this card and it is up to us to go out there and prove them wrong. He reminded us of our responsibility to represent the sport well, give the fans what they want, and show how good we are at mixed martial arts. But Dana also understands what we all put into our professions and the sacrifices we make. He knows it is a hard and lonely road at times, so one of his specialities is fostering a team environment within the most individualistic of sports. MMA was still really in its infancy as a mainstream sport and was accustomed to being attacked from all sides almost every day, so it was nice to feel like a unit at times, like we are all in this together. It was nice to lean on each other and feed off each other for ten minutes the day before war. I'd never played team sports to any great standard so I missed that spirit. I often imagined it was like Brian Clough talking to the Nottingham Forest team before the European Cup final. It reminded me of Billy Bob Thornton and his 'being perfect' speech in *Friday Night Lights* (often one of my fight-day movies) too. Dana would finish by telling us the hard work was all done, that we were to go and drink and eat and rest and be ready tomorrow. That was what every one of us was there for so his words fed into the feel-good vibe we all have at the conclusion of the cutting process, the biggest drag of most fighters' preparations. Everyone walks out of that talk with Dana with a lot of positive energy, a lot of fist bumps and mutual good lucks.

I guess I just felt very well looked-after as a fighter after years of dealing with dodgy operators and low-budget promotions such as Xtreme Brawl, Fight Club, UK Storm and Fight Fest. One of Dana's other concluding remarks was always to check that we had our contact lists and knew who to call with any issues. The most important number on that list was always that of Burt Watson. He was the glue that held everything together behind the scenes. Burt, a guy in his sixties with a lifetime in professional boxing behind him and more soul and swagger than James Brown, was basically an event manager. He loved everyone, and everyone loved him back. He had a couple of famous catchphrases that made all the fighters smile. 'If it's in here or here' – pointing to your head and your heart – 'then I want it in here' – now pointing to his own ear. 'If you're sick, or worried or whatever,' he'd continue, 'you have my number and I'll answer at any time of any day you call.' Burt kept an eye on all of us and made life as easy as he possibly could. His second catchphrase was the trigger to fight. 'We're rolling!' his roar echoed down the corridor ahead of him as he proceeded towards your dressing room when it was time to walk to the Octagon. Nothing could get me buzzing like the sound of those words from Burt. I have goosepimples now just thinking about it.

It was also nice to have a guy like Stitch Duran, perhaps the most famous cutman in the world, wrap my hands and no one ever did it as well as Stitch. Then it was into the famed and trademarked Octagon, where the one-and-only Bruce Buffer stood ready to announce me to the crowd in his own unique and exhilarating fashion. I developed a special relationship with Bruce, who has been introducing fighters since he first appeared at UFC 10. Every budding MMA fighter dreams of the day that Bruce announces them and I was no different, even commencing my visualisation training with his distinct voice roaring out my name. When I stood in my corner of the Octagon for the first time and Bruce turned to face me, my adrenalin began pumping even faster. As the words came out of his mouth I mimed along, getting more and more fired up. It became a tradition that the fans would expect before my fights and would energise them just as much. Bruce would even come up to me before the event started, offering a fist bump and saying, 'Let's give them a show tonight.' I would adapt it slightly depending on the location of the fight, stamping my foot on the canvas when I was on home soil, or growling at the camera with a mouth-guard that read 'England' across it in big letters. It was a little bit of extra theatre that I absolutely adored.

Noticing how these strong personalities had carved out their niches one way or another, it soon became clear that, as a fighter, the onus was very much on me to do the same. Very few UFC competitors will reach superstar status on raw talent inside the Octagon alone. We are in the entertainment business, albeit a particularly real, bloody and violent strand of it, and so how you carry yourself in front of the cameras or microphones when the gloves are off can be just as important as when you are kicking someone in the head or choking the consciousness out of them on the canvas. The marketing minds have an expectation that you create and work on a particular image of yourself that you wish to project and, as I enjoy the theatrical aspect to the UFC, I was only too happy to fully embrace that side of the game.

There was nothing contrived about my Outlaw persona, it was effectively just Dan Hardy with the volume turned up a few notches. As a teen, you'll remember, I was sporting long hair, black nail varnish, coloured contact lenses and fronting a Rage Against the Machine cover band, so it was in my nature to put on somewhat of a show. The bandana came first, an obvious accessory for any self-respecting outlaw, and when I had my cousin Chloe stitch a red-and-black one together for the second Izidro fight, they became my colours. The Mohawk then appeared and got dyed red so everything was co-ordinated. I never thought of any of it as a deliberate marketing gimmick, but when someone once said to me, 'Hey, you're the guy with the red hair,' it hit home how these details can contribute to a fighter first becoming a recognisable face and maybe even a household name. I remember thinking it would be amazing to look out into the crowd and see thousands of my fans wearing bandanas and the odd red-and-black Mohawk from the hard-core followers. Then I started wearing different contact lenses, sometimes coloured, sometimes animal eyes, to weigh-ins just to mess with my opponent. The eyes being the window to the soul is a rather tired cliché, but I knew I wanted to look deep into my enemy's pupils and so I guessed he wanted to do just the same to me. If a pair of wolf eyes prevented him doing this and in any way frustrated him, then it was all worth it. Often I'd wear a pair of sunglasses and only reveal the contacts when we were head to head, to maximise any shock value. By the time I was in the UFC, I'd added fang-like gumshields so it was more obvious when I was smiling during the fight, which was often. The fans loved the whole performance and I fed off the buzz all these little details created. I thrived on the energy, good or bad, that I produced. It was all fuel for me. They were all little moves in the larger psychological warfare that takes place before every big fight, a battle that begins the moment the contract is signed.

Trash-talking is probably the single most important element of any psychological warfare campaign, and so that too increasingly became a huge part of my image. I had dabbled in it earlier in my career against the likes of Berik and Thorpe, but most of the time before I signed with the UFC I had no contact with my opposition until the weigh-in, which made it difficult to mount any preliminary offensive. Then with Gono there was a language barrier, and Markham was basically invisible until fight week, so it wasn't until my third UFC fight against Marcus Davis that I really went to town and got a reputation for it. Again, it all came very naturally to me. I come from a culture in which pseudo-bullying between genuine friends is the norm. I'd grown up watching my dad mercilessly rip the piss out of his teammates and work colleagues, and the MMA gym environment, especially within Team Rough House, took it to another level altogether. Rough House was extreme and borderline nasty at times. Jokes like 'Your new baby looks a lot like me' would get taken to the limit, sometimes even the wives and girlfriends playing along. Guys were savaged for the slightest slip-up and the abuse would continue for weeks. That was our way of engendering a team spirit and forging bonds and it worked — we were soon more like brothers than mere teammates. But it is a totally different atmosphere within the big US MMA teams. I remember when I was first there and a fighter came up to me after training and said, 'Dude, you were awesome today', or 'That was amazing when you did this move', I turned on them like, 'Are you fucking with me?' From my first day of taekwondo with Mick, throughout every martial arts session I ever had in the UK, nobody had ever spoken to me like that, trainer or peer. I couldn't believe this was genuine praise and so presumed it was passive-aggressive sarcasm against the new guy. Of course it was the opposite. They really were totally innocent and bona fide compliments. It took me a long while to get used to that positive-attitude dynamic that dominates US gyms and even when I did, I still tried to introduce the barbed British banter at every opportunity. I occasionally got a taste of my own medicine, but it was always pretty tame compared to a session with the Rough House boys.

I started on Marcus 'The Irish Hand Grenade' Davis early, the post-fight press conference after knocking out Markham in fact. When asked who I fancied taking on next, I called the Irish-American out. I said he'd been coming over to the UK and Ireland recently, winning a few fights, building a little fan base for himself and calling this place home. 'But he's not English and he's not Irish,' I continued, 'and he doesn't belong here. This is my home.' It was all very calculated. First of all, Davis was a veteran with a winning record and had no reason whatsoever to get involved with someone as young and dangerous as me. I needed to provoke him into a fight, in other words. Secondly, I knew how passionate about his Irish heritage he was and so the Plastic Paddy attack was the most obvious and easiest approach to take. He took the bait almost immediately and so I kept reeling him in. A friend unearthed a bare-chested photo of him looking sultry in a kilt for some modelling shoot and it was just too good to ignore. I posted it onto the Cage Warriors forum and simply said I was sure some people on here can have some fun with this. Within hours, Davis had been photoshopped into all sorts of compromising situations, many involving leprechauns and homoerotic situations. It was a double whammy for Marcus for, as a traditional man's man, he was never going to handle very realistic-looking mock-ups of his image adorning the cover of *Gay Times* magazine particularly well. When I described his website as looking like a bomb had exploded in a St Patrick's Day gift shop, I think I pushed him over the edge.

Davis was a boxer before he switched to MMA and was very proud of his 17–1–2 professional boxing record. So to keep messing with his head, I decided to combine my training at Eddie Bravo's 10th Planet jiu-jitsu school with daily sessions in Freddie Roach's Wild Card gym, in the middle of West Hollywood. Hungry to have the most renowned pro boxing trainer in the world critique my style, I immersed myself in the sweet science for a full month. The gym was always absolutely rammed with fighters, except of course when Manny Pacquiao turned up and everyone had to clear out so the Filipino legend could have the place to himself. I sparred on Tuesdays and Thursdays with whoever was available and I remember picking up invaluable pointers from Michael Moorer, the ex-heavyweight champion of the world, in particular. Freddie didn't know what I was all about in the beginning as I just blended in with the crowd, but when the cameras started showing up to film me, he realised I was a UFC fighter and took me aside for one-on-one sessions. It was fantastic to be in the ring on the pads with him, or to have a quiet moment just to pick his brain about something. I remember one day he spent a bit of time showing me tricks for hitting with the elbow, a dark art in boxing but totally permissible in my world. He helped me with distance control, throwing a punch, leaving the arm out there a split second longer than usual, and then stepping through with the elbow. It was all good because it was a totally different technique to the Thai boxing elbows I was accustomed to throwing.

I loved every minute I spent in the Wild Card, and I certainly added to my game while there, but there is a limit to how much a pure boxing coach can help an MMA fighter. Many armchair fans, especially among the boxing fraternity it always seems to me, are apparently desperate to compare and contrast boxing with MMA at every opportunity, but they are two totally distinct disciplines under the overall combat sports umbrella. The differences are both too numerous and too glaringly obvious to spend time discussing here, but body position before and after throwing a punch is one quick example of where I always have to tell boxing trainers that I just can't do what they suggest in the

Octagon. Boxers stand more side-on in order to dart in and out of range easier and to allow their backhand punches to benefit from a full rotation of the shoulders when it lands. But I can't do that in an MMA fight for it will leave my front leg horribly exposed to kicks and will also make it easier for my opponent to shoot and take me down. What I always have to do is put advice or new skills through an MMA filter to see what, if anything, can be utilised in the Octagon. Much like the reality filter through which I began putting all traditional martial arts when I reached my sceptical teens. It was a useful perspective to have cultivated from a young age, particularly in the early days when coaches in Europe simply didn't know what an MMA fight entailed as they had zero experience in the sport. I wasn't even certain what I was preparing for at times, so how could a boxing, judo or wrestling expert be expected to know? I remember at a seminar working with an old Bulgarian wrestling coach who was affiliated with the British Olympic team and he chastised me for warming up by shadow boxing in front of a mirror. In Muay Thai sessions I had to explain that I couldn't really afford to stay on my back leg with high hands and a light front leg poised to kick out. Even traditional jiu-jitsu, with the likes of its collar chokes or throws, was not always relevant in an MMA context. I employed a constant filtration process to my learning, and plenty of hours and days of work were immediately discarded, but I always enjoyed the journey. The constant questioning and testing was necessary and I continue doing it today, for it allows me to see everything from a very analytical standpoint. Even within skill-sets that are undoubtedly applicable to an MMA fight, it is important to establish whether they are right for you.

Body shape and size, for example, must come into the equation. After all, what works for Jon Jones and his 84.5-inch reach may not be ideal for a fighter with a normal-sized wingspan.

Like Bruce Lee said, 'absorb what is useful, reject what is useless'. He did the same thing learning ancient techniques, and, by adopting his thought process and shedding low-percentage and non-realistic techniques, I like to think I am continuing that approach in the modern day.

● ● ●

Ten weeks out from the fight, I flew back to the UK. As we were fighting in Germany, the UFC wanted me to spend a week touring military bases in the country to meet the US troops, help publicise the event and strengthen our relationship with the armed forces. It is something that the UFC has always focused on, making events available for free to as much of the military as possible, and I have had some of my most inspiring experiences meeting people in various military roles. I may not agree with 99 per cent of the wars being fought in the world today, but I have no issue with the brave individuals forced to become involved in them. We were always very warmly welcomed, but it seemed inconceivable to me that someone who risks their life as a job could be inspired by a professional fighter. I felt like we were playing at combat in comparison to the unpredictability of real warfare, and the people that put themselves in those situations. I always remember the attitudes of some of the wounded soldiers, wanting nothing more than to be back in combat, watching their brothers' backs. That resonated with me as I can imagine how I would feel if I was stuck in a military hospital, and Jimmy, Paul and Andre were out in the field engaging the enemy.

I had been smoking marijuana regularly in California and, although I wouldn't be partaking back home in the build-up to the fight, I knew that after the fight I'd take few days off, and would probably want to then. So I packed a tiny amount of weed into a glass pipe, wrapped it and taped it tight, and stuffed it inside one of my wrestling boots. The whole day, while packing my gear before the flight across the Atlantic, I took the weed in and out of my bag repeatedly as my mind chopped and changed about whether it was worth the minimal risk involved. To be totally honest, by the time I caught a cab to LAX I had lost track of my constant switching, possibly because I was smoking and packing at the same time! Once in Germany, I joined up with a handful of other UFC fighters and travelled together on a coach around the country, visiting the various military bases and doing our bit. Understandably security is pretty tight at these places and at the gates of every base we were all ordered off the bus so sniffer dogs could clamber aboard and go through our belongings in search of contraband, explosive or otherwise. My heart was in my mouth the first couple of times, although I can't imagine anyone would have got too excited about a tiny quantity of marijuana, but in six separate searches the weed was never discovered. I was a little relieved that no issue arose, and that first smoke after the fight was all the more sweet because of the process endured to get it home. Not that I recommend such silliness to anyone else!

Our fight was set for UFC 99 in Cologne and, such was the level of interest the war of words had created, we were scheduled to be the big opening bout on the pay-per-view (PPV) section of the card to get the fans in attendance fired up and boost the atmosphere for the audience at home. The UFC also produced a ten-minute preview documentary that they showed on the big screens inside the sold-out Lanxess Arena. I couldn't believe it when I first saw it. There was a deadly serious Marcus Davis talking about being told as a kid that he was wrong to say he hated something because that was such a strong emotion and it meant you spent some of your day thinking negatively about the person or thing you disliked. He then pauses before continuing solemnly with, 'I hate Dan Hardy. I spend a lot of every day thinking about how much I don't like Dan Hardy ... I'm going to smash his face to pieces.' It was all music to my ears. I could see how much energy he must have been wasting thinking about all the shit I was spouting on social media about him not being a true Irishman. I had a load of T-shirts printed with *I Hate Dan Hardy* on them and wore one to the weigh-in to keep his blood boiling. I didn't even need to say anything now, just eye contact and a smug grin was enough to set him off.

Davis gave his game-plan away at the weigh-in. You could always tell how Marcus Davis was going to fight by the way his physique developed during training camp for each bout. He was always in great shape, but if he stepped on the scales with his muscles looking a little leaner, you knew he was going to come out and box. But when he took off his T-shirt and revealed a heavily muscled torso, you knew he was going to focus on wrestling. As soon as I saw him on the stage, I knew he was planning to grapple. I felt that everything was playing into my hands and I was incredibly confident at the first bell. I was always sure I would beat Davis, but now I had him angry and looking like a bodybuilder there was no way I could lose. The only pressure I felt was totally self-manufactured. Three or four hours before we headed to the arena, it suddenly dawned on me that my provocative behaviour this time around would guarantee the loss of many fans if I now went out and was beaten up. In that scenario, I'd become just another mouthy Brit who talks a good game but is incapable of backing up his words and gets found out the instant he is forced to step up a level. And as the loser, it is much more difficult to spin out the lines that it was all just part of the game, that I have huge respect for all my opponents and it was nothing personal, because Davis, the winner, will already be running the show and can shout from the rooftops how he shut up a cheeky, ignorant, arrogant loser. Looking back, I see it was a pretty big gamble on my part, but at the time I saw it as another investment in myself in terms of my future UFC career. I was going to win this one and build my profile exponentially at the same time.

When the physical confrontation begins, all the talk stops from me. I'm not one for continuing the trash-talk in the Octagon and the vast majority of my fights are fought with limited verbals. The only guy I remember encountering who never shut up was Paul Jenkins back in that smoky pub on Portsmouth pier. It was all nonsense that came from his mouth though and had zero impact on the fight. But I could see Davis still had that genuine hate in his eye when we first engaged. He took me down and controlled a lot of the first round. There is no doubt he was very strong, just a wall of muscle weighing down on me. He was already thirty-five years old and had that man strength, that solid brute force people get from lifting weights every day for over twenty years. But I was relaxed the whole time I was on the ground. I had been expecting this after I saw his shredded physique and I also knew such a heavy build would cause him to tire as the bout progressed. I never felt in any way hurried or panicked. Compared to the Dan Hardy who fought Lee Doski for the first time exactly five years earlier, I was a totally different animal. I was a much more refined fighter, I knew what I was capable of, was sure of what I wanted to do and how to do it. I had a much deeper understanding of mixed martial arts and what it took to win a fight at the elite level. I had also lost that misplaced arrogance of my youthful self and replaced it with a justified confidence. So while he had me down for a lot of the opening three or four minutes, he did no damage whatsoever. Then, with around ninety seconds left in the round, I heard a single voice cutting through the white noise of the 12,000 in attendance. It was as distinctive to me that night in Cologne as it is on the video recording available today. That "come on, Dan!" from my little sister gave me the extra 5 per cent I needed to turn things around. I scrambled and drove him into the fence and with a minute to go we were back on our feet exchanging strikes and I made sure everything I threw was heavy. I demanded his respect and from the look on his face as I landed I knew I had it. One vicious elbow on a break buzzed him, and I opened a cut on his forehead and caused a swelling at the corner of his left eye with further punches. Despite all the effort he had put into the round, I hurt him much more than he hurt me and I believe I earned the round.

We spent the first ninety seconds of the next trading blows on our feet until, sensing he was coming off second best, Davis moved in to grapple. He had already lost some of his power, however, and I easily forced enough space between us to pull his head down and into my rising knee. It landed sweet and Davis dropped. I was on him fast, raining down hammer fists and elbows, but he recovered his senses in time to survive. As I sat on my stool waiting for the third, I could hear Mark DellaGrotte, the famed Muay Thai trainer, in the opposite corner, shouting his instructions in a thick Boston accent. 'Don't make mistakes, Marcus,' he said. 'This kid's dangerous and it only takes one punch.' That gave me great confidence. Then, just in case I was wondering whether Team Davis had calmed down enough to realise this was business and nothing personal, DellaGrotte screamed, 'You're just one round away from shutting this kid up!'

In my mind I was two rounds up, but I wanted to dominate the third to make sure. It was an inauspicious start, however, as I fell to my back after Davis caught a lazy low kick at the same time as he threw a reaching left hand. His punch never landed, and certainly didn't precipitate my fall, but the judge sitting behind my back believed that is exactly what happened and it ended up costing me the round on his scorecard. After a bit of grappling on the deck, in which Davis threatened but never came close to a submission or even landing a damaging strike, he attacked a foot, allowing me a moment to break free and scramble back to my feet. Then it was my turn to take him down and secure top position. From inside his closed guard, I controlled his wrists to remove his defence and plunged the most brutal elbow of my career into his face. His head literally bounced off the canvas floor and seconds later the blood was flowing from the bridge of his nose. 'Stay out of danger,' I heard DellaGrotte shout to his man. *A bit late for that*, I thought. His face was a mess and the referee separated us to allow the doctor in to clean him up and take a look. Davis rose slowly on unsteady legs just as his coach shouted, 'You're good, Marcus, you're good.' More extremely wishful thinking from the always positive DellaGrotte. His man wasn't good and it was only going to get worse in the final minute as I punished Davis with left hands as he struggled to see through the blood and swelling.

To his credit, Davis kept coming forward and swinging to the end, and when the final bell sounded he instinctively reached out for a brief handshake. It was a shame then when he refused a proper embrace when the split decision victory in my favour was announced. Only one judge voted against me, the one whose angle of vision made it look like I'd been dropped by a left hand rather than my own misplaced feet at the start of the final round. Most people agreed that I deserved the victory, but the feud with Davis lasted for a long time. I hadn't thought it would be necessary, but I used my post-fight interview with Joe Rogan to reiterate that I had no personal problem with Marcus Davis whatsoever and it was all just a ploy to seek any marginal edge over an extremely tough opponent. I found it strange that people would honestly think I had an issue with a man self-identifying as Irish and it still amazes me that my comments riled Davis so badly. It was something that would have been laughed off as gym banter with the Rough House boys, but the cultural difference was evident and I had used it to my advantage. As soon as I was back in Nottingham I smoked that weed the military-police dogs had missed, watched a DVD a neighbour had put together of all the build-up and fight, and just laughed at how silly and hilarious it all was. There was also a huge sense of relief that the loud-mouth braggart routine hadn't backfired with a chastening defeat. But I now know Davis to be an extremely proud man, the type of guy who fights for respect. He's the fighter who hopes that years down the line people will come up to shake his hand and say, 'I saw you do such and such and you were one tough bastard.' Fame or titles or money or rankings are a distant second to those kinds of warriors. And then here was me, a kid with a big mouth, only two fights into my UFC career, swaggering about and disrespecting him in public. The Irish thing got to his heart, but I think whatever I used to disrespect him would have worked. I'm glad we got a chance to sit down briefly together the following year at UFC 113 in Montreal. Marcus had beaten Jonathan Goulet in the second round and then invited me to his dressing room. He apologised for some of his own behaviour, explaining that he was a proud and emotional man and he'd just let the whole situation get to him. I naturally apologised for my part in it all and we shook hands properly and left it at that.

● ● ●

I was now 3 and 0 in the UFC and the rest of the welterweight division were forced to sit up and take notice of the brash Brit backing up his words with actions in the Octagon. UFC 105 was scheduled for Manchester in November and I was told I'd be on the show and high up the card. The Korean Dong Hyun Kim was named as my opponent, but he injured himself in sparring and had to withdraw. That was good news for two reasons. Firstly, Kim was like a human backpack in fights, another spoiler that could make for a very boring fight. It would have been a frustrating contest and I hadn't been excited by the prospect of facing him. The language barrier would have negated my burgeoning trash-talk skills too. The second reason I was glad the match-up never happened is down to the fighter Dana White soon announced as the replacement opponent. Mike 'Quick' Swick was not only a much more exciting fighter, but he was also the number one contender in the welterweight division. That meant he was at the front of the queue to face the champ, Georges St-Pierre. It also meant that if I could beat Swick, I would fast-track myself into that title-challenger position. The magnitude of that situation, the possibility of becoming the first British fighter to contest a world title in the UFC, saw our bout bumped up to co-main event alongside Randy Couture versus Brandon Vera. Bisping was on the show as well, fighting in his home town against Denis Kang, and yet I was higher up on the card. It was an unexpected promotion to such a lofty position, arriving at least three bouts earlier in my UFC career than I had ever anticipated.

It was also a big enough fight for me to take the decision to make a change to my coaching set-up. Owen had been great for my career, but I felt I now needed a level of commitment from a coach that, largely due to the demands of his real job and his family, he was unable to give. Instead, I looked to Steve Papp, a guy I knew to absolutely live and breathe martial arts. Steve worked out of a few spit-and-sawdust gyms in the Midlands and was renowned for his ability to cultivate killers within the otherwise unassuming fighters under his wing. He was a hard-nosed Thai fighter, small, stocky, tenacious and mean, with a variety of training in other martial arts such as Jeet Kune Do. My first ever session with him was a non-stop forty-five-minute round of serious sparring. Whereas Owen was a taller, looser fighter with a lot more finesse, Steve was a rugged, march-forward-and-land-an-elbow-type guy. He was also unquestionably, totally committed to training camp preparations and I needed that consistency. I knew he was new to the sport of MMA, but he was an extremely fast learner and I was convinced his passion and enthusiasm would make up for any gaps in his knowledge.

I had my reputation now and Swick was expecting months of online trash-talking, so I decided to hold my tongue. It was a question of horses for courses and I figured that silence or platitudes might screw with his head more than Davis-esque abuse. I did change his nickname from Quick, earned via a series of early finishes, to One Trick, but it was all very mild. At the pre-fight press conference I thanked him for making the trip over and then handed him a runners-up trophy so he wouldn't fly home empty-handed. He thanked me and promised to bring it to the Octagon the following night to return it. The only person who made any effort to get under Mike Swick's skin was the cheeky fella who swiped the cap off his head as he made his way through the crowd to the Octagon in the Evening News Arena!

Swick was taller than me, had a longer reach and was fast on his feet, famed for sprinting forward while throwing a flurry of punches to catch opponents off-guard. When people panicked and made defensive errors as he charged, he also had a good guillotine attack in his locker that was dubbed the Swick-otine after he used it to beat Steve Vigneault and Joe Riggs barely two minutes into those fights. But I studied his back catalogue and a strategy to counter his style soon formed in my mind. First of all, he had a clear tell, a lift of the chin and a swelling of the chest as he rose up to launch his charge, which indicated when he was going to plough forward. I visualised this movement for hours on end every day so that I'd recognise the very first muscle twitch and be ready for Swick approaching at pace. The second part of the puzzle was what to do with him once I knew that he was coming. It was here that I noticed the natural response seemed to be to back away from him and his flying fists, but that appeared counter-intuitive to me as you simply gave him more time and space to keep building speed. Despite him having begun his MMA career as a light heavyweight, I didn't think that Swick was actually a naturally heavy-hitter, more that he generated his power via forward momentum and gained his knockouts in that fashion. If I stopped the momentum, I was sure I would negate his power. So I resolved to simply stand my ground when he came for me and time my own strikes to catch him on the way in. I would win this fight with an 'intercepting fist', as The Master would say. As far as I could see, the absolute worst that could then happen was I'd have to deal with a maximum of two punches and then a clinch as our bodies collided and his assault was smothered. Part of my preparation included watching a lot of Wanderlei Silva, famous for never wanting to give an inch to any of his opponents, and by fight night I had my game-plan perfected: I'd throw hard and, aiming directly at his lifted chin, use his momentum against him and stifle his attack.

I put it into action in the opening seconds when he made his first predictable rush towards me and I caught him flush on his jaw with a right hook as soon as he was in range. I knew I must have buzzed him, but it wasn't until we spoke later that I realised how bad he actually was. He fell forward and kind of sagged against me, but I presumed he was angling for a takedown and so I secured an underhook and basically held him up. I didn't know then that he hadn't a clue where he was and had I let go he would have likely slumped to the floor, allowing me to steal an early finish. Swick told me in the hotel reception after the event that he didn't remember a thing about the fight from that right hand onwards. For the rest of the opening round, he basically held on like grim death and it was an attritional battle of knees to the thighs and midriff. But by the end of it, I was the man with a smile on my face. That smile widened fifteen seconds into the second round when a trademark left hook buckled my foe's legs and sent him retreating backwards fast. This time I knew he was struggling, but I missed a monster overhand right by an inch and he was able to grab on, pull me close and steal some respite. I punished his body for the rest of the round, but it wasn't until the third that I really put the gloss on one of my best performances. We both stood our ground and swung for the fences but I was the man to land the big blow and Swick stumbled away on drunken pins. I advanced, struck him a couple more times, then picked him up and took him down. There, I slashed an elbow across the top of his skull that opened his scalp as if I'd used a razor blade. I leaned over him in his guard and kept piling on the misery as his blood began to stain the canvas. He sporadically made vain attempts to lock in a triangle, but I merely rose out of it and then plunged back down with a fist aimed at his face to discourage further attempts. The ref stood us back up, but Swick, with his left eye badly swollen and his shaven head stained red from his own claret, was a beaten man. With ninety seconds to go and the capacity crowd shouting *Hardy! Hardy!* I waved a hand to get them to up the decibels. I was in my element. I didn't get the finish, but the decision was unanimous and indisputable.

The champion, GSP, was cageside and Dana led him into the Octagon as I was talking to Rogan so the photographers could get a few early shots to start the publicity machine for my next outing. I had a shot at the title and was facing a legend of MMA.

THE FALL

6

My shot at GSP's welterweight title was announced for UFC 111 in New Jersey on 27 March 2010. I wasn't used to having a fight set in stone so far in advance, and all that extra time to think about what was coming down the road worked against me. I knew my body needed a period of total rest after the exertions of the Swick bout, but I was so eager to start my preparation for St-Pierre that I couldn't stop myself from training. I slowed down somewhat for a couple of weeks, but I was still running, lifting and grappling every other day during that fortnight, so it was hardly a holiday. Then, come December, I officially began what was to become a sixteen-week training camp.

It was crazy, and looking back now I can see that. My enthusiasm for training actually peaked then faded while still inside camp and that is never a good sign for a fighter. But getting everything right in terms of preparation is one of the great challenges of mixed martial arts. I was always a real planner, with everything drawn up and documented on charts and schedules and highlighted in notebooks. With the benefit of twenty-twenty hindsight vision, it was the wrong approach for me. I would keep to those schedules throughout the camp come hell or high water, and that invariably led to over-training. On days when I was carrying a knock, or just bone tired from pushing it too hard in a previous session, I still went on that run, lifted those weights, or strapped on my gear and sparred a few rounds. It is one of the symptoms of not having a specialised MMA coach to oversee everything. I was basically my own overall performance manager with complete autonomy over training. Part of the reason why I relocated to the US for my camps was to seek out that authority figure who could guide me through the process. But in reality, I was still always making my own decisions. When I first joined the UFC, I linked up with Ollie Richardson, the strength and conditioning coach of the Leicester Tigers rugby union team, and he became one of my best friends, as well as a fantastic addition to my team. There were big changes with Ollie on board, a much more professional feel. It was hard graft too, the Saturday morning sessions in particular a total nightmare. Ollie did his best to help me manage the overall schedule, but it was a big ask when my coaches were spread across three counties. In Leicester I would go and do a session with my jiu-jitsu coach and he would beast me for a couple of hours. From there I'd drive across town, or to another city, for another two or three hours with my Thai boxing coach and he would put me through the mill as well. An MMA camp is a real team effort, but often the different members of that team are not communicating enough to know what the other is doing or planning to do. It leads to every single session being 100 per cent, 100mph, when maybe it should have been dialled back a notch. It is one of the clear benefits of the MMA super-gym model that has become established in the US. Everything is under one roof in the likes of the Jackson-Winklejohn gym in New Mexico or American Top Team in Florida and so it is easier to micro-manage a fighter's routine. But even within such a system, there are always specialised coaches with their own competing priorities or ideas. When I was at ATT, Ricardo Liborio was regarded as one of the best MMA trainers in the world, but he told me absolutely nothing about the striking range. For that major aspect of the game they had the ex-pro boxer Howard Davis Junior. More all-round coaches are emerging all the time, but MMA is such a multi-faceted beast that it is hard to see anyone becoming a true specialist in every discipline needed. The more holistic the approach to preparing for a mixed martial arts fight the better, but two or three heads are still better than one as far as I can see.

The other reason why I was training flat-out a full four months before the fight was my opponent. Like every welterweight in the MMA world at that time, I looked at GSP and knew I had a lot of work to do and a lot of catching up to do if I was going to compete with him. From a totally objective point of view, it was undeniable that the Canadian was superior to everyone else on the scene in 2010. He was just an awesome athlete on top of all his specific fighting skills. He was probably the key influencer in the sport of mixed martial arts at the time. At the grassroots level, fighters were mimicking his style and getting tips on training from any footage that the UFC would put out. I know this because I was doing the same, just as I used to watch the HBO boxing countdown shows and copy Bernard Hopkins' and Roy Jones Jr.'s training sessions. When GSP was the champion we were all looking at him to see what he was doing differently, and anyone that says they weren't is either ignorant or a liar. He was the catalyst behind the evolution that now has us approaching an era in which every UFC fighter is a pure athlete, capable of competing in whatever sport they put their mind to. GSP was at that level when the rest of us weren't. I was a fighter striving to be a martial artist whereas he was beyond that. He was a genuine professional athlete with formidable fighting skills.

I didn't consider the task in such stark terms. I didn't simply accept that he was better than me. But I did acknowledge that he was clearly further along in his evolution as a combat athlete, which is where the sport was going. It was possible the opportunity had come too soon for me. At the same time, however, I always believed, and always will believe, that every MMA fight is winnable by both contestants. The beauty of mixed martial arts is that no one individual will ever be the best in every discipline of the sport and that gives every fighter hope. I could admit that GSP was above me in a certain area of the game, but that is vastly different to just throwing my hands up and saying he is better than me, full stop. If I fought him under Thai boxing rules, for example, I was confident I could knock him out every night of the week. So the challenge for me then was going to be keeping our fight in the ranges within which I could beat him or at least be competitive.

The big fear was finding myself embroiled in a pure wrestling match with GSP. The vast majority of UFC competitors have a relatively rudimentary wrestling game, so St-Pierre was the first genuine elite-level grappler I had faced. And I say that despite the fact he came from a karate background and learnt wrestling as a secondary skill-set. Some guys seem to naturally gravitate towards a particular aspect of the game and that becomes their preferred range in which to compete. Georges had a varied and dangerous striking game, but wrestling seemed to be something that really made sense to him. Much like striking makes more sense to me than most other things in life! He chained his takedown attempts together beautifully, and the transitions were so smooth that even veteran college wrestlers struggled to keep up with him in the MMA arena. Usually when I sensed an opponent considering a takedown, the steps to defend were quite clear and I'd spent years working hard to improve my speed at going through those steps. Some were still skilful enough to successfully take me down, but I knew I could hold my own with them on the floor and that I'd eventually get back to my feet, where I could start searching for their chin again. GSP was a different animal, however. What made him such a nightmare was the combination of elite-level athletic ability and fluid transitions in grappling exchanges. He would go for a double-leg and at the exact moment you began to defend that, he would instantly switch to a single leg to keep a step ahead of you. I couldn't really prepare well to counteract such an attack because, unless GSP himself was willing to spar with me, no one in my circles had the ability to replicate it, and I didn't have the money to fly around the world looking for someone who could. I understood the principles of it and how it worked, but without being able to physically practise against it for hours every day, it was impossible to teach my body to react quick enough when it happened.

So instead my focus for the camp became working on my ground skills. I can look back now and think that maybe I did misdirect my energies, that perhaps if I had worked on my takedown defence more it would actually have enhanced my striking offence. But at the heart of that debate is the fact that I didn't want to enter the Octagon already on the defensive. I didn't want to be in there fully focused on twenty-five minutes of defending takedowns. I didn't become a fighter and sign up to the UFC to be so negative. My goal is always to be on my feet offering the threat of a knockout, or on the mat threatening a submission or establishing a top position in order to ground-and-pound. And while I dedicated a huge part of my time in advance of GSP to grappling and striving to improve that side of my game, I'm happy to admit that it will always be striking that drives me. Attempting to perfect my ability to switch a human being off with one clean strike is why I am a martial artist. It is undoubtedly impressive to witness someone out-grapple another on the deck, but only if you are one of the trained minority who knows what they are looking at. With a pristine KO, on the other hand, everyone recognises that for exactly what it is. It is the ultimate way to finish a confrontation and, as far as I am concerned, the most efficient. In a real fight situation, it can be the only means of victory as well. If I'm attacked in the street on Saturday night by three different guys simultaneously, I'm not going to be able to choke all three of them out. But, utilising my ability to strike a man, I'd back myself to walk away unscathed from three sleeping bodies on the pavement.

● ● ●

When you fight the pound-for-pound number one fighter on the planet for the UFC's welterweight title you expect a little more media attention than the norm, but nothing could have prepared me for the overwhelming intensity of the scrutiny I felt under ahead of the GSP fight. I have always enjoyed the media side of the fight game. It may not have been quite the monster it is today, flying around the world for mass press-conferences and the like, but I received a lot of requests from the moment I signed for the UFC and I was happy to meet all of them. Sometimes the UFC would rent a studio for hours of radio interviews and I would sit there patiently through every one. In the early days it was still more like an introduction to mixed martial arts and answering a long list of basic questions. It was more like a morbid curiosity from the media outlet rather than any educated interviews or desire for informed analysis. But I understood the value of it all, to me as an individual and to the organisation and sport I was representing, so I said yes to every TV programme, radio show, newspaper, magazine and website that came knocking. More than that, I wanted them interested in me, both for the value of the promotion it would provide and from a posterity point of view. I want to be able to look back on records of my fighting journey in forty years and share them with the grandkids.

But, even so, handling the media obligations that came with the GSP fight became a major battle in itself.

The UFC needed footage for three episodes of their Primetime series, which was then their major promotional vehicle. That meant that for four full weeks, in addition to all the standard media work that comes with a PPV title fight, I had a UFC camera crew all over me, around the clock. They were nice, professional people as you would expect, but the nature of the work meant it was the most intrusive and exhausting experience of my life. Aside from the unsettling feeling of having cameras following your every move, there was a constant stream of little demands that soon began to wear me down. *Could you just walk back through the door, please? Could you just do that again but look this way, please? Would you mind just changing your T-shirt for this next part, please?* One night I got a call at 1am from an apologetic director who said they needed a shot of me coming out of the lift in my apartment block. It had to be done right away ahead of whatever deadline they were working to in the US. On another occasion they had me in the gym in the dead of night with the main lights off, hitting the heavy bag and doing pull-ups while they sprayed me with water for effect. It was deep mid-winter in England at this time and absolutely freezing but, as always, I obliged. It felt like I didn't have one minute of the day when I could just switch off and relax. Years later I asked GSP how he dealt with it all and I could see him looking at me like, *it's hardly that big a deal*. But as we talked I realised that he didn't have to endure anything like what I went through because they already had so much footage of him in the can from his previous sixteen UFC bouts. 'They just called up when they needed something,' he told me. 'And if I didn't want them around that day, we just rearranged another time.' I wish I could have had that luxury.

Then, just when I felt it couldn't get any worse, Grandad Derek died. He'd fallen seriously ill over Christmas and had been hospitalised ever since he took a real bad turn. For weeks, my routine was train, hospital, rest, and repeat. I spent hours at his bedside and on occasion had to excuse myself for five minutes to conduct an interview over the phone with one media outlet or another. I hadn't mentioned anything about my grandad's situation to any of the media, but one evening talking to a Canadian website they asked me where I was and what I was doing and, without really thinking, I answered that I was in the hospital. They immediately jumped to the wrong conclusion and started worrying about my own health and whether there was any risk to the fight, so I decided to explain the situation. I told them how influential my grandad was in my career. How he'd driven me to Taekwondo and back for all those years and even joined me in the classes for a period. How he'd always found a way to get me any book or piece of kit that could help my evolution as a martial artist. How I would go to him ahead of a fight just to listen to how proud he was of me. How I could do no wrong in his eyes. How he'd been the one closest to me along every step of my journey to the UFC. How he'd seen me as a kid on the bad days when I'd fail and cry and lash out at Mick and swear I'd never be back. How he'd been there on the good days too when I'd overcome a hurdle or reached a milestone and walked away with an extra spring in my step. How I valued every second I ever spent with him. Basically, what he meant to me and how much I loved him. When the interview finished I walked back into the hospital room and stood beside my mum, dad, sister, grandma, cousin, two aunties and an uncle. Ten minutes later, we all looked on as Grandad took his final breath.

It was so hard to lose him. And the fact that I was barely a month out from the biggest fight of my life and had cameras following me everywhere exacerbated the nightmare. I remember my coach having to start asking them to turn the cameras off in the gym because between rounds of sparring I would sit on the stool, let my mind wander to Grandad, and just start crying. They asked to go to the funeral to get some footage as well, but I had to draw the line somewhere. Like I say, they were all nice, professional people who were just doing their jobs, but some moments in life are too personal and painful to be used to sell a few more PPVs.

● ● ●

A couple of days after Grandad's funeral, and without feeling that I had in any way processed losing one of the most important figures in my life, it was time to fly to America to complete my training camp. I had everything meticulously planned as usual. With my striking coach Steve Papp I flew to Newark, New Jersey and met up with Alder Hampel, a jiu-jitsu black belt friend of mine from 10th Planet who was going to assist with that side of things. We hired a cheap and cheerful Dodge Caliber, stuffed all our gear into the back, and hit the road for the town of Saddle River, thirty-five miles to the north. This part of the world was chosen for one reason and one reason only: Joe DeFranco. DeFranco became famous off the back of his documentary *Strong*, but he had been well known in strength-and-conditioning circles for years. Since the year 2000, DeFranco has been preparing top college football players for the make-or-break NFL Scouting Combine with an unrivalled success rate. His speciality is the so-called Cinderella story, taking guys you wouldn't expect to perform well in the tests and evaluations and having them add reps to their bench press, inches to their vertical leap, and shave seconds from their forty-yard dash, to excel at the Combine and get drafted into pro football. As far as I was concerned, there was no better man in the US to pick up my strength and conditioning prep from where Ollie left off in Leicester, and it was Ollie who reached out and set the meeting up. Joe also knew a guy nearby who had wrestling mats in his garage and had secured the services of local high-school wrestlers to keep me sharp until it was time to taper off the training. If I needed it, there were also a couple of boxing gyms in the area that could provide adequate sparring at the drop of a hat. I was happy and confident I was in the right place to get into peak condition for GSP.

When we arrived at our hotel in Saddle River, the UFC cameras were already there and waiting. They followed us up to the one room I had booked for the three of us, a spartan affair with two single beds and a fold-out sofa for whoever drew the short straw. To nobody's surprise, I ended up on the sofa – number one of the 48 Laws of Power: Never outshine the master! I could see the UFC crew looking a little puzzled by the scene, and when they saw the wheels I had hired and the garage I was planning to train in, I sensed them stealing eyebrows-raised glances at one another. About an hour later my phone rang and it was Dana White on the other end of the line.

'Hey, Dan,' the UFC president began, innocently enough. 'How's it going, buddy?'

'All good thanks, Dana. Just getting settled in Saddle River.'

'Right, right. Here, Dan, what car did you get by the way?'

It struck me as a peculiar question, but I described our humble motor.

'Okay, yeah,' he continued. 'I tell you what, Dan. Give the keys to one of the crew there and they'll go change that for you.'

'Eh, okay,' I replied.

'And, Dan, where are you planning to train for this?'

'Here in Saddle River, Dana. I've sourced a garage with mats and there are a couple of local gyms—' I began before the president politely cut in.

'Okay, buddy. Listen, what you're going to do is get into the new car that comes back for you and drive to Long Island. I got a guy there waiting for you.'

By now the penny had dropped that my low-budget version of a US training camp was not exactly what the UFC had in mind for its welterweight title challenger. Dana and the Fertittas had drastically overestimated the size of my bank balance at this point in my career. The runner from the camera crew was soon back with quite the upgrade, a massive, top-of-the-range cream Escalade. In working-class Saddle River, where everyone drives more subtle and nondescript vehicles, it stuck out like a sore and garish thumb, but the UFC had TV to make so what could I do? I clambered aboard my pimpmobile and we started the two-hour journey to Long Island. Once there I waited for the cameras to get in place and then stepped out of my ride like 50 Cent, strode through the doors of Serra's Gym, and dramatically clasped hands with the proprietor, à la Arnold Schwarzenegger and Carl Weathers in their famous 'Dillon! You sonofabitch' scene in *Predator*.

Matt Serra was the last man to beat GSP, having spectacularly and surprisingly knocked the champion out in the first round of their meeting at UFC 69 back in 2007. He had been given about as much chance going into the fight as I was being given this time around, and the UFC was keen for us to link up and build that storyline into the hype. Serra was pretty much retired by that point, but he had his own MMA school and it was doing well. He is as talented a coach as he was a fighter and he was extremely generous with his knowledge as he helped me prepare. People may think that it was all a superficial partnership manufactured by the UFC for the benefit of the cameras, but Matt really dedicated a huge amount of time and energy to me. He had been in pretty much the same boat as me before he fought St-Pierre, in that his only hope of victory was a big one-in-ten punch landing. But he had also identified all the problems GSP would pose him and he now applied his learning to me. For three weeks I tirelessly worked escapes and positional considerations with his three best black belts and I truly believe I wouldn't have survived his arm-bar attempt if it wasn't for those sessions. It was actually nothing revolutionary, but I simply couldn't have replicated that intensity anywhere else. In three short weeks, Matt equipped me with everything that he thought might be useful from a grappling point of view.

Matt Serra is also a hilariously funny and entertaining guy. He's very

Long Island, which for the uninitiated means he's like a brash New Yorker but even louder and more to the point. Everyone is given a nickname, and my training partners for the few weeks I was there were Monster, Bam-Bam and He-Man. Ray Longo works closely alongside Serra and he is a great character himself, famous for saying to Chris Weidman in a thick Italian-American accent, 'I want you to punch a hole in his fucking chest,' between rounds against Anderson Silva. Weidman stood up and knocked the great Brazilian out a minute later. It was just great fun being around personalities like that – they deserve their own TV show.

All my best-laid plans were in disarray, however, and I had to make a slightly awkward call to Saddle River to explain I wouldn't be needing that garage with the mats on the floor. But it was all good. Matt's entire team were so accommodating and I couldn't turn down the chance to learn from a guy of his quality and experience. The UFC also rented us much nicer individual hotel rooms in Long Island, but I kept doing the daily four-hour round trip from Saddle River and back to see Joe DeFranco and call in on the hotel room I'd already paid for upfront.

By fight week, although the training had tapered off, the media and publicity demands were still pretty intense. The main press conference was at the famous Radio City Music Hall in the Rockefeller Centre, and from there I went to watch the New York Knicks from courtside in Madison Square Garden and was interviewed at the half-time break. It was all a bit surreal, as was looking up in Times Square and seeing a massive poster of myself adorning the side of a building. Well, most of me anyway ... I was told different reasons why it was necessary, but Mike Swick's stomach was photoshopped in to replace my own. The problem was my tattoo of a Tibetan prayer in intricate Sanskrit lettering: it either made the event information difficult to read or was offensive to the emerging and important Chinese market. Either way, I had Swick's toned and pristine stunt-stomach in place of my own.

But as fight night drew closer, I became more and more relaxed. It was nearly time to do what I was born for, what I was truly good at. It was also nice to be in among the fans now the UFC cameras had been switched off. I may get my fair share of abuse online, but face-to-face 99.9 per cent of the public are warm and friendly when I meet them. Perhaps it helped this time that the trash-talk was kept to a bare minimum and the one-liners I did come out with were clearly tongue-in-cheek banter rather than anything resembling personal attacks. Some of the highlights were claiming I was going to knock the fake tan off GSP and that I had no idea how he managed to get his jeans on in the morning with so many people hugging his nuts. When he made a comment about being a true martial artist, something I apparently couldn't understand, I fired back that he knew nothing about me and that walking to the Octagon in your pyjamas (GSP wears his karate gi for his entrances) didn't mean anything. Like I say, more humorous than venomous this time around.

Being the main event, and my first UFC world title fight, didn't weigh heavily on me at all. It may have been a little new and a little different, but I certainly didn't feel under extra pressure. This was probably due to the fact I was such a huge underdog with pretty much everyone who voiced an opinion on the fight. But that negativity didn't bother me, in fact it fuelled me. I function better when I have that fuck-you mind-set after listening to everyone say I'm going to get submitted in the first round. I respond much better to that than to being told how great I am and how easy a night it is going to be for me. What did sting a little, however, were the frequent accusations that I didn't deserve this title shot, that it had been somehow gifted to me. There were fans, media and jealous rivals like Josh Koscheck all beating that drum. The week after I destroyed his teammate Mick Swick, I sat cageside at UFC 106 to see Koscheck defeat Anthony Johnson and then take the mic and claim I didn't deserve to fight GSP. The camera immediately zoomed in on me and I responded in jest with the boo-hoo face that still appears as a gif on my Twitter timeline at least once a month. Like many people who meet him, I don't like anything about Josh Koscheck, but his words pissed me off more than usual this time. I had worked so long and so hard for everything I had achieved in mixed martial arts. I knew that I absolutely deserved whatever came my way for all the blood, sweat and tears I'd left in the gym and cage and Octagon over the past decade or more. There is no doubt that it was a stacked welterweight division in the UFC back then, but Swick was the established number one contender and I beat him convincingly. Rankings are always subjective and should be consumed with a pinch of salt, but I was already well positioned and rising in any list available before the Swick fight. The other names in the top ten were Jon Fitch, Thiago Alves, Paulo Thiago, Nick Diaz, Matt Hughes, Paul Daley, Martin Kampmann and Koscheck. GSP had already beaten Fitch, Alves, Hughes and Koscheck, and I was ranked higher than Diaz, Daley and Kampmann by everyone whose opinion counted. Paulo

Thiago certainly deserved a shot, but I beat Swick before he did, and when I beat Swick it was an official title eliminator so it is a bit of a moot point. There is no doubt that plenty of the criticism sprang from my nationality as well, suggesting that my elevation to title contender was simply a nod to the expanding British market, but I had a wise enough head on my shoulders to realise I couldn't do anything about that. All that mattered was that I and those around me knew I belonged where I was and that I was ready to prove all the naysayers wrong.

Backstage in Newark's Prudential Center, I shared a dressing room with Frank Mir, who was battling Shane Carwin in the co-main feature. Frank is a great guy, super mellow. With the clock ticking, his coaches were eager for him to begin his warm-up and he was shooing them off as he tried to finish whatever game he was playing on his phone. I know that elite professional boxers automatically receive their own individual dressing rooms but in the UFC we pretty much always share, at least two in one large space. And I prefer it that way, being in with someone else who is fighting. I also like the fact we always have a TV screen in the room so I can watch the other fights on the card, something else that boxers apparently rarely do. I can't tell you the difference between us, but I know it would be odd for me to be sitting alone and isolated with my team, just twiddling my thumbs and waiting to hear Burt Watson cry, 'We're rolling!'

The UFC had a camera installed high in one of the corners to keep an eye on us at all times and we soon realised it must be controlled by some guy in a truck somewhere. You could walk from one side of the room to the other and back again, and the lens would mechanically swivel to record your every step. At one point, just to kill some time, I waited until it wasn't focused on me and leapt across the room to squeeze into the corner underneath it and the only square foot which it couldn't cover. Above my head I could hear it going mad, spinning this way and that looking for me. I liked to imagine the controller had just turned away for a drink of his coffee for a split second and when he turned back I was gone. Maybe he radioed Dana or Lorenzo saying, 'Sir, we've lost him.' It was like a scene from Orwell's *1984*.

Mir's wife was there the whole time too and she decided to stay with me in the warm-up room and watch her husband in action on the TV rather than take her seat octagonside. As wives or partners or family members tend to be, she was incredibly nervous. Her state of mind was to deteriorate pretty fast, however, as Frank got knocked out midway through the first. Mrs Mir was an absolute mess and, when I really should have been focused on the mammoth task I had in hand, I was consoling her as Frank was struggling to his feet on our TV screen. It was just another bizarre quirk that formed part of the unique build-up to this one.

● ● ●

Looking across the Octagon at GSP, I knew I could win. But I was also strangely and soberingly realistic about how that would play out. On the basis I had no intention of even trying to submit him and I never fought to win a decision, my means of victory would have to be a knockout blow, most likely my counter left hook. If I did manage to land that punch and put him to sleep, I'd be treated like Matt Serra. I'd be forever told that it was nothing more than a lucky punch and that he'd destroy me in a rematch. Said rematch would soon arrive and, as per the accepted script, he would then defeat me and reclaim his title. In the end, the fight went as it was meant to.

Within a round, I knew this was a different beast to anything I had ever faced before. I'd had loads of conversations with myself, saying that people lose to GSP because they are frightened to let their punches go, that they merely stand meekly by and wait to be taken down. I wasn't going to do that, I swore. If I was going down, I was going down with all guns blazing. But when you are in there with him, it is incredible how powerless you feel as an offensive force. The way he puts his wrestling together is so slick and tight that it makes you tentative about trying anything. You soon realise that you might get one shot away at best and then he is shooting in on your legs. Combinations are basically impossible. It is certainly not a fun fight for a guy who is predominantly a striker to find himself embroiled in. His ability to take a fighter down was unrivalled, incredible when you think he was never a wrestler in high school. He covered distance so quickly, and was explosive enough to switch his attack and power through an opponent, slamming them to the canvas. His balance and posture was always so on point that creating space to scramble was almost impossible and, because he didn't open up to strike a great deal, it wasn't until he would commit to a submission attack that I would find a space to get out.

But at the end of each round I found myself still alive and I sat on my stool and thought, *we're back on our feet now, I always have that puncher's chance*. Then, invariably less than thirty seconds later, I was on my back expending all the energy and strength I had just to keep him off me. The cold hard fact is, I didn't land a meaningful punch in the entire twenty-five minutes we were in the Octagon. He just shut me down, nullified me. He totally took the fight away from me. I didn't even feel like I was in a fight to be honest. All I felt was frustrated and bored as I spent the entire bout on the floor defending. He was in total control of practically every second of every round, but he progressed his positions so slowly. I'd make such a huge effort to get to my feet, but halfway there he'd change his tack and bring me down again. I remember thinking that this must be what it feels like to be slowly drowning. To keep breaking the surface to steal half a breath before sinking back into the murky depths. There was barely a mark on my face at the end. Sometimes I think I'd rather just have been beaten up by him like Koscheck and Fitch and Alves were. I think he landed one clean elbow on me, but even when he had the opportunity to strike me he didn't. It is an incredible level of discipline to have, but he simply never opened up, never risked allowing any space for me to operate whatsoever. GSP had that frightening level of single-mindedness that all legendary champions in sport are blessed with. He formulated a strategy to win and stuck to it with almost religious fervour. I always wanted to win as well, of course, but it was also about the act of fighting to me. To Georges, it seemed like it was all about winning and nothing else. As much as I can respect that mind-set, I'm made of different stuff and will always roll the dice and take a chance to clinch the victory before the final bell.

There are two moments in the fight that everyone likes to talk about, the only two moments in which I was in real and immediate danger. The first is the arm bar that GSP locked on in the final minute of the opening round, and the second is the *kimura* he manufactured in the fourth. I let both submissions get much deeper than I would have preferred, and I'm not going to pretend that my shoulder in particular didn't ache for a few days, but at no point did I consider tapping out. I'd worked a lot with Serra, who knows the intricacies of GSP's game in a real-life scenario and had the knowledge from years of Brazilian jiu-jitsu on exactly how to escape these situations. That involved many hours practising arm triangle, arm bar and back defences on the mats of his Long Island gym. I am also blessed with highly flexible shoulders and contrastingly inflexible elbows, which helps when you have a guy trying to twist your arm out of its socket. During the arm bar I was able to keep it moving, even if just millimetres, while he tried to keep it still and crank it to hyperextend my elbow. It looked pretty gruesome, but I was always able to rotate it a degree or two which was enough to ease the tension and keep it just short of unbearable. The *kimura* was much more uncomfortable but, despite hearing my friend Joe Rogan scream, 'He's going to rip his arm off here!' submitting didn't enter my mind. I think I probably would have let him wrench my shoulder from its socket or snap my arm in two before tapping. Straight after the fight, Georges came over to me in the Octagon, prodded at my arm, squeezed it gently, then asked whether it was made of rubber. 'No,' I replied with a smile on my face. 'I'm just very stubborn.' There was no way I was ever going to give all those who said I would submit the pleasure of watching me tap out.

I was naturally disappointed to lose, but the feedback I received picked me up pretty quickly. I guess people saw my level of commitment to MMA and respected my determination as an underdog. They saw that I always give everything and never take the easy option out of a situation. That I would never quit. If anything, my stock grew in defeat and I gained a whole army of new fans. I always say that, for where I was in my life and career, the fight went as well as it could have gone.

Maybe I should have gone straight home to the UK after the fight, but I wasn't ready for that. I just wasn't ready to face the fact that my grandad was gone. I still hadn't begun that process. It had hit me that he died and it was incredibly upsetting, but I didn't have the chance for a prolonged period of mourning and reflection to truly process his death and the impact it would have on me. So instead my fiancée and I set off on a four-week road trip down the east coast of America to Florida, smoking a lot of weed and generally blowing off some steam along the way. I felt like I needed a break from MMA for the first time in a decade and that the saccharine environs in which Mickey and Minnie rule would provide that. On the way we stopped off in Charlotte, North Carolina, for a UFC event featuring a couple of my friends. It was nice to see both Ross Pearson and my Rough House teammate Andre Winner take unanimous decision victories over Dennis Siver and Rafaello Oliveira respectively. I also had time to get a memorial tattoo for my grandfather from my good friend Matt 'Skinny' Bagwell.

I got recognised a lot on that holiday, much more so than I ever had before. The fight had been shown on the big screens of a major cinema chain and apparently a life-size cardboard cut-out of me took centre stage in the lobby of every one. My large red Mohawk then did the rest in guaranteeing that my image stuck in people's heads. Once more, absolutely everyone I encountered was kind and complimentary if they had watched my performance. Every single day I was told by at least one individual a variation of, 'Dude, he was so scared to stand and trade with you. If you just work on your takedown defence and a bit of wrestling, you'll be the champ no problem.' Of course I realised that this was a grand over-simplification, but when you hear something every day, and it continued for months after I returned to the UK too, you can't help but start to believe it a little. I started thinking, *Yeah, you're right, that's all I need to do, and it's an easy thing to do, and then I'll force everyone to trade with me. I'll improve my takedown defence while I'm knocking out these other bums, fight my way back to another title shot, and this time the result will be different.* It was then that my arrogance peaked. And it was then that I ran into Carlos Condit's gloved left hand.

● ● ●

I had watched Condit during his time as World Extreme Cagefighting champion, before the UFC swallowed up that particular American promotion, and knew he was a talented fighter, but in my arrogance I didn't see him as a threat. After surviving twenty-five minutes with GSP, I simply didn't respect Condit's ability enough to be concerned about anything. He was a good kickboxer with strong submission skills, but he wouldn't try to take me down and I didn't fear his power in a stand-up striking contest. I felt that our skills were in similar ranges, but I was stronger across the board. He always looked untidy to me, was not technically impressive, and I saw lots of holes in his game that I expected to exploit. On top of all that, the fight was scheduled for London and I viewed that as a clear sign the UFC was immediately looking to build me back up and into title contention again as quickly as possible.

So I entered camp over-confident and that soon spilled into complacency. I had beaten everyone until I ran into a legend and I fully expected to beat everyone again and then this time defeat whoever stood before me with the UFC welterweight strap. I still put in a couple of months of great preparation and arrived at fight week fit, sharp, strong, bang on weight and feeling good with my game, but the difference was in the mental preparation; that is where the complacency lay and it is every bit as dangerous as complacency in the physical preparations. We've seen it recently in Brazil when Fabricio Werdum basically sambaed to the Octagon, smiling and waving like he was on a Rio Carnival float, before getting sparked out by Stipe Miočić. I believe it was a big issue for Conor McGregor ahead of the first Nate Diaz fight too. The Irishman strutting onto the stage to weigh in rubbing his belly was severely lacking in the intensity we expect from the Notorious one the day before battle. I was in a similar frame of mind to McGregor and Werdum. My stock was so high after GSP and here I was in the British capital getting lauded as the local hero who's going to bring the title back to the UK for the first time. I was enjoying the whole process too much. Condit then failed to catch his flight across the Atlantic and wasn't there for the pre-fight press conference and so I missed out on the energy or rage boost which that whole charade provides. I felt invincible as I walked to the Octagon in the O2 Arena that night, totally bereft of anxiety. In truth, I was already looking well past the immediate challenge in front of me and towards an anticipated title shot two years and four more victories down the line.

The fight didn't even go one round. Condit certainly landed more strikes, but mine were much more damaging. Nothing he hit me with got my attention, whereas I saw his eyes open wide every time I connected a fist to his jaw. I had zero fear of or respect for Condit's power going into the fight, and by the midway point of the opening round absolutely nothing had changed. I was convinced that if we just stood toe to toe and swung, he would be the one out cold on his back. I swung my trusted left hook with all my might. Then another. Then another.

Then I woke up.

I have never understood the knocked-out guy who comes to on the canvas and starts flailing wildly at the referee and onlookers. Nor the guy apparently lost in total confusion, unable to comprehend what the hell is going on. Logically, as a professional fighter, it is not difficult to figure out what must have happened. You will probably not remember what has transpired, but you always have the pieces of the puzzle and it isn't hard to fit them together. The only time I had been knocked out before Condit was the sucker punch in the ATT gym and, although I didn't even know where I was, common sense allowed me to make an educated guess that the guy with the gloves standing over me had played a large role in the affair. It was similar that night in London. I opened my eyes and saw the doctor and, behind him, Carlos Condit celebrating. I just sat up and shouted *fuck*! Later I watched it back and it all became clear. I committed the schoolboy error of throwing the same punch three times in a row. By the third, Condit was waiting and the shorter, tighter arc on his hook, coupled with my momentum pushing my head towards his oncoming fist, ensured he cracked my chin a split second before I would have his, and that was all she wrote.

I felt different as soon as I got up off the canvas. It was as if all the arrogance that had been accumulating over the previous six months was smacked out of me with that one left hand. I immediately realised that I had got away from myself. My thoughts then turned straight away to my family and, in particular, my mum. It must have been very tough on my dad and sister too, but during the action Mum used to hide behind the English flag they brought with them, so being told her boy had just been knocked unconscious would have been a nightmare for her. I apologised to the fans, but I knew they wouldn't turn against me. So long as you go out on your shield, the support will always be there. It was all massively disappointing, but it was what it was and an hour later I was sitting in the hospital with Steve Papp laughing about it. He was taking the piss out of me, and in typical British self-deprecating manner, I was giving myself as good as I got from Steve. I knew where I had gone wrong and I knew I'd be back.

● ● ●

It wasn't long before Joe Silva was on the phone with the news I was to fight as the co-main event on the Tito Ortiz versus Antônio Rogério Nogueira card in Seattle on 26 March 2011. But when he told me who

I was to face, for the first time in my life the immediate reaction was less, *fucking right, I'm gonna kill him*, and more, *Oh, shit. Really?* My opponent was Anthony 'Rumble' Johnson, an absolute mountain of a man and the terroriser of the welterweight division. We were on friendly terms and every time I saw Anthony I would look him up and down and joke about how we could possibly be in the same weight class. A few weeks before the announcement I sat beside him signing autographs at a fan day and he was 235lbs, a full 65lbs over the UFC welterweight limit! He was a monster who knocked out every 170-pounder he faced. And they weren't your run-of-the-mill knockouts. I had sat cageside to watch him many times in the UFC and when he starched someone I genuinely wondered whether they would get up. And if they did, I knew they would never be the same again. They were just brutal, violent knockouts. And here was me coming off the first knockout loss of my career and getting matched with a killer. For the first time ever there was a small voice of doubt in my head questioning whether the UFC was actually trying to get rid of me rather than steer me towards another title shot.

With the fight taking place in Washington State, I took the opportunity to visit Bruce Lee's grave in Seattle's Lakeview Cemetery. It was a pilgrimage I had always wanted to make, but I went at that particular moment of my career in order to correct my perspective on fighting. I had somehow wandered away from a disciplined mind-set in the Condit fight and I wanted to reconnect with my love of martial arts. 'Your inspiration continues to guide us toward our personal liberation': these words are inscribed on a marble book on the grave and it is true that Lee had always led me through my journey and relationship with martial arts. I also watched *Enter the Dragon* several times and re-read all of Lee's writing during the Johnson camp. Part of the rationale behind looking to Lee for guidance at this time was that he often spoke of being outmatched in size or number and that you have to adapt your offensive for the situation with which you are presented. Although we would step on the scales at the same weight, Anthony Johnson was naturally a bigger human being and I knew that his size and strength were additional obstacles to overcome before the technical aspect of the fight would even come into play. I had been the clear underdog against GSP but it was a fairly matched fight between two similarly-sized athletes. He may have been technically superior to me in a particular range, but I could always attempt to do something to counter the advantages he held. But in facing Johnson, I felt a little like I was fighting natural physical advantages that I couldn't do much to counter. I could train for twenty years and he would still be much bigger than me, much stronger than me, and would punch much harder than me. Lee spoke and wrote and taught a lot about finding a way to win when outgunned and I knew I would benefit from some of his spirit. I looked to his adaption philosophies and his famous words of wisdom on water had a particular resonance:

Empty your mind. Be formless, shapeless. Like water. You put water into a cup, it becomes the cup. You put water into a bottle, it becomes the bottle. You put water into a teapot, it becomes the teapot. Now water can flow, or it can crash. Be water, my friend.

It was a very emotional experience to visit my hero's last resting place, much more so than I had anticipated. Although I had always recognised Bruce Lee as a pivotal character in my fighting story, I guess I hadn't completely appreciated his impact until I sat there looking at his headstone. I suddenly realised how much I had to thank him for and it was pretty overwhelming. While I was wiping away the tears, Taki Kimura approached and was kind enough to stand chatting with me for almost an hour. Taki was Bruce Lee's best friend, his best man at his wedding and a pallbearer at his funeral, and someone that spent most days training with and learning from Lee. He visits the grave every other day just to tidy the place up and talk to whoever has come to pay their respects. Hearing all the stories about training with Lee, what he was like as a man, and what it was like to be around this phenomenon in the sixties and early seventies was just an unreal experience. I left Lakeview Cemetery that day fully recharged with a renewed focus on my martial arts career.

With Anthony Johnson and I liking and respecting one another there was never going to be much in the way of vitriolic trash-talk, but I did make sure to comment upon and draw as much attention as possible towards his weight cut. I always saw the fact he killed himself to try and make 170lbs as a mental weakness on his part. It was like he needed to be sure he would be the biggest and strongest in the Octagon in order to manufacture self-confidence. It was also no secret that he struggled big time to torture his massive frame down to the welterweight limit. Twice before he'd missed weight, and they became catchweight bouts at 177 and 176lbs, forcing Johnson to forfeit a percentage of his purse to his disadvantaged opponent. When I heard he spent hours of every night during fight week sweating off excess pounds in the sauna, and was allegedly found on the floor of a hotel lift in an exhausted state after one session, I knew there was a genuine chance he could miss 170lbs again. So I did everything in my power to verbally coerce him into punishing his body to make weight. I knew the process would wreck his cardiovascular output and cause him to burn out faster than usual over the course of our scheduled three rounds together on fight night.

It was all crucial to the game-plan we had formulated to beat Johnson. In essence, I go into every fight with three distinct but interconnected strategies that can be generalised as follows. Plan A is to get in and out with a victory without leaving my comfort zone or absorbing damage. Plan B kicks in if Plan A is not working and states that my opponent must be doing X to counter my Plan A and so I now need to do Y to beat his X. Finally there is Plan C, which is very simple: neither A nor B is working out for me and so I need to bite down on my gumshield and go toe to toe until one of us is unconscious. The specific Plan A for Johnson was to stay out of trouble early but in a way that kept him busy so he'd run out of steam and I could take control in the second half of the fight. Plan B was to counter the fact that he mustn't be engaging with me by being more aggressive a little earlier until he's breathing heavily. Plan C was the same as always.

The strategy was based on two vital theories. Firstly, that AJ's cardio would be nowhere near the level mine was always at and he would inevitably tire and slow down as the fight progressed. His extreme weight cut ensured I could take that assumption to the bank. The second theory was that Johnson was going to trade on his feet and try to spark me out. Now, living up to his nickname Rumble, he had knocked out guys for fun in all his previous victories, and I was seen to be vulnerable, having just had my lights turned off by Condit, so my team and I felt we were on safe ground with this prediction too. That confidence then grew when an injured Tito Ortiz withdrew from the main event and was replaced by Phil Davis. Davis was a great athlete but he had no real venom in his work and no real love of fighting. The fans didn't warm to him because of that and he would eventually become the only fighter in UFC history to be cut from the roster when actually ranked in the top ten of his weight class. A draw like Ortiz he certainly wasn't and AJ and I immediately recognised our opportunity to steal the show. We began trading private messages on Twitter in which he talked about going to war, throwing bombs for as long as it took, winning the Fight of the Night bonus and putting on a spectacle that fans would talk about for years to come. 'We should be the main event,' he said, and I agreed wholeheartedly. There was no doubt in my mind that Johnson was going to try and take my head off as soon as we were instructed to fight.

He didn't actually appear that big when I saw him stride to the stage and step onto the scales. And when we went head-to-head for the cameras I was quietly pleased that there didn't look to be much between us in terms of body frame. But twenty-four hours later when I stood opposite Anthony Johnson in the Octagon, it was like they'd switched him for a different, much bigger man. He had piled on 44lbs overnight to arrive at 214lbs and he looked every ounce of that and then some. A year later he failed to make 195lbs for a catchweight bout with David Branch, before breaking Andrei Arlovski's jaw in a heavyweight contest, and he now campaigns in the UFC as a 205lb light-heavyweight. Having shared the Octagon with this monster for fifteen minutes, none of those three facts surprises me in the least.

What did surprise me on the night were his tactics. After all his messages about fireworks in a toe-to-toe brawl, the big man proceeded to take me down and smother me for three rounds. I couldn't believe it; he had played me for a chump. I always thought I was smart enough to get the best of any mind games in the build-up to a fight, but AJ sucked me in and I fell for it hook, line and sinker. The most adventurous move he pulled was a head-kick in the opening minute that I blocked with my arm. But my feet were crossed at the time and the sheer weight of his leg knocked me over. From there he charged me into the fence and I dislocated my thumb as we landed on the floor. I remember looking at it while he was on top of me and thinking, *that's not right*. He was in my guard and so I tried to reach around his back to force my thumb back into place, but I could barely link my hands together. He was so massive that I felt completely eclipsed. Daniel Cormier recently told me he felt the same against Anthony and Daniel is a full-blown light-heavyweight. I finally managed to pop my thumb back in, but from that point on it was of little use in terms of holding and manoeuvring a giant. I was trying to use a *kimura* to sweep him, but I just couldn't get a decent grip on his huge arms and back with a damaged digit. Aside from the beginning of each round or when the ref ordered us back to our feet, I spent the entire night under Johnson's considerable bulk, struggling in vain to move the battle into a range I could compete in. I was furious with myself for failing to read his bluff and thus finding myself caught in a trap from which I had not prepared an escape. I just didn't consider the possibility that a knockout artist would hold me down for fifteen minutes. His nickname is Rumble, for fuck's sake! I launched into Plan C at the outset of the third round, but I was too exhausted to land anything hurtful and he just shot and took me down as soon as he could anyway. He stuck fast to his strategy until the final second, exploiting my weakness all the way, and earned the unanimous decision.

I saw him four years later in a hotel lobby in Stockholm a couple of hours after he had beaten Alexander Gustafsson senseless in three brutal minutes and joked that I was glad he didn't do that to me. AJ just smiled that easygoing smile of his and replied, 'Yeah, but I like you, man.' I half-seriously wondered then whether he kept shooting against me just so he didn't have to knock me out and risk seriously hurting someone he had no wish to seriously hurt. Did he decide to kill me with his own warped view of kindness? To be honest, I'd rather be knocked out inside a minute than spend a quarter of an hour being smothered. And more importantly in the grand scheme of the UFC business, so would the paying public. Fans want dynamic striking exchanges and knockouts and the UFC has structured its fight-night bonus scheme accordingly.

If every fighter fought the way Anthony did that night against me, the UFC would be dead within a couple of years. Though impressive in its own right, attritional wrestling matches will never appeal to a mass live or televised audience. I have no problem with wrestlers using their skills to win a fight, but when they use them just to basically shut down or avoid a fight I think something needs to be done.

I have two perspectives on the debate. The first is that the fans will respond to the intention of fighters regardless of what they understand in terms of the intricacies of grappling on the ground. I have no love for Matt Hughes as a person but as an athlete he is the perfect example to illustrate this point. He took people down, held them down, beat them up and there was no booing because the crowd loved it. They could clearly see that Hughes' intention was to win the fight by hurting his foe and drawing blood. AJ did not do that against me though. He took no risks, caused me little damage, never looked like he was on the point of finishing me and that's why he was booed during and after our contest.

My second belief is that the scoring system must be modified so that negative wrestling approaches are not rewarded. Matt Hughes was always trying to end the contest, he wasn't thinking about what he needed to do round by round to emerge a points victor. But a smart coach like Greg Jackson, who is building a team of athletes rather than fighters, knows exactly what to do to win with minimal risk. It's the intelligent approach and to watch a talented athlete in any sport is impressive, but when it comes to fighting there is something deeper at play. Especially when considering how the fans gravitate towards a fighter. They want to connect with that chaotic, primal endeavour taking place inside the Octagon. But a high-level MMA coach will be able to look objectively at a fight, identify without bias the safe and danger zones for his athlete, and prepare them accordingly. A paint-by-numbers game-plan is written out and, as long as it is followed, the risk of injury or defeat is kept to a minimum. A fighter can thus take the current system and play by the rules to score points, earn a round, and win enough rounds to win a fight. One of the most blatant demonstrations of this thinking is ensuring you score a takedown in the final seconds to steal a round. To my mind, that is not a tactic we want to see dominate MMA fights. The system should encourage and reward aggression, risk-taking and the intention to finish the fight in any given second. Fighters shouldn't be going into battle thinking, *Okay, I've got three or five rounds and this is the scoring system, how do I fight according to that system to emerge victorious?* It should be much simpler than that. It should be, *This is a fight, how do I beat this man?* It is why I liked many elements of the old PRIDE scoring system in Japan because it placed more weight on what happened towards the end. If a fighter got off to a slow start but spent the entire second half chasing and getting closer to a knockout or sub-mission, he would be favoured and scored more heavily for doing so. It eliminates the chances of a fighter simply holding an opponent down to nick the first three rounds, then clearly losing the final two but still having his hand held aloft at the conclusion. To be honest, I think the type of fighter that shoots for takedowns then clings on will be, and probably already is being, phased out of the sport, but adapting how we score fights now would undoubtedly expedite that process.

It would also make it interesting if someone like GSP made a return to the Octagon. There is a real clamour for Georges to make a comeback now but I think a lot of people are looking back in time through rose-tinted spectacles and hold a rather romantic memory of how St-Pierre fought. He was obviously a phenomenal fighter and champion, but if you actually watch footage of his later contests, plenty of fans are booing out of boredom. He began his career more aggressively and attack-minded, but after he paid the ultimate price against Matt Serra he started playing the percentages more. I spent twenty-five minutes in a cage with the undisputed best fighter of my weight class on the planet, and I left without a scratch on me. Something isn't right there in my opinion. It also goes against what I see as the raison d'être of martial arts. Bruce Lee said it himself: 'defeat your opponent as quickly and efficiently as possible', and that is my own perspective every time I step into the Octagon. GSP and AJ both beat me fair and square, but neither could be said to have done it quickly and efficiently.

In the dressing room after the AJ fight, I looked over at my cornermen, Steve Papp and Roy 'Big Country' Nelson, and realised I had lost confidence in their ability to improve me. To be fair, there weren't many genuinely slick, organised and professional corners in operation at that time. Jackson, who coached GSP and cornered Condit against me, probably stood out from the crowd. He went as far as mimicking the cadence or inflection of a foreign fighter's accent to replicate someone with their mother tongue speaking English as a second language. But the vast majority of fighters were just making do with the corners they had and not really gaining anything from them between rounds. Owen Comrie had been with me for every bout before Steve, but Owen could be very intense and when he got worked up he even slipped into his native Jamaican Patois which I found hard to follow at times. Nathan Leverton was normally alongside Owen. Nathan was very technically-minded and because of this, always had a lot of information to impart between rounds. When my heartrate is up and my adrenaline is pumping, I found that a more relaxed and positively-minded corner worked best to calm me down and reset me for the next round. The frantic atmosphere in that old corner team set-up gave me the information I needed, but the way in which it was delivered made it difficult to digest in the short sixty seconds of allotted rest. Steve then came in for the Swick match-up and I loved working with him. He was fully committed, always had a smile on his face and gave me 100 per cent no matter what else he had going on outside the gym. He also had great Muay Thai and general striking knowledge. But Swick was Steve's first time cornering in an MMA fight; he was a novice in this world. His lack of expertise shone through at times, like when I had GSP in a brief side-control and I heard him urge me to knee him in the head. He was still learning the intricacies of the sport and thinking in a street-fighting sense. Nelson then joined the camp after the Condit fight. I met him at the North Carolina show I attended during my road trip after GSP and he did a good job convincing me we would make a great team. The idea was that I would settle in Las Vegas to help him with striking and conditioning and in return he'd help me with jiu-jitsu and wrestling.

Nelson is a black belt under Renzo Gracie and he wrestled all through high school so I believed he could certainly improve my game. He had lots of experience against top guys and I also felt I could benefit from a new voice and fresh perspective within my circle. But the relationship deteriorated soon after the move to Nevada and by the time the AJ fight came along I had little time for Roy. I just didn't feel he was as committed to my career as he could have been, considering how much I invested in this during camp. The sum of all those moving parts was that I always felt I was merely working with what I had in terms of a corner. When I went to train with GSP before he fought Condit in 2012, his coach, John Danaher, told me I had been winning throughout my UFC career *in spite of* my coaching. That was a big moment. It made me stop and think and I saw that he was probably correct. If I could do it all over again, and I had the resources to make it happen, I would move to the US, sign up with one of the big teams, and settle there on day one. But back then I had neither the money nor the contacts nor even a working visa so I got my head down and worked with what I had.

But sitting there with Steve and Roy after the AJ fight, I had never felt more defeated in my life. With my thumb in a bucket of ice I listened to Steve tell me that the journey wasn't over, that I'd get another chance and there was lots we could improve on. I wasn't convinced. 'I'm done, Steve,' I told him. 'I'm just not enjoying this any more. It's time for me to do something else with my life.' I meant every word of it too. If I'm honest, I presumed the UFC were going to get rid of me anyway. That was my third strike and it is extremely rare that a fighter gets given another life after a trio of consecutive defeats. I had always said that my plan was to ride the UFC rollercoaster until the wheels fell off. There was no way I was going to grind away out of the spotlight in front of a few hundred drunk, bloodthirsty fans on a lower circuit, praying each time my phone rang that it was Lorenzo or Dana inviting me back into the big league. I was ready to move on. As far as I was concerned that night in Seattle, the Outlaw had retired.

● ● ●

The UFC didn't cut me, however. Part of the reason for that is down to the gauntlet of killers I had lost to: there was disappointment but certainly no shame in losing to GSP, Condit and Johnson and that bought me some leeway. But I was no longer so naive about my standing within the organisation and I understood that everything was a business decision. The UFC had invested a lot of time and money in me as a brand and I was still marketable due to my fighting style, so the last thing they wanted was for the Outlaw to go and be successful with a rival promotion. I was also easy to work with, never turned a fight down, did all the media work required, and never tried to renegotiate my contract or demand more money. I guess I was the consummate corporate employee, a by-product of being more interested in fighting than riches. And yet I no longer felt treated as such. In fact, I no longer felt particularly valued by the UFC at all. Part of the problem was undoubtedly due to my naivety in the early days when I was winning every fight and everyone was being nice to me. I felt they were building me and allowing me to develop without being rushed, like they were matching me perfectly with exciting bouts that would challenge me in various aspects of my game, yet were within my capability if I gave it my all. I then got my title shot without a delay, lost it but was immediately back in the mix versus Condit. At that time I still thought I was one of the golden boys and that Condit was the perfect guy for me to beat and get straight back into contention. But looking back I see it more as a no-lose situation for UFC. If he won, he was the new fresh contender. If I won, I was back looking for an eliminator again. The UFC would win either way and probably had little preference as to which man advanced. When I then got AJ I really started to understand that the organisation wasn't interested in me on any personal level, that their interest was in me as a commodity and nothing more. This was a desperately discouraging insight, but the seeds of hopelessness had been sown even earlier than that.

I felt like I had done more than my fair share of the promotional duties ahead of the GSP fight. There was little interest in it when it was announced as most said I couldn't win and didn't even deserve to be there. So I worked my ass off for the Primetime show and all the rest to sell PPVs, PPVs that only GSP as the champ would see a penny of. Amidst it all I lost my grandad and didn't let that affect me outwardly. I didn't bat an eyelid when the UFC effectively took over my camp and scuppered all my plans. And I survived twenty-five minutes with a legend. I knew how well the PPV had sold and so when I later got my cheque and it was nowhere near the level of compensation I believed my endeavours deserved I felt truly undervalued. GSP spent five times my total cheque on his training camp alone. Okay, he'd fought his way up the ladder into a position to be able to do that, but I was hoping that after facing him I'd be rewarded enough to be able to make a similar investment in my own career. But it hadn't worked out like that. Apparently, in some people's eyes, I hadn't progressed at all from my first fight in the UFC. Up to then they'd looked after me and met my very humble expectations with their discretionary bonus cheques, but that was no longer the case. Having spoken to other title challengers I had an amount in mind for what I would receive after GSP and the final number was way less than I hoped. I felt I had busted my balls for nothing other than a loss on my pristine UFC record. I felt disillusioned, like I was a cash cow they'd fully drained. I felt like my investment, in terms of money, time, my entire life really, was never going to pay off as I had once imagined it would. Then I was punched unconscious in London by Carlos Condit and I began questioning whether this was all worth it from the point of view of what I was putting my family through. My head was spinning a little, with everything feeding in to a grand sense of disillusionment with my career in MMA.

But rather than show me the door, it wasn't long before Dana was asking me to headline a show in Milwaukee against Chris Lytle. Lytle had starred on *The Ultimate Fighter* season they called 'The Comeback'. It featured guys who had previously been cut from the UFC and the prize was a shot at GSP's welterweight title. Lytle fought his way through to the final, where he lost a very close split decision to Matt Serra. We all know what then transpired when Matt fought Georges, but it was also a turning point in Lytle's own career. From that point onwards he decided he would just go out and brawl, force the pace, give the fans what they wanted and fight for bonuses. And he was hugely successful with his fresh approach, eventually accumulating ten of those bonus cheques and becoming the first man to win the Fight of the Night, Knockout of the Night, and Submission of the Night accolades. *Fuck it*, I decided, surprising myself a little with my gut reaction. *Why not?* I had already mentally checked out but it did bug me that my final minutes in the Octagon had been spent bored to death under the weight of Anthony Johnson. I couldn't stop thinking about the fans that had paid a lot of money and travelled huge distances to watch that disappointment. Against Lytle, high-octane action was guaranteed so *fuck it, yeah*, I thought, *let's do it one more time and put on a show*.

Despite the reservations I now held about the team I had surrounding me, I stuck with Papp and Nelson one more time. The call to fight had arrived much quicker than I had anticipated and I simply didn't have time to start making massive changes concerning my fight preparation. But it wasn't a good camp and I was over-trained and exhausted by the time fight week arrived. My mind was wandering to life beyond the UFC. I was already thinking about what was coming next, not like versus Condit in relation to getting another title shot, but in terms of a totally different life far removed from fighting. I'd investigated university courses and was pretty excited by the thought of signing up to the first semester in September. I viewed Lytle as my last hurrah, as the all-out war I was supposed to get with Johnson. I just wanted to brawl. I wanted a fight that the fans would come up after and say, 'Wow that was wild, that was so much fun to watch, thank you, man.' And so a crude and brutal war is all I trained for. There was no real game-plan. I didn't think Chris was particularly outstanding in any specific range. I knew I was faster, younger, technically more rounded in striking and I believed that he didn't have the wrestling game to take me down and hold me down. I was training to have a high cardiovascular output to stand in the pocket to throw bombs for fifteen minutes. I was training to fight, not to win. All I wanted was the adrenalin of violence coursing through my veins. I felt that, even if I did win, my UFC career would be short-lived anyway and I was ready for a new chapter. Lytle was in the same boat, actually announcing his retirement at the final press conference, and as a natural brawler it was clear what he was going to do. I just gave him the fight he wanted; he even said exactly that to me after when he thanked me. I could have fought at a longer range, could have used my footwork, could have kicked him, could have done anything else to win that fight. But I just stood toe to toe in a primitive shoot-out that he managed to get the better of after my lazy last-minute shot and attempted slam to break the rhythm of the fight and land some ground-and-pound. It was the most ignorant fight of my life. I had engaged in more astute and cerebral physical confrontations as a drunken seventeen-year-old on Saturday nights outside pubs in Nottingham than my performance in Wisconsin against Chris Lytle. With perhaps just my debut against Lee Doski aside, I had never fought so crudely in a professional fight. It was Plan C without even bothering with an A or B first.

I sat in the post-fight press conference with sore knuckles and a black eye, ready to say my goodbyes and do something else. I'd lost but I was smiling, and I never smile after I lose. But this smile was laced with a sense of resignation, it really was time to move on. Whether I wanted to or not, my ride on the UFC express was over. And then it all changed with one tweet from Lorenzo Fertitta. The journalists in the room picked it up and I was soon told what the UFC kingpin had said: 'Will not cut Dan Hardy! I like guys that war!' It was a small, yet massive gesture. It came from Lorenzo the individual rather than the overall UFC business, but it effectively amounted to the same thing. As far as I know, nobody before me had ever lost four in a row and kept their name on the UFC roster. It was a hell of a vote of confidence to receive and I guess I instinctively felt like I owed it to Lorenzo not to throw it back in his face by walking away. He had stuck his considerable neck out for me, if not financially at least in a reputational sense, and there was an instant spark of desire within me to repay and validate that faith. I definitely needed a break to reassess and recalibrate, but I knew my UFC journey hadn't reached its final destination just yet.

7

MY REPTILIAN SELF

It was a full nine months before I stepped back into the Octagon, and when I did so I was a different man from before. I'd had some good people around me in Los Angeles in terms of training, but so many elements of living in that city weren't working for me. I was trapped in an old routine and an outdated mind-set that wasn't doing me any favours. It was actually causing me to disconnect from my natural and deep-rooted love of martial arts in a way I had never thought possible. Somewhere along the line it had become all about building my career and less about growing as a martial artist. With the losses mounting it was difficult to see any light at the end of a very long and dark tunnel. MMA is an all-consuming profession and when things are not going well, it negatively affects every single part of your life. For a while I woke up feeling like shit and went to bed feeling like shit and all my personal relationships suffered along the way. I felt like I couldn't get away from the negativity either. I was in the public eye and a lot of the public had apparently decided that I wasn't good at my job and should be sacked. With the likes of Twitter and Facebook in full flow, that meant every time I went online I was reading about how bad I was and why I didn't deserve to be earning a living. There seemed to be a growing movement that wanted my UFC contract torn up and my head on a spike. Having thousands of people demanding in very public forums that the job I loved and had been dedicated to for over a decade be taken from me was tough to stomach to say the least. I equated happiness in life with my success as a martial artist back then so it was a horrible place to find myself in. I was angry and frustrated that all my hard work and sacrifices were being discounted, it was just, *Get rid of him, he doesn't belong any more*. There were supportive voices in among the critics, of course, but for the first time in my career I suddenly had to search a little harder to find them. A lot of people look to live vicariously and be inspired by sports stars, but the flipside is that as soon as the star stops being successful, those people must move on and find a new athlete to feed off.

Basically, I felt very alone. I was rarely back in the UK now so I had lost the consistent support network of Rough House and the contagious positive energy that flows out of Steve Papp. They had always been there for me and provided a major source of strength at times when I may have been feeling a little sorry for myself. I had training partners and good friends in LA, but never that feeling of brotherhood that created such a strong bond within Rough House and made us feel like we had a team in an individual sport environment. In LA everyone had their own agenda and their own issues to deal with and a clear focus on themselves as individuals. Rough House, on the other hand, was always a genuine team. We worked towards a common goal and were there for each other when there was a need. If one of the boys back home lost a fight, all the others would be keeping in contact, saying we're training here or there, and making sure the guy who needed it most at that moment was there in the thick of it. There was never any sense of abandonment like I felt after each loss when I was living in the US. Returning to England wasn't really a viable option, but I decided I needed to wipe my slate clean, step out of where I currently was in my life, and continue with an entirely new chapter. I needed something to refresh and recharge me and the only way I could see to do that was to change everything. With my mind made up, I packed all my possessions into the back of a U-Haul truck, loaded my old Pontiac Hot Rod onto a trailer, and set off in a north-easterly direction, destination Las Vegas, Nevada.

Now I was in a new location, it was time to change the nuts and bolts of what constitutes daily living. One element I knew I needed to revise was my interests outside of MMA. For a few years I had been getting bogged down in some really heavy and depressing issues. I've always enjoyed reading, but I found myself drawn to subjects like animal rights and political corruption. I was researching factory farming and the US dog-fighting subculture one week and then lost in books like *Confessions of an Economic Hit Man* by John Perkins the next. As subject matter I knew it was all too dark to be immersing myself in while preparing to fight in the UFC, but I still struggled to walk away from it. I started becoming more outspoken on certain issues and this in turn led to a lot of people bringing more of humanity's woes to my attention. After a while I couldn't separate myself from the cruel, selfish and often ignorant actions of people all around the world, and it burdened me with negative thoughts that weighed heavily on my shoulders. So the move to Vegas was like drawing a line in the desert sand and I took the opportunity to put some distance between myself and massive, global issues I could do little to influence at this point in my life.

I found the likes of Howard Zinn and Noam Chomsky relatively light relief after years of unadulterated doom and gloom glaring out from every page. Chomsky is so intelligent and to the point with his ideas, but he's amusing along with it. He reminded me of my grandad in many ways. Reading his thoughts actually made me quite positive about the human race again. I began appreciating how resilient we are as a species and saw that if we could just open our eyes a little wider and band together, we could stop a lot of the awful shit going on in the world. I felt like there were millions of people out there from different walks of life and distinct schools of thought who were all moving in the same direction. In a weird way it took a load off me as I realised that the stuff I thought I had been carrying on my shoulders alone was shared across the globe.

My old friend and training partner in LA, Mac Danzig, then recommended the work of Terence McKenna. I immediately connected with his outlook and really began to open my mind to new ways of viewing the world and my own consciousness within it. That led me on to other revolutionary thinkers such as Timothy Leary, Albert Hoffman and, later, Dr Rick Strassman and Graham Hancock, who have all contributed immensely to my current operating system. I wouldn't say they necessarily changed my thinking in any dramatic way, but they certainly enthused me about life at a time when I was in danger of losing interest. They also gave me back that feeling that there is something more to life, much like kung fu and the other traditional arts did for me back in my college days, and faith in religion does for millions of people around the world today. In terms of traditional religions, I've always been a little too questioning and cynical about the intangible and therefore find it hard to be satisfied without some evidence or a source that I can go to and see for myself, as I did with China and kung fu, for example. But as well as something that I was able to reach through meditation and natural substances, gaining a better understanding of consciousness involved a lot of scientific research. I was excited by the idea of going on a journey of self-discovery and, although I'd been pursuing it for a number of years with the martial arts, this seemed to be all-encompassing and far more powerful on a personal basis. That excitement carried over into my training camp, and I used that positive energy to drive me through my fight preparations. Often when I got back from training in the evening I was just too tired to keep my eyes open and read a book, so I started listening to McKenna's audio recordings. He has such a gentle voice and a comedic way of putting things that it's perfect for relaxing and absorbing simultaneously. I would fall asleep listening to him talk about the benefits of psychedelic plants and his

The finishing touches of my knockout victory over Chad Reiner,
the win that got me my UFC contract.

Above: UFC 95 at the O2 Arena, London. One of the most surreal moments of my career, walking up to the front doors and seeing my name in lights.

Below: With my proud parents after a successful first round knockout over Rory Markham.

One of the best punches I've ever thrown.

Opposite: Great face-offs don't always turn into great fights, but Anthony 'Rumble' Johnson was one of my toughest and most frustrating contests.

Above: Mike Swick showing a lot of heart in our three-round fight for a shot at Georges St-Pierre. He took some big punches and elbows and would not go down. Tough dude.

Right: The elbow in round three was what really sealed the deal on my split decision win over Marcus Davis. I'm glad this one lived up to the hype and trash talk. Definitely a big turning point in my career.

Georges St-Pierre. An educational twenty-five minutes with one of the greatest champions the sport has seen. It was an honour and I just wish I knew then what I know now so I would have had more to offer in the fight.

The infamous armbar escape. Stubbornness, determination, and three weeks of hell on the mats at Serra Jiu Jitsu was what saved my arm on that night.

The aftermath of the best punch of my career. Unfortunate that it was my friend Duane Ludwig on the receiving end, but it snapped a four fight losing streak and saved my spot on the UFC roster.

In my new role as a commentator, sat next to Jon Anik at a Fox Sports event in Melbourne, Australia.

Interviewing Brett Johns in Belfast after his successful debut.

On stage at the UFC Fight Night Belfast weigh-ins at the end of 2016, with top middleweight contender Gegard Mousasi.

Above: Race start of the Clipper Round the World yacht race, on the bow with my watch leader, Andrew Hendley. This was the first hour of the most challenging month of my life, sailing from London to Rio de Janeiro.

Right: With my beautiful wife Lacey, in Los Angeles in 2016.

theories on their impact on our evolutionary journey. Those lectures lifted me out of a hole: *here was something I could really explore*, I thought.

One of the more depressing thoughts that would drag me down in those days was the realisation that man has totally taken over the Earth and there is nowhere you can go to be free. I have always had a real struggle with not feeling free. It partly explains my love of pirates dating back to when I was a kid. I was always very jealous of that lifestyle, not the raping and plundering and pillaging, but the anarchy and absolute freedom of a group of outlaws banding together and living under no monarchic or governmental rule. There were captains, of course, but they tended to be elected and agreed upon by the crew and would never stay in control for very long if they weren't fair and just in their leadership role. Freedom today is an illusion. There is nowhere you can make money legally and not be required by law to hand over a portion of what you have earned to someone else. And there is nowhere you can go where you won't be standing on land owned and controlled by someone else. That inescapable fact, that there are no frontiers for man left on Earth, is a real killer to me. Bar the depths of the ocean or launching into outer space, there is nowhere on my planet to explore, nowhere undiscovered and unmapped. I really identified with Kevin Costner's character in *Dances with Wolves* when he arrives at the last outpost and tells the general he wants to go to the abandoned frontier outpost and rebuild it. 'Why?' the general asks. 'Because I want to see the frontier while it still exists.' It also explains why I've always been fascinated by famous explorers like Sir Francis Drake, Captain James

Cook and Sir Ernest Shackleton. Imagine setting off in a ship and believing there is every chance you'll sail off the edge of the world. What a perspective on life they must have had. Or imagine taking a pack of dogs and going to the South Pole, in an attempt to reach a destination or make a crossing that had never been done before. I loved reading about Alexander the Great marching his armies into Asia and describing tribes of little men living in trees. He meant monkeys, of course, but they had no concept whatsoever of what a monkey was until they saw it. It was depressing to admit that, visits from alien life forms aside, there is nothing left like that for me to discover. Even if I saw a T-Rex crossing Shepherd's Bush Green in London tomorrow, although I'd be equally amazed and terrified, I'd instantly recognise it for what it is.

Listening to McKenna speak, however, I realised that he had found something that worked for him and I was eager to know if I could reap similar benefits. Psilocybin could offer me the means to be an explorer. Psilocybin could take me to places and show me things that my mind was as yet unable to imagine or fathom. It would provide access to my own subconscious which, like everyone else's, is unique and personal to me and would help me find ways to better myself and improve my human experience. It wasn't long before I grew convinced that psychedelic experiences were what I needed to emerge from the pit I had been languishing in, and get back to a state of constant evolution. I also heeded McKenna's words on the importance of 'set and setting', and was determined to follow the respectful method he employs when working with psilocybin. It is crucial to appreciate that this is an organic substance that grows in nature and can be somewhat unpredictable. This means that even the most seasoned veteran of the psychedelic realm can find these experiences difficult or challenging and should approach each ceremony with great care.

• • •

In my new home on the fringes of Vegas close to Red Rock Canyon, I created the MushRoom. This was my own personal and private space, a room in which I could stretch, meditate, smoke joints and, most weekends, have a dose of psilocybin in a ceremonial setting, in the hope of having a powerful psychedelic experience. With friends growing the raw material in California and Colorado and topping up my supply every time they passed through Nevada, I was able to consume as much as I liked, but as the body builds up a resistance to the toxins that cause the psychedelic experience, more than once a week is pretty pointless. On a very basic level, the ceremonies became my escape from the pressure I was under in my career. Where others turn to alcohol or prescription painkillers or gambling or another vice, I had mushrooms to break the monotony of training camp. But unlike the vast majority of consciousness-altering substances, they were massively more beneficial to me than simple escapism for a couple of hours. The common misconception that so-called magic mushrooms are for a crazy party experience has always seemed a little ridiculous to me, especially in the amounts that I work with. The correct dose for a deep psychedelic experience will not make you act a fool and dance to music that you would usually hate, but will take your pineal gland and fire it off into the stratosphere with your consciousness still attached. It is not always an easy or enjoyable process, but it is always a helpful one, allowing me to explore problem areas in my behaviour and issues in daily life and find the clarity I need to move past them.

My relationship with marijuana, something I introduced into my lifestyle a couple of fights before I signed with the UFC, can be thought of in similar terms. It began when I was having trouble sleeping and maintaining an appetite throughout training camps, mainly due to being uncomfortable, sore or injured after a day in the gym. Other than myself, a chiropractor friend in LA was the only person regularly monitoring my health and physical condition at that time and, aware that it had been a long time since I had used any pharmaceutically produced medicine, he suggested I try marijuana.

I always prefer to stay connected to my body, even when it is in pain, and I quickly found that marijuana and what I refer to as medicines help me not only connect with myself but also communicate with others. Fortunately, good-quality weed isn't hard to find in the City of Angels, especially with all of the 10th Planet friends I had in the area. I discovered that a couple of hits in a small glass pipe not only helped me relax, deal with pain and increase my appetite, but it also sparked my creativity, which had been largely absent since putting university on hold for a prize-fighting career. These renewed creative impulses brought about balance and gave me another way to relax when I had to stop smoking in the build-up to a fight.

I usually worked on the eight-weeks-before-a-fight rule, but after a couple of fights in the UFC that shifted to four weeks. That change came about because I found training camp to be so much more enjoyable and, contrary to popular stoner law, my motivation to train considerably more pronounced when I was consuming marijuana. It also provided some much-needed relief from the battering we take during fight preparations. Over the course of more than a decade within professional sports, I have met many athletes messed up or struggling with pharmaceutical painkillers and opiates, and not one for whom marijuana was not beneficial in some way or another. Sure, a few of them will get a little fat between fights, but we all deserve a break from the grind, especially when the grind involves kicking and punching every day. In recent years the limit for marijuana metabolites has been increased and I think in time the athletic commissions will realise that it is a far healthier and safer way to manage a lot of common problems that athletes experience. It certainly helped me over the years and kept me from needing anything stronger and potentially more damaging. If it were up to me I would take marijuana off the banned list altogether, particularly in light of the clear shift in opinion towards the plant that is taking place all around the world. Not everyone is so educated, however, and I find it disappointing that there are still many who subscribe to the archaic opinion that a plant should be regulated and maintain outdated laws enforcing that point of view on the general population. It echoes what I was saying about the apparent lack of true freedom in the world today. As the popular saying goes, if nature is illegal, freedom doesn't exist.

I always follow a routine when I eat mushrooms, and the ceremonial aspect of the experience is very important to me. In Vegas I would wake up on a Saturday morning and go to the gym to work up a thorough sweat. I then wanted to get out into nature and, living where I did, I was in complete wilderness a twenty-minute cycle from my front door. Out there hiking alone in the canyons I'd ground myself by walking across the rocks and streams barefoot to connect with the Earth. Then I returned home to clean the house and prepare my space. I laid out bananas, Brazil nuts and bottles of water in the kitchen, and in the MushRoom I organised my crystals and prayer beads and had a large mirror in place in case I wanted to interact and converse with myself during the ceremony. I normally had a sketchbook and notepad with pens and pencils at hand too. Finally, I set up whatever music I wanted to listen to later on, rolled a couple of joints, and walked around the house with burning white sage to seal the space for protection, much like the ceremony at the beginning of a Muay Thai fight. When everything was ready I would then meditate in order to set my intentions for the ceremony, another recommendation of Terence McKenna's. The idea is to focus on the things that you want to explore or need to confront so they are in the forefront of your mind when the mushrooms take hold. This could be anything from issues in personal relationships, uncertainty in plans for the future, or psychological preparations for a fight, all the way to questions on the very nature of our existence. The important thing was to go into the ceremony with clearly-defined questions and a specific aim in mind.

As the sun began to set, it was then time to take, using McKenna's terminology, a heroic dose. That means five grams of dried mushrooms and upwards, basically enough to pin you to the floor and take you to another dimension. I found that pushing past seven grams would make me feel a little overwhelmed, losing total awareness of my physical self and experiencing nothing but intense love and light. Although beautiful to experience the complete separation of body and consciousness, I found that it wasn't as productive to work with. Once I had discovered my ceiling I was able to play with amounts until I could manage the experience better and get the most out of it. Although it's an organic substance and can still be powerful in small doses, the price of my ticket was usually about five grams dried. With three grams I could be quite functional and have a conversation with someone or go out hiking, but a heroic dose is designed to push the boundaries and take you as deep as possible. That meant it was important to feel secure in my environment: hence the routine to make everything as safe and comfortable as possible. It is hard to say I am in complete control of what is happening, but certainly it always feels manageable and safe, and I always came out the other side feeling like a new, improved version of myself. It re-established my connection to the Earth, allowing me to identify with it as a living entity of which I am a part instead of an inanimate rock where we live very separate, disconnected lives. I guess it is a controlled chaos and I have the option whether to step in or out and can choose whether to turn the volume up or down on the experience. Five grams is just about perfect for what I needed. It rockets me out of my physical being for a few hours but there is a sense of familiarity with where I find myself almost every time I enter a psychedelic space. The effects are similar to those caused by dimethyltryptamine; I once heard the state of being that DMT induces being described as the waiting room between death and rebirth. To this day I haven't heard a verbal articulation of the experience that makes as much sense. Even from the first journey into that space, it felt like I had been there many times before and I always felt very nurtured and safe. So safe that I was usually a little disappointed when I could feel the medicine delivering me back into my body and the MushRoom.

With the mushrooms digested, I keep meditating until I feel it coming on and then I lie down and will be gone for four or five hours. When the psilocybin begins to wear off, I eat my snacks and drink my water and grab my sketchbook and notepad. There'd be times in Vegas when I would wake up the next day to find the house covered in notes and drawings scattered on the floor and taped to walls. In Nevada I'd also go into my backyard and stare at the sky. It is much easier to connect with the natural environment around you in Vegas, it is inescapable really. In the UK I still enjoy spending time in nature but it is generally overcast and feels sort of enclosed. That serves to shrink our perspective on the universe and can make us a little ignorant of the vastness of everything. But on the edge of Vegas where I lived, I could see all the way across the valley to the distant mountains defining the horizon and the invariably clear sky ensured the stars shone spectacularly. Everywhere in the UK is cultivated and controlled in some way, but much of Nevada is still untouched and fairly barren wilderness. In an environment like that it is easier to build a relationship with the Earth. I know that sounds a little hippyish, but it's true. It granted me much-needed perspective on my life and my place in the world.

Around that time I developed a regular meditation that I turned to during times when I felt consumed by the negatives I was facing. I used to zoom out and visualise myself from above. Then I'd zoom out again and see the house and backyard. Then Las Vegas and the valley, then the North American continent, until eventually I was looking down on planet Earth. I could then appreciate how insignificant I was, and how unimportant the stress and drama I was dealing with were in the bigger picture; that felt very reassuring. All I needed was to feel connected to the bigger picture and that was easily achieved by standing barefoot on the Earth and acknowledging that this is what I have come from and this is what I'll return to. Anything I experience between those two moments in time is temporary and inconsequential. It simply doesn't matter. I learnt similar lessons from reading Albert Hoffman's *LSD and the Divine Scientist*. As well as discovering LSD, Hoffman cured his own depression with logic after having a conversation with a tree in his garden. He told himself that on a molecular level there was little difference between himself and a tree, so why is he struggling and the tree was doing so well?

After snacking and taking on some water, I would then return to the MushRoom, turn on my music and meditate. This would often allow me to step back into the psychedelic experience. It was now a bit more manageable and I could direct it somewhat. I found that there were doorways in my mind that I could access using psychedelics. Music played a huge role in the process, often guiding me through a particular psychedelic journey. Massive Attack's *Mezzanine* album and *Subconscious* by Phutureprimitive were influential, but *The Dark Side of the Moon* by Pink Floyd was made for the psychedelic experience and I turned to it a lot. It spoke to me personally because it is very British in a lot of ways and I could easily relate to the subject matter David Gilmore and Roger Waters sang about. It is as if the language used is very familiar to me and when they talked about time passing you by and life moving too quickly, it resonated with where I was at that time. I was approaching thirty and my career was not panning out as I had expected. There were issues in my personal life too and I had a real sense that I needed to grow up and take responsibility for everything. *The Dark Side of the Moon* captured a lot of those feelings, with its lyrics about not being told to run, and missing the starting gun. Pink Floyd also tended to take me back to my childhood and to memories stored in my subconscious that I had never revisited. During one ceremony I saw my own birth from the point of view of my family members waiting in the hospital for news of my arrival. I remember that it was specifically through the eyes of my auntie, my mum's eldest sister, that I watched the drama unfold. I was old enough to recollect my sister and cousins being born, but I was still a child too through those arrivals. To witness the birth of a baby into the family from an adult's perspective, and then be there to see that baby grow and develop into an adult themselves, was something totally different. I saw it all through my auntie's eyes and understood what I must mean to her and the love she has for me.

Sometimes I would let the music play out and then sit in front of the mirror and have long internal conversations with myself. I discovered during these dialogues that there was a definite disconnect between me and my physical self. The first time I looked in the mirror during a ceremony I didn't recognise my body. It was as if my skin and flesh and bones were just a suit I was wearing. That what I saw wasn't really me but just a form and a space I am currently occupying. It was a truly weird sensation. I wondered then whether my pupils were dilated and so I leaned in close and looked deep into the black of my eyes. *Oh, there I am*, I remember thinking. Only in the blackness of my eyes did I recognise myself.

An experience with salvia, a psychoactive plant from Mexico, reaffirmed this disconnect between my physical and real self. In the parts of Latin America where it grows, locals just grab ten or fifteen leaves from a bush, stuff them up into the roof of their mouths and use their tongue to squeeze the juices out for the full experience. Unfortunately I had to make do with a dried version of the leaf in Vegas, and that meant smoking a hell of a lot more to achieve a similar result. But I'd been reading all about it and wanted to go as deep as possible, so one day I stuffed as much as I could into a bong and took three or four huge rips until I felt something happening. To be honest, it was a bit of a creepy and uncomfortable feeling for me. I lay down on the sofa and had the sensation of expanding until I filled the whole room. Then I saw images of all my cells, looking like miniature versions of me, linking arms and marching along together as I felt my skin crawl all across my body. About ten minutes later I opened my eyes and sat up. I stayed seated for a while until I was sure I felt normal again and then stood up and walked to the kitchen to get a drink. I got as far as the corner of the sofa before I collapsed. Sometime later, I have no idea how long, I woke up with incense oil, which I must have somehow taken from the back of a shelf, stinging my eyes and burning the inside of my nose and mouth. The taste and sensation were absolutely foul. But as I was lying there on the carpet looking across the room, I became aware of one question in my mind. *Which one am I?* Not *who am I?* But *which one am I?* It was like I was in the scene from *The Matrix* when they are sitting in the chairs plugged in through the back of their heads. I felt like I was in a room of eight bodies with one plug. The plug was my consciousness and could be inserted into any of the eight physical forms and I wasn't sure which vehicle for the human experience I was in. It was as if my consciousness can occupy other bodies and have entirely separate human experiences from the one that I have been living since my birth. A few minutes later, as I was leaning over the kitchen sink trying to wash the oil from my eyes, nose and mouth, I began feeling like myself again. It was a strange and revealing experience, but I will wait until I have the actual plant before engaging with salvia again.

Staring at my Self via my pupils in a psychedelic state was a mesmerising experience. I was reading Carl Sagan's *The Dragons of Eden* around this time, learning about the triune brain and Paul D. MacLean's theory that our forebrains added two additional structures, a limbic system and a neocortex, to the initial reptilian complex as our species evolved. Suddenly it was clear that the various driving forces within me had their own distinct agendas and the ceremonies helped me understand these different influences. What interested me most was the reptilian part of my brain whose job it was to keep me alive. It is from this R-complex that our propensity for aggression, territoriality and social hierarchy arises. It was very much applicable to Las Vegas life where so many of the population are hardwired into their reptilian complex. Vegas does strange things to the people that live there for any length of time. It is as if the energy of the city affects their operating system and forces many of them to rely on reptile to get through their days. I guess it is down to the surrounding natural environment being so bleak. It is such a harsh way of living, things aren't meant to survive in the desert. You can build a city, populate it with humans and provide everything they need to survive, but the mentality of desert life is still in operation. It's an every-man-for-himself-type vibe. If there was a water shortage I wouldn't be surprised to see people shooting each other in Walmart carpark within hours. Around 4,000 people move to Vegas each month so there is a constant feeling that everyone is out to get each other, to take what you have. The ceremonies helped me connect with the people around me and helped me understand the lives they were living and the internal influences that were guiding their decision-making. This in turn allowed me to let go of any frustration I felt towards them, and forgive them for the poor decisions they made. They also helped me understand a little better my need to fight. When I looked into the blackness of my eyes, it was like I was looking directly at the reptilian part of my brain. Or rather, like I was entering through my pupils and stepping right inside my brain. I started communicating with it directly, reassuring it, strengthening it, feeding it, talking to it, getting to know it better. If there was something I was struggling with technically or from a motivational point of view I was able to assess it and pull it apart and put it back together in a way that made more sense and helped me get over the bump in the road. I was communicating with my true self in a way that had been impossible without a psychedelic experience. And I sensed my reptilian brain was now coming to the fore because my career appeared to be dying and it had to help save it. I knew I needed to make some changes to rescue myself, but I felt confident knowing the reptile in me had my back. The practice felt almost like I was cultivating a relationship with a powerful animal that would step up and defend me if I was ever threatened.

Then, when the sun was starting to rise and I was feeling the effects of having the equivalent of about a gram or a gram and a half in my system, I'd go out into the canyons for a trail run. I can function perfectly at this point, but I am still in an altered enough state that connecting with the space around me comes naturally. I would just hare down these trails in my Vibram Fivefingers, and occasionally I'd wipe out and end up bloody and bruised, but that rush was part of the attraction for me now I had no fight in the immediate future to train for. At that time of the day there was no one else around so I could just blaze down as fast as my legs could carry me. What I realised was that with this gram or so I could read my environment so much quicker and more clearly due to the psilocybin compound enhancing my edge and depth perception. Despite the velocity of my descents, I could see exactly where my feet were going to go and read whether it was solid rock or gravel. I could sense what might cause me problems and I felt more balanced and agile in order to deal with it. Basically, I just felt more switched on. It was like having adrenalin coursing through my veins at the absolute height of that sensation, but without the tremors or fear or anxiety that accompany that experience. It was like the mushrooms allowed me to log into my R-complex and function at my physical and mental peak. It is an incredible feeling, one that provides supreme confidence. McKenna talks about it in his book, *Food of the Gods*. He describes our ancestors clambering down from the trees as the rainforests depleted in Africa, becoming foragers on the plains, consuming psilocybin as they came across it in mushrooms, and benefiting from the enhancement in their visual acuity to increase chances of avoiding predators and catching prey. They also became more sexually active and so, effectively, better survivors all round. He goes on to hypothesise that the psilocybin also triggered neuroleptic seizures that would eventually lead to speech and imagination and intelligence and everything that is human. In essence, McKenna concludes, our higher consciousness was reached via eating mushrooms. But it was the first point, the avoiding predators and catching prey that immediately attracted my attention. Imagine if I could get into that state inside the Octagon. Imagine if I could grant my reptilian brain total control over my movements and actions in an MMA fight. The possibility fascinated and re-energised me.

Psychedelics undoubtedly got me back on track with my life. They provide me with a greater sense of balance and perspective. I always use them with purpose. For me, it is not about taking a handful of mushrooms and going to a party. I use them to learn about myself and understand my life better. Who I was and why I had become that person.

It is very difficult to explain the psychedelic experience with words. As a race we have become so estranged from it and our languages fail us. No one has yet developed the vocabulary to fully articulate what happens in a psychedelic state. But what I can say is that those ceremonies in Las Vegas reopened my eyes to how much I love martial arts and how privileged I was to be doing my passion as a job and making a living from it. They showed me how lucky I was to be able to dedicate my time and energy to something I loved, when going into the Lytle fight I had forgotten all of that. They reminded me that life as a mixed martial artist is supposed to be challenging, but it is very rewarding too. I saw that I always have options to move forward and it is up to me to choose the correct ones. I was ready to fight again.

● ● ●

The permanent move to Vegas naturally precipitated a change in my training team. I welcomed that, feeling I would benefit from some new eyes on my game. Seeing less of Nelson didn't bother me, but I still feel guilty that I created distance between Steve Papp and me. Looking back, I didn't explain things particularly well to Steve, but in all honesty I didn't really understand what was going on in my head at that time. My partnership with Owen Comrie had fizzled out naturally as he was being pulled in so many directions by his family, full-time job and other fighters under his charge, but Steve had always been totally committed to me. We worked well together and it was tough to leave him, but I was convinced that a new direction was required. I wanted a team that already worked well together. I no longer wanted to manage my own schedule and try to piece everything together myself.

I began spending a lot of time with the UFC veteran heavyweight Frank Mir. Frank, a true legend of the sport still going strong a full fifteen years on from his debut at UFC 34, had opened his own gym in Las Vegas and built a team around him there. It is a set-up more akin to what an elite pro boxer enjoys and I was happy to be able to stay out of the MMA factory model and move into Frank's more intimate arrangement. As I was tall and long enough to replicate a smaller heavyweight's reach, I started as his sparring partner, doing rounds one and six when he wanted a session of six five-minute rounds. We are style-opposites in many ways and that ensured we could learn from one another. I am quick and good on my feet with a countering style and high work rate. Frank, like many heavyweights, slows down quicker than lighter athletes when fatigue sets in, but he's immensely strong and when he takes you down he can snap your limbs off with ease. We made a good team and I could be trusted to be controlled while in there with him. Other sparring partners, through either ego, eagerness to impress, or fear, get into the cage with a superstar and go all out for a KO. There are plenty of guys like that in the MMA world. I find them all the time while travelling around dropping into gyms for sparring or when teaching seminars. In seminars you can do thirty rounds with a different person each time, and there'll always be one who tries to take your head off or rip your arms out so they have a story to tell when they get home. It is hardly ideal when what you are looking for is someone controlled and respectful who understands the point of a sparring session and won't let ego take over. The danger posed by unknown quantities is part of the reason some gyms now insist on fighters donning headgear, sixteen-ounce gloves and an array of padding over shins and arms before stepping into the cage. I respect the rules of every gym I walk into, but I prefer not to use headgear if there is any way I can avoid it. The fact is, I get hit far more often with the protection on. My style is built around slipping punches and that means becoming adept at letting a fist whistle an inch or less past my skull. With the headgear adding an extra couple of inches all around, those slipped punches tend to land as glancing blows that can upset balance. Another problem I have with added protection is that opponents often throw heavier against a guy with headgear because they treat it like hitting a punch bag. The only time I choose to wear extra gear is closer to a fight when I'm working at close quarters doing a lot of clinch work and want to avoid head clashes or getting nicked or cut.

The beauty of being part of Mir's team was that I had my coaches around me all the time. It wasn't like before when I'd work with a grappling coach, then a different striking coach in a different gym, then go searching for sparring by walking into a gym full of sharks with no one from my side looking on at all. The three main men I was now working with were Jimmy Gifford, Ricky Lundell and Shawn Yarborough. Yarborough is a vicious and excellent Muay Thai specialist, while Lundell is a grappling wizard and an immensely strong athlete, and both men were a good size to double up as training partners for me. Giff then assumed the head coach role, overseeing everything and formulating fight strategies. They were able to put their three heads together and say, 'Okay, today we're going to work on this, I want Dan doing this, and we're going to achieve this.' It took a lot of the pressure off my shoulders and allowed me to concentrate solely on improving myself as a martial artist, which is exactly how it should be.

I love working with Giff because he is so passionate and committed. He started life as a boxing trainer, working pro corners in South Boston when he was only thirteen. He began a life-long friendship with Dana White when they were both young men, and later became Lorenzo's personal boxing coach. When they brought him into the UFC, they sat him in a hotel room with every UFC ever recorded and told him to watch and learn. Giff absorbed it all like a sponge. He enjoyed working with me because I came from something of a traditional boxing background and had the natural footwork and head movement you associate with prizefighters. In comparison with ex-wrestlers, who can sometimes struggle to grasp those basics, I was a fun project for him. He described his approach to me as throwing a bag of toys on the floor and watching what I instinctively picked up and played with. He would take me on the pads, but his real genius is figuring out game-plans and putting them into operation. I believe that part of the reason Giff is so good at his job is because he never had his own fighting career. That can be a problem for coaches for two reasons. Firstly, there is always the danger of a lingering jealousy if the pupil ends up surpassing the master's own achievements. That risk never exists with Giff because he has always wanted to teach and nothing else. It takes a special person to excel in this way, and I think that with the grappling arts at least you need to have had your hands on people to understand how things work, but

Jimmy has certainly succeeded. He doesn't crave the spotlight and never has an agenda. Every move he makes is decided upon with his fighter's best interests at heart.

The second potential issue with ex-fighters coaching is that many fall into the trap of trying to teach how they fought when that may not be the best style for their fighter. Both Owen and Steve taught me the styles that suited them, some of which clicked immediately while the rest simply didn't suit my physical attributes and strengths. Steve, who I still train with when I'm back home, recently discussed this with me as we reflected upon our training camps together. He also said that now I'm not so fat he can see how long my arms are and would do things differently to maximise my reach! Giff naturally takes each fighter on their own merit and designs a game-plan specific to them without being influenced by a previous life in the ring or Octagon. He is very open-minded and always wanting to learn himself. He is also very analytical and obsessed with how each fighter should approach a bout, and the fact that he is free from ego and honest about his own strengths and knowledge means he is happy to call for help from other specialists when necessary. If he devised a tactic for me to uti-lise switching my stance, for example, he'd then call Ricky in to drill it with me until it became second nature. I loved everything about Giff's approach to fight preparation.

I also loved just being around Frank. He is such a family man: part of the reason he built his own gym was so his wife and kids could always be there with him. Plenty of neighbours and friends were always milling about too. It was rather hectic and chaotic at times, and I sometimes found it difficult to cope with it close to fight time as I am more reclusive than Frank, but it was an environment that worked for him and I could only respect that. I sometimes wish I had had the resources to create my own space and fill it with whatever I needed to fuel me before a big fight, but unfortunately I never reached a point in my career where I could afford it. I often think back about what it would have been like to be able to truly explore my potential. If there is a target for us to aim for as a species, it must surely be to create a social structure where people have the freedom and resources to explore their true potential in whatever endeavour they choose. I much prefer that to the reality of life today where the vast majority simply work to help drive a lopsided economy and line the pockets of a select few. Nevertheless, I had a team around me and was grateful to them all for taking me in and being so generous with their time, knowledge and resources. It was also nice to be preparing with another fighter that would share the card with me at my next fight. I was ready to compete again. I felt like a new person both physically and mentally.

● ● ●

I was now training to face Duane Ludwig, a guy who had been a real inspiration to me throughout my career. Back in the early days when MMA footage was hard to come by, I would send off for DVDs of fights from some obscure events in Japan and South America, or the likes of King of the Cage and Gladiator Challenge where Ludwig was busy making a name for himself. I felt like I had watched his career progress in this way and was delighted for him when he made it into the UFC in 2003. I loved watching Duane fight and saw a lot of my own style in his game. He came from a kickboxing background and was trained by the one-and-only Bas Rutten, the first European UFC champion and a personal hero of mine. I liked how Ludwig represented Muay Thai in the MMA world and held him up as an example of the success I could achieve in the game. Back then, most of the main guys in the UFC came from wrestling or jiu-jitsu backgrounds, so seeing his polished striking skills on display was a joy to behold. I remember watching him bite down on his gumshield and blast away at someone against the fence or stepping to the side to find angles like a championship boxer too. He looked devastating in any striking range and that was exactly how I envisaged myself fighting if I ever reached the Octagon.

One thing I'll never forget about that fight week was the support I felt from everyone linked to the sport. We were fighting at the MGM Grand Garden Arena in Vegas, which effectively made it a home fixture, but the warmth of feeling towards me ran deeper than affection for an adopted local son. From fellow fighters to fans to media to everyone connected with the UFC organisation, it felt like they were all pulling for me. I was just about keeping my head above water in the riptide of a four-fight losing streak and if I lost this one, not even a tweet from Lorenzo would save me from going under. You always receive a lot of good wishes from all and sundry in the run-up to a bout, but this time they were heartfelt. All the behind-the-scenes staff that work tirelessly to make the UFC what it is paused and took a moment when they approached to wish me luck. Often their kind words were delivered with a direct look in the eye and a hand on the shoulder too. They weren't the bog-standard platitudes I had grown accustomed to and I had the impression that people were genuinely willing me on, as if they were invested in me winning as much as I was myself. They all gave me strength and I'll be eternally grateful for that support.

Ludwig was famous for recording the fastest knockout in UFC history when he sparked Jonathan Goulet inside a handful of seconds in 2006. It was with his signature punch at the time, a compact right hand starting with his fist close to his chin and thrown straight out with a twist at the end as it connected with an advancing opponent. The way he kept his elbow from flaring out and minimised the body rotation meant it was a very well-concealed punch. It was almost like a jab that nobody saw coming and he relied on his innate and exquisite timing to ensure the blow did maximum damage as he placed it perfectly on the tip of his opponent's chin. I respected the threat, but was intent on using his biggest weapon against him. I knew he'd keep looking for it because fighters always tend to revert to what has worked for them in the past. I made similar errors, trying to land my left hook too often at times. It all becomes too predictable and an opponent can anticipate and exploit it if they have a sharp eye and are paying attention. So I thought if I could draw this punch out of Ludwig on my terms, I'd be able to sneak my counter left around the corner and onto his exposed mandible. It didn't take long, in fact he caught me with it almost straight away in our first real meaningful trade. It really rang my bell and for a few seconds I felt unstable on my legs, so I grabbed hold, turned him and ran us both into the fence.

This was the point when my mushroom ceremonies connected with the fight. I had just spent nine months talking to the blackness of my eyes, connecting with my inner reptile, and I fully appreciated the potential value of engaging that element of my consciousness. It is about deactivating the sections of the brain that are over-thinking things like, *shit, if I hit that rock and fall there I could knock myself unconscious and never be found*, and trust the part telling you, *that piece of ground is solid, hit it with certainty at full pelt and continue down the trail*. I knew I would benefit from being in that space during a physical conflict, but the challenge was how to get there when a psilocybin ceremony backstage clearly wasn't an option. I had enjoyed some success with prolonged fasting and meditation because I knew the feeling I was looking for and could allow myself to pass into that state, but food deprivation isn't viable before a fight and it is tough to meditate in a fight environment when surrounded by other stimuli pulling your consciousness in different directions. I required another key to open the door.

There exists an old cliché that some fighters need to be hit with a clean shot before they start fighting, and that is effectively what happened to me against Ludwig when he landed his right. I was happy about that because it gave him confidence to use it again and again and I only needed to be waiting once to punish him. But it was a good shot and I was buzzed. It felt like I was under water. It is a sensation of floating and then sinking as your hearing grows muffled and distorted. The body's temporarily disturbed equilibrium then provides the sensation of being dragged by a current in various directions. That's how I felt pressed against Ludwig and the fence for a few seconds, but then I started having an internal conversation with myself. *I'm in a fight*, I said. *He's moving and I'm reacting to what he's doing. But I'm not even thinking about it, this is all automated now*. It dawned on me that the punch had switched my reptilian brain on and, having gone through so many repetitions in the gym that I now trusted that part of my subconscious to make the optimum move in any given combat situation, I decided just to let it take over. From that point on it was as if I was a passenger. I was still conscious of a thought process computing data and reacting accordingly, but it was independent of what my body was physically doing in the fight. I was still mulling over the thought of getting caught with that first clean shot and thinking I probably shouldn't let it happen again, and all the while my body was reacting to his movement and stifling his efforts to get off the fence. I was present, but as a spectator at my own fight. Then the second time I clinched him up against the fence, I remember very calmly and rationally thinking, *Okay, maybe I should try and draw that right hand from him now so I can land my left. So, I need to feint a jab and see that right hand come away from the chin to try and counter me. Just a few centimetres of movement is all I need, so I know that he's committing to it. Okay, good, he took the bait . . . now I'm gonna pump a jab to draw his counter a second time, and throw my left hook at the tip of his chin where his right hand should have been and clean his clock*. It was totally surreal, but that was the conversation with myself taking place in my head as I was fighting. I was full-reptile.

Now that I have a better understanding of myself, I look back at recordings of old fights and I can see in my eyes the moments when I was full-reptile. I can see it in other fighters too. Wanderlei 'The Axe Murderer' Silva and Robbie 'Ruthless' Lawler are two good examples. They get into that reptilian space and it is beautiful to watch them fight. I've seen it in other sports with the likes of the legendary Thai boxer Ramon Dekkers, who Ludwig actually fought, or Mike Tyson in his prime. Theirs is more of an internal, instinctual rage that needs an outlet, but I can identify with that feeling too. I've seen it with my dad on occasion and in myself when I used to drink and the alcohol had the undesirable effect of turning the volume up on my reptilian brain. The problem with alcohol is that it introduces raw emotions into the decision-making process. In full-reptile you are only interested in number one in the purest sense. Once in a nightclub I looked across the dance floor and saw three guys targeting a friend of mine. Logic would have told me to ignore it, that there's three of them and I should probably fetch help. But raw emotions originating in the limbic system and fuelled by the vodka I had consumed overrode those safety mechanisms and I piled in. My sense of brotherhood with those close to me and the innate desire to protect them when danger arose meant that full-reptile took over, which isn't always helpful. The alcoholic rage then ensured I still had one enemy by the hair, smashing his head against the floor when I was pulled off him. That's why combat sports are so important to provide an outlet to guys who would otherwise be menaces to society and to themselves. The dominant reptile inside them will manifest itself in some way, so we are all much better off if that happens in a ring or an Octagon. You can see it in plenty of other walks of life too. Wall Street and American politics are riddled with characters operating in full-reptile most of the time. Guys like Kissinger or Cheney or even Trump and Hillary Clinton today. They would walk over you and everyone else to secure more power. It is a very dangerous state of being when left uncontrolled.

My hands shot up in jubilation as soon as my left hook detonated on Ludwig's chin. As a fighter, you just know when you've landed one that signals the beginning of the end. A split second later, however, I realised I needed a killer blow to force the referee to call a halt. Because of all the respect I had for Duane, I just wanted to land one clean shot on his jaw to seal the deal without damaging him, but as I threw it he was beginning to sit up out of instinct, and my punch whistled past his head. The position we were both then in meant I had no option but to drop elbows, which opened a large cut on his forehead, before the ref dragged me off. It hurt me to leave him bloodied, but that is the nature of our sport. I stood up, walked to the centre of the Octagon, dropped to my knees and kissed the canvas in relief.

There must have been a line of forty journalists waiting to interview me backstage. Duane and I were the final fight of the preliminaries that night because it was a special show featuring five heavyweight bouts. Frank Mir, Junior dos Santos, Cain Velasquez, Stipe Miočić and Roy Nelson were all in action, but rather than watch the first of the main events, virtually all the press corps were waiting patiently in line for me. One after another they expressed their genuine elation for me. Having not felt particularly valued after the GSP fight and throughout subsequent match-ups, it was great to get that love from media, fans and all the people behind the scenes within the UFC machine. For the first time in a long while, I felt appreciated again.

● ● ●

Win, lose or draw against Ludwig that Saturday night in Vegas, I had a trip already booked well in advance which I wasn't going to miss. I returned to the MGM Grand to see Van Halen in concert the following night, travelled to California to meet my friend Beto on the Monday, flew to Peru on Tuesday, and on Wednesday I was deep in the Amazonian rainforest, ready for my first ayahuasca ceremony. Ayahuasca, sometimes translated as spirit vine or vine of the soul, is a potent brew that the indigenous peoples of the Amazonian region have taken as a traditional spiritual medicine for millennia. Made by combining the fibrous body of an ayahuasca vine with a companion plant containing the potent hallucinogen dimethyltryptamine, or DMT, the foul concoction is imbibed as a religious sacrament and a means to view ourselves as we really are, stripped of personality traits like ego and pride that often obscure true introspection. I first came across this teacher plant in the work of Terence McKenna and his brother Dennis, but it was a chance meeting with an old Rough House teammate at a MMA show in London that convinced me I needed the spirit vine's help.

Nick Ospiczak was a naturally talented guy who could seemingly turn his hand to whatever held his attention. His interest in MMA peaked and his life took him in a different direction but he had been good enough to fight four times in the UFC. A loss by split decision to Ludwig in Germany in 2010 eventually put paid to his career in the Octagon, but his mind always seemed to be going a million miles an hour, as if constantly searching for the next chapter. I hadn't seen him for a couple of years before I bumped into him in London, but I had been told he was a very different character now after taking part in an ayahuasca ceremony and I was eager to ask him all about it. I remembered him as this pretty hyper guy who always seemed a little restless in his mind, but he just looked at me serenely and smiled. I asked him about his experience and he sort of shrugged his shoulders and quietly told me that all he knew now is that everything was going to be all right. Seeing that calmness of energy and apparent peace of mind, particularly from a character like Nick, really struck me. I wanted some of that. And I was prepared to go to the source, to the Amazon, to find it.

The experience began long before I crossed the Equator and entered Peru, however. I adhered to a special diet in the two-week-long build-up to my first ceremony that was effectively vegetarian with the additional requisites of no oils, spices, seasoning, excess fat, salt, caffeine, acidic foods or sex. The idea is to cleanse the body physically before accepting the spirit vine but, just to be sure, we all endured a tobacco ceremony when we arrived to fully purge ourselves of toxins. This involved drinking copious amounts of a heavily-sweetened mix of tobacco and coffee that left a bitter aftertaste and caused you to sweat and vomit everything out of your system. It wasn't pleasant and there were a lot of tears and shivering uncontrollably in the corner as the foul mix did its worst. The following day it was time for ayahuasca. I fasted for six hours after a light lunch, and then took my place in a circular wooden structure, ironically about the same dimensions as the UFC Octagon, known as a *maloka*. From around waist height up to the leafy, thatched roof there is nothing but netting to keep the worst of the insects at bay, so it really feels like you are just sitting in the jungle. That night a full moon cast a ghostly, silvery-blue sheen over the forest and as we fell silent the chorus of frogs, toads and weird and wonderful insects created a cacophony like nothing I have ever heard before. At one point we even heard the high-pitched roars of two jaguars fighting in the distance and it all added to the intensity of the situation. I was nervous, scared even, but that is exactly how you should feel before you embark on an ayahuasca journey. The shaman, or *ayahuasquero*, then began blessing the space and reciting some prayers. He sang chants of protection called *icaros* – term deriving from the Quechua verb *ikaray*, meaning to blow smoke in order to heal – which were his way of communicating with the spirits and energy around us. He keeps these icaros up throughout the five or six hours of the ceremony and uses them to set the mood and tone of the night.

I deliberately sat on the opposite side of the maloka from my friend Beto because this was a very personal quest for both of us and we were there to work. Having shaved my Mohawk off before leaving home so as not to draw attention to myself, I entered the hut with no psychedelic paraphernalia whatsoever. All I had was a bottle of water, a torch, my prayer beads and a warm jumper for later. I sat in silence and tried to prepare myself mentally and spiritually for what was about to happen. It is necessary to go into an ayahuasca ceremony with specific intentions, just as I did with psilocybin. I had four main questions I hoped would be answered. First of all, am I still a fighter? Second, do I still want to fight? Third, why do I fight? And finally, with a silent nod to Nick Ospiczak, will everything be all right? I was keeping myself to myself, focusing on my intentions and listening to the icaros when, just as we were about to begin, the guy to my right leaned across and whispered, 'I just want to let you know I'm a big fan.' As much as I will forever appreciate it when someone makes the effort to say something positive like that to me, there is a time and a place and that just wasn't the right moment to wrench me from a semi-meditative state and back into Outlaw mode! But I thanked him, refocused and the ceremony began soon after.

The shaman worked anti-clockwise, calling each participant up one by one, beginning with the person seated on his immediate right. He handed out a dose in a cup, the quantity determined by a combination of his judgement and personal requests from those who had drunk before and knew what quantity they needed. The receiver accepted the cup with both hands and drank the gritty, repulsive concoction, before returning to their place in the circle. Even as I waited for my turn, I could see the medicine begin to take effect as it worked its way around the room. Everyone to my left was gradually hit by the toxic mix and commenced crying, sweating, writhing, retching and vomiting in equal measure. *It's coming for me*, I remember thinking. *There is no turning back now.* When I had the cup in my hands I was more anxious than ever, but I kept concentrating on my intentions and telling myself: *Accept the medicine, surrender to it, be with it, allow it to work, allow it to take over, I am open to this.*

I drank the rancid tea and suffered like the others. I then sat in the dark and waited for around an hour for the medicinal effects to take over. With mushrooms, it feels like the information and knowledge is already inside me and the psilocybin simply allows me to open a few doors, have a dialogue with myself, and discover it all. But with ayahuasca, it was more like my whole mind was opened and the knowledge was poured in by the gallon from another, independent source. It began with the sound of popping and fizzing all around my head. It felt like all the myriad noises of the jungle were right in my ears. I kept looking all around me to double-check I wasn't somehow attracting all the insects and animals from out of the nearby foliage. Then my eyes started to stream and I became really cold so I put on my warm top. Minutes later I was sweating and too hot so I took it off. I was yawning like crazy and then I suddenly felt sick and grabbed my purge bowl and violently puked an oily, black liquid into it. I continued dry retching long after even my reserves of stomach bile were exhausted, but this is encouraged as a means to rid the body of spiritual as well as physical poisons. Finally I set the overflowing bowl to one side and sat back, heavy-limbed. As I did so, it felt like someone grabbed me from behind and was dragging me deep into the jungle. All the leaves and branches were flying past, brushing against my face, and then they changed to a stream of geometric patterns, fractals and psychedelic colours. I realised that I couldn't physically move and I remained in that paralysed state for what seemed like hours although it is difficult to tell for sure. It was all very intense then as the strange visions began. I was outside a circular building that appeared to be my house, standing in the back garden with a woman and two girls I presumed to be my wife and daughters. I could see all of my family around me, laughing and smiling, and generally looking well and happy. That was my reassurance that everything was going to be all right. I took a deep breath and pushed on with my other intentions about being a fighter. It is basically the same questions every fighter, whether they care to admit it publicly or not, asks themselves before walking into the arena. *What the fuck am I doing this for? I could be any one of those 20,000 sitting there with a beer and nachos in my hand, laughing and enjoying this spectacle, instead of being the guy about to put his life on the line for their entertainment. What the hell am I doing?* I wanted to know what drove me to fight.

The ceremony then took me on a very emotional journey through what felt like past lives. Even now, recollecting some of what I saw causes me to well up. When I was thirteen or fourteen I had three dreams on consecutive nights that I now recognise to be similar visions. In the first I was a British Redcoat in the American War of Independence, standing in a line with my rifle facing a battalion of blue-uniformed American soldiers. We opened fire on each other in the violently senseless way battles were then conducted, and I died. In the second dream I was a miner somewhere in England who perished in an underground tunnel collapse. The third was probably the strangest of all. In it I was a Jewish woman in what I assumed to be France during the Second World War. I was running through wet-cobbled streets, trying to escape the SS, with four young children in tow, two of whom were mine and two were orphans from a family close to my own. We huddled in an arched doorway and as the kids stifled their tearful sobs I realised it was a church and pushed the door ajar. We ran inside and downstairs into a crypt where we hid on the dusty floor of a long room with no other exits. Minutes later, the Nazi soldiers found us, lined us up against the wall, and shot us all dead.

But while these teenage dreams felt rather remote to me at the time, the emotions in my ayahuasca visions were viscerally real. What I saw in the ceremony was not essentially me, Dan Hardy in 2012, but I connected so profoundly with the emotions that it felt as if they were experiences from past lives that still echoed in my subconscious. I started off as an old samurai warrior in ancient Japan, wilting under the weight of personal disappointment and shame that I hadn't died an honourable samurai death while giving my life to a cause. It seemed I had let everyone down and was going to drift away and die as a disgraced and lonely old man. From there I became a dragon and was immediately slain by St George with a spear through the heart. Then I became the last wolf in England, tiring as I was chased through a forest by a gang dressed in medieval clothing brandishing spears, bows and arrows, and nets. I could already feel the pain of losing every member of my family, and the ache of loneliness was unbearable. I stopped running because there suddenly didn't seem to be any more point in continuing. *If it is not this group of humans today that kill me, it'll be another group somewhere else tomorrow or next week. And there are no more of my kind left alive so what is there to live for anyway?* Panting, I decided to make a last stand. *If I have to die, I'm taking at least one of these bastards down with me.* I ran, and it truly felt like me inside this wolf's body, on all fours surging through the forest undergrowth, and leaping onto one of the men. I mauled the arm that held the spear and then turned my attention to savaging his throat. Just as he spluttered his last bloody breath, another arrived and drove a spear through me, followed by two arrows that were fired into my body at close range. The final vision was the most vivid and detailed. My skin was dark and inked with the traditional markings of my South American tribe and I was standing in the corner of a huge pit around eight feet deep. My wife and daughter were pressed against me and we were all packed in tight alongside the rest of my community, about fifty of us in all. I looked up and all around the perimeter of what was to become our mass grave stood Spanish conquistadoras armed with swords and spears and muskets. I was a warrior of the tribe and I had failed to protect my family. Sitting in that maloka in Peru, I intimately felt the pain of anger and frustration and despair as the European invaders opened fire and slaughtered us all. It was very, very real.

At last I had an answer to my question, why do I fight? Because I never really knew before. My life had been pretty comfortable growing up. I had been blessed with a close, loving, loyal family unit. We weren't rich but I was certainly never conscious of wanting for anything. And yet, from very early on I seemed to find myself in situations where I felt persecuted, either by a person in a position of authority or a group who didn't like the look of me for whatever reason. When I passed a certain age I began responding aggressively, refusing to be pushed around and making no effort to appease anyone that took issue with me. It was as though I sought to test people's discriminatory inclination to see if they would react to me. If they judged me based on my look or personal tastes I would bite back, and their breaking point always came before mine. Now I understood that I could be carrying this fighting energy either from past lives that I couldn't fully recall but experienced in psychedelic dream states, or a collective consciousness that we can all access on different levels. Not only that, but I had failed to survive the circumstances and protect my loved ones. In this current life I am a fighter and although the winning and losing isn't a case of life and death, it provides me with an arena to confront these things and learn about what drives me. But the message that was coming through was that everything in this life would work out fine. Soon after this realisation I started to come round and become aware of the others in the maloka with me. It was then I met my wolf.

When I arrived in the jungle retreat a few days before, one of the first things I did was take a look at the books on the shelf in the communal area. I find I can learn a lot about people before I've spoken to them if I can see what they have been reading, or, in this case, encouraging us to read. I must confess I was a little disappointed when most of the literature on show was about spirit guides and spirit animals, supernatural beings out there in the ether guiding someone through their life. I was searching for an authentic, tribal ayahuasca experience and the idea of a kindly animal appearing to hold my hand felt a bit too out there and more fitting in a Harry Potter book. So when I looked to my side towards the end of my first ceremony and saw a wolf sitting to attention beside me, my first thought was that someone was playing a prank on me. I thought someone must have let an Alsatian into the maloka and it had made itself comfortable next to me in my altered state. But the strange part of the animal's appearance was that my eyes were open and I could also see the other people around me who I knew were definitely there. I was used to weird and wonderful visions from regular mushroom ceremonies, but I always had my eyes closed when they appeared. Here I was awake and alert with a wolf apparently sitting beside me. I reached out and touched it. I ran my hand along its back to its neck against the grain of its fur and when I took my hand away I could feel the oil from its skin on my own. *That wolf is there*, I decided. *I don't care what others can or can't see, but that wolf is really there.* And it never left me. For every minute of each ceremony from that point onwards, my wolf was present. On another night I looked across the maloka and saw one of the group struggling with the medicine. There was an ugly red energy surrounding him and he was lying on his side in a lot of discomfort. I remember thinking that my wolf should go and help him, and immediately it rose, strode across the room and sat beside him. Just like that, my perspective on spirit animals changed beyond all recognition.

When everyone in the group had returned to a manageable state, the shaman lit a candle to signal the end of the ceremony and advise that it was time for us to go to bed. The next morning we all returned to the maloka to share our experiences with one another and get feedback or interpretation from the ayahuasquero. In the two weeks I spent in Peru, I took part in three such ceremonies and two San Pedro ceremonies, in which a drink made from an Andean cactus containing mescaline, another powerful medicine native to South America, is consumed. They were all similar, but unique in their own particular ways. The second time around I was more prepared for what was coming and that certainly helped in terms of the purging if nothing else. I took a larger dose of the brew and actually walked outside into the jungle in my underwear. I was fire-breathing and shape-shifting and all sorts. The shaman, who just pointed and said the Spanish word *luchador* (fighter) the first time he saw me, also spent a lot of time working directly with me during that ceremony. My overriding memory is a strong vision of myself as a tiger with a litter of cubs to protect. A friend that I met there made an audio recording of that night and I was able later to listen back and have Beto, a fluent Spanish speaker, translate the shaman's words when he was alongside me. There was a lot of protection stuff and he was placing defensive iron on my chest, arms, hands and legs. He then began striking my body with the ceremonial branch and leaves while chanting, 'Spirit of the tiger, spirit of the wolf!'

My third and final ayahuasca ceremony of that trip was the toughest. Such was the feeling of pain and fear, I actually crawled to the door midway through to escape. As soon as I got outside I felt better and made my way to the sleeping quarters to lie down and forget about that one. But the night watchman saw my pupils dilated to the size of dinner plates and sent me back to the maloka for safety reasons. Immediately the feeling of dread and physical pain returned and I just sat down and waited for the candle to be lit. Just before that happened, the shaman gave permission to an Irish fella called Niall to play a few songs on his guitar. He did some Dylan, some Marley and a Beatles track and some people were singing along and I guess it was quite nice. But I was still feeling terrible until he began his fourth and final number. As soon as he strummed the first chord it was like a massive weight had been lifted off of me and a surge of relief coursed through my body. It was as if I could breathe unrestricted and was immediately myself again. I knew the song well and as soon as I woke up the next day I began scrolling through the tens of thousands of songs on my iPod in search of this track. I knew I had it somewhere but although it felt more familiar to me than the classics by Dylan, Marley and the Beatles, I just couldn't identify what artist had written it. I went looking for Niall and asked him what it was. 'It's called "Stillness",' he told me. 'I only wrote it last week in Argentina and that's the first time I've played it in public.' I couldn't deny that it was impossible I had heard it before, but I knew that song. He made me a copy and I still listen to it today. I also have a tattoo of the main lyric, 'stillness is how you breathe', around my wrist.

● ● ●

As always with psychedelic experiences, it is difficult to articulate the impact the ayahuasca ceremonies had on my life. I guess what they did was to help me take a step back from certain issues and look at everything more clearly and from a fresh perspective. It then became easier both to identify the relevant pieces of a puzzle and be able to fit them together. Sometimes I think of life as being a computer game in which you need to keep completing levels to move forward. A bit like forcing your own evolution along. The ceremonies helped me remove a good chunk of my ego and be more honest with myself and this in turn helped me raise my level of consciousness. No one knows me better than I do, so as long as I'm being honest with myself, I have all the answers in front of me. I always say that ayahuasca, or any natural substance that induces a psychedelic state, doesn't necessarily change you, but it will help you know who you are so you can change yourself.

My trip to Peru proved to be a watershed moment in my life, a two-week period within which I was able to let go of a lot of baggage and find some answers to questions that had been eating away at me for years. My problems used to leer at me in front of my face at every turn like the corks on an Australian hat, and now it was as if I could simply remove the hat. For want of a more original turn of phrase, I found myself. I was able to connect to all these different parts of my personality and, even more importantly, understand what each part needed. I had a moment of realisation about how to live within my means and not encroach upon nature or other people, a more conscious approach to living. And I can now read other people and their emotions much better than before. It is all about enjoying each day as it comes and finding a peace and balance within myself, a balance I never had before when fighting was dominating everything. At times I still feel aggressive and want to fight, but I can now hear the conversation going on between different competing forces in my mind. My reptilian brain, who I now feed and nurture and control better than before, will be screaming, *Hit him! He deserves it*. My higher consciousness will then counter with, *He probably does deserve it but if you hit him then you become the arsehole in the room*. The key for me is balancing the needs of my higher consciousness with the animal or ego inside me. And sometimes I believe that physical aggression, or rather the threat of it, is still necessary and justified. As a strong, fighting man, I see my role within the community as one of maintaining order and discipline. So when I see a guy pissing in the street where I live, or a jackass hitting his girlfriend in a car on Vegas Boulevard, or a drunken idiot bothering my wife and a UFC ring girl in the lobby of a Swedish hotel, I need to act. To this end I've developed my seven-out-of-ten theory, with one representing total passivity and ten meaning someone is going to hospital for a very long time. My trick is to appear to be at seven, when in reality I'm probably only at three or four out of ten. The appearance of seven is invariably a sufficient stance to defuse most situations or, at worst, compel the aggressor to make a first move which I, in my calm internal state, can comfortably deal with without the need to call the emergency services afterwards.

John Kavanagh talks about the need to update our software without damaging our hardware, which is a thought-provoking phrase, in reference to intelligent training methods. Years before, Terrence McKenna had his own IT analogy for self-improvement. McKenna believes that humanity is working with an outdated operating system and that psychedelics are the key to advancement and finding peace within ourselves. Some have success with the likes of meditation, fasting and sensory deprivation tanks, but psychedelic plants provide the most powerful, spiritual and potentially rewarding experience. I truly believe that the world would be a better place if everyone, when they are ready for it, took part in an ayahuasca or psilocybin mushroom ceremony. But at the same time, I acknowledge that I can only speak from my own personal positive experiences with the medicine and for that reason I never advise others to experiment.

● ● ●

I flew back to the US and within a week the UFC announced my next fight, a late-September date with Amir Sadollah in my own home town. It was an awesome feeling to be the guy who brought the UFC to Nottingham. It was also totally unexpected as, with a capacity of just over 7,000, the city's main venue was a little shy of what the UFC usually expects to host a show. Birmingham and Manchester are more obvious options for that part of the UK, so it was a tremendous personal honour that the organisation had decided to visit my city. I was thrilled for my family, friends and everyone who had followed my career as well. I had only fought twice in the UK in the previous three and a half years so it was great they'd be able to walk to the arena rather than fly half way across the world.

I couldn't wait to get back into training with Giff, Ricky, Shawn and Frank, but I also had a new weapon up my sleeve. Another thing I left Peru with was a belief that I needed to introduce yoga into my routine. I couldn't explain why exactly, but all of a sudden I was overcome by the feeling it was vital for me. My previous yoga experiences had involved sitting around with a bunch of old ladies doing breathing exercises and watching them trying in vain to touch their toes, so I was keen this time to find a more challenging form of the ancient Indian discipline.

Hot yoga, ninety minutes of postures in forty-degree heat, fit that bill and I soon integrated twice-weekly sessions into my training camp. It helped add more balance to my training regime. Even during supposed downtime in previous camps, my mind was always focused on the fight and I felt under pressure to be continually doing something directly connected with the battle ahead. Hot yoga became another escape of sorts, albeit one that was entirely relevant and very beneficial in terms of affording time for injuries to heal, improving my flexibility, and keeping my weight in check. It also surprised me by providing another avenue to explore in terms of accessing those inner reaches of my subconscious that lie dormant and untouched throughout the monotony of daily life. It was during a deep spinal stretch that I worked a particular muscle which released an emotion from my taekwondo class when I was six years old. The instructor Paul, the half of Eagle & Hawk that could be gratuitously mean, often forced us past our pain thresholds while stretching in a misplaced attempt at having us push beyond our limits. For twenty-five years I had locked that memory away without thought, totally unaware that my hatred of stretching probably stems from that evening in the village hall. It was an incredible revelation, all the more so because the physical act of manipulating a muscle in a meditative state a quarter of a century later was the trigger for me to figure it all out. I was used to psychedelics helping me to delve into the past but now I had another key to unlock some of the doors within my mind.

Camp went perfectly for the Sadollah fight. I felt calmer than ever and, partly thanks to the hot yoga sessions, I only needed to shed 6lbs during fight week. I was so excited to be fighting in Nottingham, but the home-field advantage brought its own unique pressures. On the morning of the fight I woke up and looked out my living room window to the arena. It suddenly dawned on me that if I lost in there, I'd never be able to live it down. It isn't like losing in Canton, Ohio and walking away safe in the knowledge I'd never return to the scene of the disappointment. This is my town, my home, my family's home. We all go regularly to watch the ice hockey in the Nottingham Arena. It's a happy place for us and I was now risking tainting all of that with a potentially very unhappy memory.

The pressure to create a happy memory built throughout the day and right into the first round. It was hard to keep my emotions in check when almost 8,000 people were chanting my name over and over again. My grandma was there as well, a little old lady who looks like the Queen, sitting in the front row offering everyone boiled sweets from her handbag. The first round passed in a bit of a slow-motion blur as we felt each other out and when I sat down I remember apologising to my corner, saying I just needed to get that five minutes out of the way. Giff's mother in Boston was sick and so he couldn't be there, but I had Ricky and Shawn and I invited my old teammate Dean Amasinger to come along and help out too, so I was in very good hands. I then went out and dominated the last ten minutes. In truth, I never really felt threatened by Sadollah. He made his name winning season seven of *The Ultimate Fighter* and he was a busy, fast-paced, Muay Thai specialist, but I knew plenty of guys who had held their own with him in sparring so I wasn't particularly concerned about what he would bring. I actually viewed him as an opportunity to practise some moves and improve ahead of future, juicier match-ups. I looked to try out some takedowns I had been working on in the gym, shooting from a clinch or against the fence or by level changing under one of his punches and exploiting his forward momentum. Just as Ricky and I had drilled, I also wanted to show my ground-and-pound game too, something I felt I had neglected since I signed with the UFC as my advantage was normally on the feet. I was basically experimenting when I possibly should have been concentrating on knocking him out. But the Condit fight was still fresh in my mind as well and I was adamant I wasn't going to get swept up in the British atmosphere again and get caught by a stupid shot. It was in many ways a very mature showing in which I displayed more facets to my game than usual and won by unanimous decision at a relative canter. I was pleased with the performance, not so much in itself, but for what it promised was coming. Afterwards I remember telling journalists about how good I felt about my career, how I was focused upon dedicating the next eighteen months of my life towards getting everything I could out of fighting in the Octagon. I saw how I was still evolving as a mixed martial artist and I was convinced that my best was still to come.

8

I was matched with Matt Brown for 20 April 2013 in San Jose, California, and I couldn't wait to get back in the Octagon. Brown was on a roll, racing along in the midst of a seven-fight win streak that included plenty of bonuses, and I knew his striking style would guarantee a fun and explosive night. Matt was also the perfect opponent against whom I could showcase my continuing evolution as a mixed martial artist and beating him would be a major stride towards title contention again. Now fully settled into my new surroundings within Frank's gym and training under the watchful eyes of Giff, Ricky and Shawn, camp was going great. Five weeks out from fight night, I was called to attend the usual UFC pre-bout medical check-up and I had never felt as fit, strong and ready for combat in my whole career. Few MMA commissions in the world require fighters to take an ECG test but California is one of them. So with this being my first outing in the Golden State, I was a little surprised but totally unconcerned when the doctor began attaching the electrodes to my chest. My only previous ECG test was the one conducted in that nightmare build-up to the Pat Healy fight in Florida back in 2004. The local doctor at that weigh-in believed he had picked up something irregular through his stethoscope and wanted a second opinion to cover his own back. I took the test and was cleared, anything irregular the first doc heard being put down to the fact my body was in a state of stress from making weight, and I had never given my heart a second thought since then. But sitting there in the medical centre in Las Vegas, I could see from the doctor's face that something was up. 'Unusual' was the word he used as he watched the needle trace my heart's activity onto the scroll of paper feeding out of the machine. Little more was said that day, but I was asked to return soon after to discuss the results. It was then the bombshell was dropped on me from a great height: I was diagnosed with Wolff-Parkinson-White syndrome.

The way it was described, an additional electrical pathway had formed somewhere in my heart, meaning I effectively had two heartbeats. The doc went on to explain that this extra group of cells generating their own electrical impulse produced a risk of a short circuit, or cardiac arrest, and death. So despite the fact that as a professional athlete I had been pushing my heart to the limit for over a decade without having any symptoms like chest pain, palpitations, shortness of breath, fainting or anxiety, the medics were concerned. Further investigation was required so I took a stress test, basically running for eighteen minutes as the speed and inclination was gradually increased and my heart activity was monitored. I then had a special ultrasound done which produced a three-dimensional model of my heart in order to look for the additional, unwanted cells or anything else enlarged or abnormal. The replica unearthed nothing sinister, but the stress test did produce something that surprised even the experts. The two beats were clear, the first maxing at 197 per minute and the second at 186, but what was odd was that the extra beat was consistent rather than sporadic, as is the norm with people living with WPW syndrome. It was as if I had been born with a back-up and it led me to later joke that the UFC wouldn't let me fight because my two hearts gave me an unfair advantage in that you had to kill me twice. In jest of course, but I also mentioned that every change in a species' evolutionary journey begins with an anomaly. If that anomaly or so-called abnormality proves to be advantageous to a living organism's survival, then it gradually becomes the norm in the species. But despite my attempts to put a positive spin on things, the cardiology specialists had refused to pass me fit to fight without first undergoing some sort of procedure.

The proposed solution was exploratory heart surgery to ascertain exactly what was going on in there. That meant cutting open the carotid artery in my neck and the femoral artery in my leg in order to feed microscopic cameras through my body and into my heart. *If* a secondary group of cells could be found, and *if* they were in a safe place, a surgeon could then *try* to burn them away via a technique known as ablation. There was no guarantee of success, and the risk of permanent damage and needing a pacemaker for the rest of my life was ever-present. Incredibly, the doctor also said I'd be able to fight in just three weeks' time if the operation went smoothly: a declaration I found very hard to believe.

I had several other issues with what I was hearing. There were just too many *ifs* in the equation for my liking and not enough certainty. I was never told anything definitive. Never, *this is the problem and this is what needs to be done and this is how we're going to do it*. We weren't talking about an ingrowing toenail here so I wasn't comfortable with so much guesswork surrounding poking about in my most vital organ. If I am honest, I simply didn't trust the American doctors' judgement on this one. I always had a fear that, within the dynamic of the extortionate health care system in the US, some of them had one eye on the next payment due on a luxury yacht docked out the back of a beach house somewhere in southern California. My heart had always been strong, it had never let me down, and I was presenting no symptoms to suggest I was in any danger. If it ain't broke, then don't fix it, right? I pushed back, reluctant to let anyone rummage about in my heart on a reconnaissance mission.

I had my mum speak to our GP back in Nottingham, who knew our family medical history intimately. My grandad had had a metal heart valve fitted in his fifties, a knock-on effect from his own father contracting rheumatic fever when he arrived back in England at the end of the Great War. The intervention helped Grandad regulate his heartbeat, although it also ensured he was dependent on medication to manage the thickness of his blood and ensure the valve was never blocked. Getting the balance of the medication right was an ongoing battle and the cause of several ambulance rides to the hospital like the one before my Lee Doski rematch. Grandma always said that in the silence of the dead of night you could hear it ticking quietly in his chest, and now if you tilt the box that holds his ashes you can hear the tiny metal device rattling about inside. I was wary of such risks, of opening a Pandora's Box and embarking on a lifetime of meds, and my family doctor agreed. He couldn't see any sense whatsoever in operating on the heart of a patient who was presenting zero troubling symptoms. This was the key consideration for me. When my condition became common knowledge, plenty of people were getting in touch via social media urging me to get it done and assuring me there was absolutely nothing to worry about. But they missed the point because they had all experienced symptoms and there was therefore more of a requirement to undergo the procedure. The son of a gym mate was the same. This kid would be sitting on the sofa and his heart rate would suddenly shoot up from 60 to 140 for no reason whatsoever. There is an inherent and obvious health risk there and so, of course, he went in for surgery. I also read that some professions demand that action is taken upon diagnosis. Air Force pilots in charge of multi-million-dollar aircraft and flying with multi-million-dollar weaponry and missiles attached, for example. That makes sense to me, but the absolute worst-case scenario if Dan Hardy drops down dead at work is people being sad for a while. I did more investigation and discovered that WPW syndrome is not at all rare, with as high as three in every one thousand people affected according to the NHS. Without symptoms or a random ECG test, the vast majority never even know and live full and healthy lives before perishing of natural causes. On the other hand, those that do discover the condition and have the catheter ablation procedure often need to return again and again for the same intrusive surgery because the extra cells either reproduce or appear elsewhere in the heart.

My mind was effectively made up, but a trip to Lorenzo's private physician in Beverly Hills sealed the deal. Lorenzo's doctor was actually suggesting the same as the previous las Vegan medics, but fortunately he had brought in a specialist from UCLA who he had presumed would back him up. On the contrary, this guy, one of only seven doctors in the entire US who specialise in electrical currents in the heart, made it very simple for me. There are only three possible reasons for you to consent to surgeons embarking on a scavenger hunt in your heart, he said. Firstly, because you are presenting worrying symptoms. I was not, and that actually meant that my condition is WPW pattern rather than WPW syndrome. Secondly, because you have a fear of sudden death. I did not. Thirdly, because it appears to be the only way you will ever be allowed to fight in the Octagon again. Number three was the only consideration to provoke a slight pause for thought, but it was still clear to me the decision I had to make. There was no way I was going to undergo what I considered to be unnecessary heart surgery just for a chance of a couple more fights with the UFC. *I'm fine as I am, thanks*, I thought as I drove out of Beverly Hills that day.

Before I left California to return to Vegas I had a stop to make, however. I had driven in from Nevada in a pretty foul mood that morning. Knowing your career and passion was being taken away from you is not a nice mental state to be in. For miles and miles I was cruising along behind a large truck with, as is an American trucker's wont, a selection of bumper stickers on the rear. One caught my attention and I stared at it for almost an hour. 'No Bad Days', it read. I called in to see a tattoo artist friend named Chris Stuart and there and then had him ink *No Bad Days* onto my leg against the backdrop of a California sunset and palm tree. It acts as a constant reminder to stay in the present and appreciate the fact that I am alive and, in my opinion, perfectly healthy.

● ● ●

I found little comfort back home in Nevada where the apparent demise of my UFC career mirrored the very real breakdown of the relationship I had been in for seven years, the final twelve months of which were spent engaged to be married. Looking back I can see we had been on separate paths going in very different directions for a couple of years, but as the wedding day approached our incompatibility began to shine brighter. My fiancée was very much focused on her career and setting herself up within the traditional social construct of modern-day America, whereas, partly influenced by my experimentation with psychedelics, I was more interested in the metaphysical dimension of life. She also showed little or no interest in my career, perhaps always a little jealous of the easy access I had to recognition or appreciation by just logging into a social media account while she was bogged down in the rat race, trying to keep busy as a graphic designer. I remember leaving the euphoria of the MGM Grand the night I beat Duane Ludwig and, still on a high, walking into our front room to be greeted by absolutely nothing. She hadn't watched the fight and didn't even get off the sofa to congratulate me. We were due to be married the week before the scheduled Matt Brown bout, but with a fortnight to go we sat down and agreed we couldn't go through with it. Family and friends were already flying in to Vegas so we decided to have the planned party without the actual wedding ceremony, but it was an uneasy time, with neither of us really knowing what was around the corner. The pressure, expectations and attitude of her family didn't help in the slightest either. Her mother in particular never really warmed to me and always had an arsenal of handy tips on how I could improve myself.

One was the suggestion that I get a real job which, given the fact my apparently fake job had recently done close to a million pay-per-views for the GSP fight, was as ridiculous and uneducated as it was insulting. Another was that I fix my teeth, particularly the front right central incisor, which has admittedly seen better days. Back in 2005 I was shadow-boxing in the small ring of the Majestik Gym when I heard a commotion emanating from the big ring on the mezzanine floor. Tony, the sixty-something Jamaican guy who ran the boxing side of the Majestik, was up there with a group of eight or ten so-called troublesome teens from the local estates, trying to instil some discipline in their lives. Tempers had flared in the midst of a body-sparring session and Tony found himself struggling to keep two of the larger kids apart as they swore at and threatened one another. I got there just in time to see one throw a punch so I grabbed him to control him until everything calmed down. Unfortunately, just as I got my arms around him, the return punch from his foe arrived and caught me square in the mouth.

I was holding the kid against the ropes as he continued struggling and screaming blue murder, and all the while I could feel my mouth filling up with blood. When it was safe to release him, I walked to the mirror, spat out the blood, and saw that my tooth had been knocked back and was now lying flat against the roof of my mouth. I pushed it back into place, held it there with my tongue and drove straight to the dentist, but by that stage the gums had reclaimed my pearly white and it was stuck fast. It was discoloured due to the blood seeping into the enamel, and clearly not exactly where it should be, but it was secure enough for the dentist to suggest we leave it as it was until it started causing me discomfort. It never did and so to this day it maintains its prominent position in my winning smile.

Further distaste was shown towards the tattoos that were quickly spreading to encompass most of my arms, back, front and a significant portion of both legs. The idea of them being lasered off was even floated at one point! Needless to say I didn't even dignify that one with a response. I always knew I would have a lot of body art and as a kid I was either scribbling on my skin during lessons at school, or sketching and designing ideas. It is true that I have a lot, but each and every one has a personal and very important symbolism attached. There are two wolves on my chest for my two heartbeats. One is calm and mellow and the other is snarling intensely, like my vision of the last wolf on the British Isles during my ayahuasca experience. There are antlers representing strength and a part-human, part-reptilian eye looking out from the centre of my torso to represent the beast inside that I had grown so close to during those late nights in the MushRoom. On my right arm I have a Japanese sleeve inked by the LA artist Sung Song. Within it, a coy fish swims up a waterfall cascading out of the mouth of a skull to represent the importance of keeping focused, motivated and determined until the end. The cherry blossoms dotted around the falls embody the fleeting nature of life and remind me to live in the moment and enjoy each day. The artist Tim Hendricks then inked my other sleeve. Britannia is scrawled down my left forearm alongside a clipper sailing out into a storm. I also have a compass on my elbow and inside my bicep a bluebird flies over the White Cliffs of Dover. This arm is all about my origins and leaving the British Isles on adventures to face danger and eventually be guided back to the place I will always consider home. I have skulls and crossbones on each leg and inside my lip as a nod to my love of the anarchist ways of olden-day pirates. Then there is a mug of tea on my left calf in remembrance of my grandad, and a little Ska man from The Specials' album cover on my opposite calf because I have great memories of listening to that music in the back of my dad's Ford Cortina as a young boy. My most recent work is a chameleon on an ayahuasca vine which symbolises my adaptability and growth, and I've plenty more ideas in my mind before I cease having my body inked, if ever that day comes. The process of getting tattooed always feels very ceremonial to me and is essential if I am to feel true ownership of the permanent, skin-deep art. After a few hours in the chair, when the adrenalin has worn off and your body has become hyper-sensitive to the pain of the needle, it can be truly excruciating. Just like lengthy fasting and self-flagellation, it is another way to put your body through extreme stress to reach an almost psychedelic state.

I'm also very selective about who I go to for the tattoo. They need to have their own style, to own their art and appreciate the ceremonial aspect as much as I do. I don't want to walk into a high-street studio with a picture and ask if they can replicate it. I prefer to discuss ideas and themes and see what unique vision the artist comes up with. In a nutshell, my tattoos mean a great deal to me and no potential mother-in-law could ever force me to remove them.

It was a huge relief when the faux-wedding day was over. With the uncertainty swirling around my heart condition and future as a fighter, I just felt like I had bigger things to worry about. Unfortunately my ex didn't agree and she rarely asked about what was going on. With my family over 5,000 miles away I could have done with her support, but in these months I was increasingly finding it from another source, my yoga instructor Lacey. She was the only person totally removed from the mess my life was then in and as we spent more time together we grew closer and closer. When I came out of a hospital test and checked my phone, the only messages asking how it had gone were from Lacey. A few days before I should have been entering the Octagon to face Brown, Lacey and I attended an ayahuasca ceremony together and quite a few things clicked into place in my mind. I saw that she was in line with where my life was heading and she was giving off the type of energy I needed. I knew that my time with my ex had passed and the only thing to do was to make a clean break there and then. A fortnight later I was sharing a house with Lacey, nineteen months later we were married, and two and a half years on we are settled back in the UK and still a constant source of motivation for each other to continue our personal journey of growth and understanding of ourselves as beings.

● ● ●

I kept myself busy in the immediate aftermath of the diagnosis and was still in and around gyms every day. It was hard walking into Frank's gym in Vegas because it was almost like pretending everything was okay, so I spent a lot of time in California and helped coach my friend Mac Danzig for his upcoming fight. But it was strange, going through the motions without a definitive personal target to aim for. I enjoy simply expanding my skill-set within martial arts, but there is a different urgency involved when the reason for doing that is to save your face in a cage. Without that looming threat, the willingness to put myself through pain and discomfort while training drained away. I grew frustrated and a little bitter at times too, becoming secretly jealous of others working towards their next fight. Worse than that was the frustration at seeing training partners not giving their all when they were in a position I was dying to be back in. To be around someone preparing for a fight but not taking it seriously infuriated me. I'd seen it before when I was fighting but just dismissed it: *They can do what they like with their lives and it's no skin off my nose*, I always thought. But now I took it personally. My frustration peaked one night with my old Rough House teammate and friend Andre Winner after he was beaten in London. It was a fight he should have won ten times out of ten, but he just sat back and gave it away.

'What the fuck was that, mate?' I demanded in the changing room.

Andre just shrugged and offered a lame reply. 'It was all right,' he began. 'I did some things well, it's not too bad, I'll learn from it and move on.'

Inside I was stewing. I was thinking, *You don't know what you've got. I would love to just shrug and move on to the next one, but there is no next one for me*. The fact that it was Andre, a guy with all the natural ability in the world, magnified my exasperation. He is an incredible athlete with speed and power and agility I'd kill to have. I was looking at him thinking, *You have everything you need to fulfil my dreams, and yet you don't even seem bothered*. It was so frustrating.

At this early stage, there was still a part of me convinced that the heart thing was something I was going to quickly overcome. I was still expecting to simply speak to some doctors in the UK, get the all-clear from them, and be back in the Octagon before the end of the year. But reality gradually descended over me and it hit me pretty hard when I had to finally face up to the fact that the UFC were not going to take any chances based on what their doctors were telling them. I struggled badly with it all for a time. I was obviously disappointed, but I felt truly lost as well. For the first time in my life, I did not know what was coming next. There had been uncertainty before, particularly while the consecutive losses were mounting, but even then I felt like I was in control of my own destiny to a large extent. Now I was just being told I couldn't fight any more. I couldn't stop thinking of the ayahuasca ceremony only a few months earlier in Peru. Of the visions of a previous life as the last wolf in England or the shaman chanting, 'Spirit of the wolf' while beating my chest with his ceremonial branch. Then there was the wolf sitting next to me throughout each ceremony. Even my nickname, the Outlaw, chosen many years earlier, became scarily prophetic. *Caput gerat lupinum* was a Latin term used in the old English legal system which translates as 'Let his be the head of a wolf,' the wolf in those days a feared and hated beast whose skin could be used to pay taxes. It referred to anyone the law considered an outlaw and basically allowed for that person to be killed on sight as if they were a wild animal. It was almost too weird and coincidental to be true, but I was reassured by it in a way. This is who I am, I decided. All of this is part of the person I am. I started referring to my condition as Wolf Heart to make a distinction in my head between the people who suffered with symptoms, and myself, healthy and asymptomatic.

I distanced myself from MMA for a few months and began doing a lot more yoga and trail running in the canyons. I also spent a lot of time in a CrossFit gym in Las Vegas, powerlifting and generally pushing myself to the absolute limit there. It was only in the midst of an interview that I realised what I was subconsciously doing during this time. After giving so many interviews in and around the same topics, I often find that my answers to repetitive questions become delivered as a stream of consciousness. I begin speaking on auto-pilot without first having thought it through, and sometimes it is only when I hear myself make a particular statement that the penny drops. I realised that, because I had been told I was defective and unable to fight, I was pushing myself to find a breaking point, searching for that moment when my heart would fail me. Because I was so convinced that it never ever would. I became so appreciative of that pulsing organ in my chest, of all my body in fact. It sounds very narcissistic but during mushroom ceremonies around that time I got into the habit of sitting in the bath and moving my focus from one joint and limb to the next, thanking it and appreciating it. I'd rub my knees and think of all the wear and tear I had forced upon them, and yet they'd never failed me. I thanked them. *And you, my friend*, looking at my hands and fingers and knuckles and marvelling at the damage I had caused them and the risks I had taken with them, and yet they were always there for me, healthy and ready when I needed them. Everything, ankles, wrists, brain and lungs. Even things that had been injured and went wrong. My jaw for example: *Thank you for healing yourself*, I said. *It was my fault for not being utterly focused in sparring one day, I was responsible for that, and yet you repaired yourself for me.*

● ● ●

One day during that summer of 2013 I called into the UFC headquarters in Vegas for a meeting with Lorenzo. It was just a catch-up really, a chance for me to tell the boss where I was in life and what I was thinking. As with every meeting I have ever had with Lorenzo, it went well and he still appeared to be very positive about my ongoing relationship with the UFC. On the way out the main doors I bumped into Dana, who was in his usual excitable, loud and swearing self.

'I've got the perfect thing for you, my friend,' he started. 'I'm so fucking excited about it.'

He went on to explain his plan. I was to move back to the UK and become the main media face of the UFC in Europe. Basically, he wanted me to do all the commentary, analysis and interviews for everything this side of the Atlantic. I was going to be his English Joe Rogan with some added responsibility and a few more strings to my bow. My gut instinct told me this was as good a way as any to bridge the gap while I sorted my future out so I immediately expressed interest in the proposal. One thing I remember saying is that I would need some media training before I could get in front of the camera as anything other than a fighter.

'Fuck that!' Dana shouted in reply. 'I want you exactly how you are!'

I flew to London for a couple of screen tests with prospective partners. I was to be the colour commentator, so we needed a play-by-play guy who I could dovetail with. The first, a well-known radio personality, didn't really understand exactly what his role would entail. He had little knowledge of mixed martial arts or the UFC, other than being a casual fan, and his questions were rather elementary. The second candidate, John Gooden, called me the night before to introduce himself before turning up on the day suited and booted and ready to nail a job interview. With many years behind him in a similar role with Cage Warriors, he knew his stuff and we clicked right from the off. He asked good questions which allowed me to do my thing and, since he's a naturally funny and charismatic guy, we quickly developed a nice chemistry on and off the screen. John would be working the position usually held by Mike Goldberg, but with his deep understanding of the sport and his genuine love of martial arts, I was confident that he would raise the bar from where it had been set previously.

Along with Andy Friedlander, an announcer recruited from Wembley Stadium, the three of us flew to Las Vegas in February 2014 to sit beside Rogan and Goldie for Rousey versus McMann and undertake a bit of a trial run. Joe and I are good friends, but I never really asked him for advice. My role overlaps with what he does for the North American audience, but there are many differences too. It is also a case of horses for courses. I couldn't be the type of personality that Joe is, and my audience doesn't want that anyway. The UFC recognised that the average European MMA fan is more discerning than their American counterparts. Europeans seem to prefer a calmer, more informative approach to sports commentating, but with Joe being so synonymous with the original UFC brand, his voice and hype have become a part of the UFC experience. Much like the distinctive tones of the 'Veteran Voice of the Octagon', Bruce Buffer. A more considered and cerebral approach is what I was aiming to achieve, akin to what Jon Anik is now bringing with his commentary, and I think that's why the organisation hired John and me in the first place. Our first gig then took place at the O2 Arena in London in March 2014, and it went pretty well. The constant voices in my ear-piece from the production truck providing feedback and guidance throughout the show were distracting at first, but three years on I'm beginning to get used to it. I wasn't really nervous because in my mind I'm just a fighter watching a fight and talking to other fighters. This is my domain and I feel entirely qualified and prepared to do the job. What also helped quell any anxiety was my perspective that, having once been knocked out cold live on air in front of millions, nothing can be more embarrassing than that.

I was excited to have a new challenge and a direction to walk in again and, although I'd never considered it before, I soon recognised what a great opportunity I had with this new role. My obsessive nature ensured I immediately dedicated myself to becoming the best MMA analyst I could possibly be. I threw myself into it, watching hundreds upon hundreds of fights to appreciate and critique and know intimately each UFC fighter's style. Our *Inside the Octagon* series soon became a fan favourite, but I imagine few viewers have any idea of the amount of preparation I do before I allow those segments to be recorded. In advance of breaking down a fight or particular fighter, I spend hours putting myself in the shoes of the protagonists. I'll stand in front of the gym mirror, mimicking their styles and envisioning what their opponent will be thinking and doing. I then flip it round to become the opponent and repeat until I have the best vision of how I believe the fight will go in my mind. I may not get it wholly correct every time, but I don't think there is anyone out there putting in as much effort as I do to be as accurate as possible with their analysis and predictions. And even if there is someone that dedicated, it's unlikely that they have enjoyed the rollercoaster ride of a UFC career that I have had. I do feel that in a short ten-fight stint in the UFC I experienced most of what a fighter could experience in and out of the Octagon. A quick rise and a four-fight win streak, a title shot against one of the best ever, then a losing streak that would have ended most UFC careers. I've knocked out guys and been knocked out, I've had quick fights and bonuses, and long, frustrating bouts which I found quite boring. I've fought smart, and I've fought recklessly, and I did every bit of media work that the UFC put my way. With all that under my belt, I believe I can speak authoritatively on MMA.

The more I do the media stuff, the more I see it as a real service to the sport of mixed martial arts. In fact, I believe I am providing a more important service to MMA as an analyst than I ever did as a fighter. It may not have been the same had I left the sport on my own terms, but I got the opportunity while still very much immersed in the UFC and I simply redirected my passion and drive and obsession towards this new chapter in my life. All thoughts of fighting again were soon pushed to the back of my mind so I could concentrate all my energy on the new role, but I can't pretend that there wasn't always a part of me wishing I was driving to the arena to fight rather than talk. In fact, every time I commentate I still have my gumshield in my pocket just in case. I know I am commentating because someone has told me I can't fight and it is impossible to escape that fact, but I truly enjoy this role and it's a close second to stepping into the Octagon to compete. One thing that has changed, however, is the realisation that if I do return to the Octagon it will be a very selfish act. I now acknowledge that no one can benefit from me fighting again except me. Dana doesn't understand why I would want to fight again and it is interesting to note a creeping change among fans as well. When I first attended fan days or open question & answer sessions after my diagnosis, I was always being asked when I was coming back and almost everyone I encountered told me they couldn't wait to see me back inside the Octagon. But suddenly, a year or two on, I began to get messages asking me to stay retired. 'Save your brain for commentating,' I am told. 'We love your analysis too much to want to see you back fighting!' It is a strange scenario to find myself in, and I have no idea where my media work will take me, but I am content with my lot for the time being and know I will have fun finding out.

● ● ●

By 2015 my working visa to stay in the US had expired and I was back living in England full-time. One day I sat and watched the documentary *180 Degrees South*, which tells the story of a guy named Jeff Johnson retracing the steps of a Chilean expedition that Doug Tompkins and Yvon Chouinard, the founders of US outerwear companies North Face and Patagonia respectively, made in the late 1960s. At one point, Johnson is on a boat on the way from Mexico to Chile when the mast snaps, leaving the three-man crew stranded in the middle of the South Pacific Ocean. I couldn't help wondering how I would react in such a helpless situation, knowing that I wouldn't be able to get myself back to safety on my efforts alone. The thought of it was terrifying and I imagined I would panic, but the vulnerability and isolation of being adrift on a tiny vessel, thousands of miles from dry land, somehow appealed to me. I decided then that it was a necessary addition to my bucket list, and a fear that I would have to face at some point in my future. So it seemed like it was meant to be then when a few months later the UFC called to say that the organisers of the famous Clipper Round the

World Yacht Race were keen to add me to the crew of *Team GREAT*, that year's British entrant in the competition. The sponsors, GREAT Britain, the UK government's international marketing campaign, were keen to have a British athlete for each of the eight legs of the race and, in addition to me, the rugby player Ollie Phillips, the badminton player Nathan Robertson, the rower Bill Lucas and the Paralympian Charlotte Evans were among those who would take part.

I underwent four weeks of pretty intense training to learn the necessary skills and prove myself capable of surviving a month on the open seas in a seventy-foot yacht with twenty-four strangers. The vast majority of that training took place on the boat, either docked in Gosport or out on the Solent, the strait separating the Isle of Wight from mainland Britain. I learnt the necessary terminology as well as an array of technical skills like how to choose a sail set according to the prevailing wind. There were also plenty of safety, recovery and survival drills. Week two was spent totally at sea, either at anchor or sailing through the night, and was particularly challenging. We were effectively put through the wringer in order to weed out those who wouldn't cope with the exhausting routine during the length of a race leg. We worked in watches on a rough schedule of four hours on and four off, but trying to get some rest in the cramped and uncomfortable living quarters was more of a challenge than learning all of the skills I would need on the Atlantic crossing. We were out in the English Channel and the waters were rough and choppy the whole time. Prolonged seasickness was everyone's big fear, but as I was accustomed to working through pain and injury I thought I would conquer it with mental strength alone.

When it came, it hit me much harder than I expected, however. It really is incredibly debilitating and, having never experienced any kind of motion sickness before, I had underestimated how much of a test of mental fortitude that would be. It struck a few of my crewmates pretty hard too and some pulled out less than halfway through training. I think the worst point for me, and the closest I came to withdrawing, was at about 2am a couple of days into our second week of training. One of our propellers got caught in a lobster pot ten miles off the coast and left us bobbing helplessly around in a circle in a shipping lane on a wet and windy night. The solution to seasickness is to focus on a point of reference, normally the horizon, in order to give your brain a location from which it can set its bearings, find equilibrium and basically calm everything down. Unfortunately this was the middle of a pitch-black night and distinguishing between sea and sky was an impossible task. I don't mind admitting it was tough to function, so much worse than just a headache and a bad case of nausea on dry land.

Stepping onto the boat with the rest of the people who would make up my entire world for the month of September 2015 was a pretty surreal moment. I have never been one for team sports, so the sudden reliance on a group of strangers for any success we might have in the race was going to be one of the many new challenges I had ahead. The idea of competing twenty-four hours a day for thirty consecutive days, even while I was asleep, was yet another new, weird and wonderful concept for me to get my head around. Sailing down the River Thames for the ceremonial journey to the starting point at Southend-on-Sea was an absolutely beautiful experience. It was a big part of the reason why I really wanted to do that opening leg of the race. We had the privilege of Tower Bridge being raised to let us pass underneath and there were people lining the Thames, cheering and waving Union Jacks, practically the whole way to the sea. I stood on deck and imagined what it must have felt like being on one of Sir Francis Drake's ships as it sailed the same stretch of water in the sixteenth century. I felt well prepared and confident but there was also a tangible fear of sailing out into the unknown. The other reason I wanted the first leg was the route and destination. Crossing the Atlantic, catching the trade winds to South America, and sailing into Rio de Janeiro with all its links to mixed martial arts; what could be better than that?

As each vessel in the race is absolutely identical and gets passed to a new sponsor every two years, the official names of the boats are functional rather than romantic. Ours was technically called *CV27*, but the superstitions of the true sailors on board dictated that she was rechristened 'Grace' with the aid of a small bottle of whisky, the only drop of alcohol on board. Then, as we stood on deck, waiting for the noon start in the hammering rain at the very end of the pier at Southend-on-Sea, a rush of adrenalin surged through my body. We were all in our foul-weather gear and I was shouting and banging on the mast to get everyone fired up. It was competition time, fight time. The first few miles are all about jockeying for position but can go some way to dictating your position in the entire 45,000 nautical-mile race. It might be the only time each boat is in sight of one other, and the only chance to see how other skippers react to circumstances as everyone chases or tries to maintain their advantage. I saw the French boat blow their spinnaker and the kite sail fell into the sea. We passed them as they were all scrambling to recover it and pull it back aboard. We were flying as we swept by the White Cliffs of Dover and I was loving it. When the sun set we still held an early lead, but suddenly we were competing against opponents we couldn't see. Out of nowhere, the French boat, which was supernaturally quick at times, steamed past us in the murky night like a ghost ship and disappeared. 'Grace' chased her for the guts of a year, but never managed to catch her.

Life on a racing clipper is not easy. Everyone is on a rota for shift work and the timeslots are: 6am–noon, noon–6pm, 6pm–10pm, 10pm–2am and 2am–6am. One day you would be on a six-hour shift and then two four-hour shifts, and the next day one six-hour and one four-hour. The only change was when it was your turn to be on full-day mother watch. That meant preparing all the food for everyone for twenty-four hours and was, in my opinion, by far the worst job on the yacht. I did it three times, rising at 5am to begin cooking porridge for twenty-five people in a dark galley. It was so cramped and hot in the galley, with a nearby toilet concealed by a curtain forever leaking and stinking the place out. The boat is invariably sitting at a 45-degree angle in the water for long periods of time, and that makes even the simplest task an ordeal. Try chopping vegetables, or boiling water, or going to the toilet at an unsteady 45-degree angle! After preparing the final meal of the day in time for the 6pm changeover, there was technically a small window to rest, but you needed a lot of luck to find a spot on which to lay your head. There were sixteen bunks on the boat, and twenty-five tired bodies hoping to use them. Our skipper, Peter Thornton, and the two camera crew had their own, so that left thirteen in circulation for the rest of us to bunk-hop. Hygiene was hardly a priority on board, so the sleeping quarters soon became pretty gross. You either went to bed cold and wet or hot and sweaty, so either way the bed space was going to suffer. I shared with a big six foot four Scotsman called Ken. He was a great guy and, as he was doing the full circumnavigation, he always got priority when it came to using our shared bunk. It was cramped for me, so how he dealt with it for the full eleven months still amazes me. At times I had to make do with the emergency bunk in the sail locker where people were always coming and going and waking you up. It had the additional drawback of lying just inches below the ceiling when it was winched into place which resulted in a sore face every time the boat bounced off a wave. Never before have I had to sleep with my guard up to protect my face, but bruised elbows and forearms are always better than a bloody nose!

It wasn't long before the boat and the elements combined to teach me a few lessons about how unpredictable and potentially dangerous life on a clipper in the ocean can be. During training, people were frequently losing bits and pieces and personal possessions overboard. It became a bit of a running joke that everyone must sacrifice something to Neptune. I had kept a watch in a case at home for years, waiting for a specific expedition to wear it on. I only put it on in Southend-on-Sea, but just twelve hours later it was somehow wiped from my wrist as I pulled on a sheet and I watched it sink into the murky depths of the Channel to join the wrecks of hundreds of boats and galleons that had found their final resting place there. Not long after the demise of my only time-telling device, and as we watched the French vessel speed past us in the 3am darkness, our skipper ordered the two head sails down and the spinnaker to be readied for launch. Half the crew were in bed, one was on deck at the helm, and most of the others were down in the sail locker getting the spinnaker ready, so I ran onto the foredeck to open the hatch and start pulling the sail up. Luckily I clipped the strap of my life jacket onto the jackstay with a carabiner before running towards the front of the boat. Out of nowhere, a huge gust of wind hit a sail which whipped a heavy rope up and struck me under the chin. The force of the impact was so strong that it knocked me up and off my feet and only my connection to the jackstay prevented me from flying over the side. At the speed we were travelling, and in the darkness of the dead of night, I would have been miles behind before anyone even realised I was missing.

On another occasion, I actually managed to sleep through one of the big storms we hit just north of the Equator. Depending on what side of the boat you were on, gravity was either trying to drag you off your bunk or squeeze you into the wall. I had adapted to life at 45 degrees by this point, but on this night we were keeled over at an even more extreme angle than normal. I woke suddenly, lying on the wall, looking at my bunk almost perpendicular beside me. The only window I could see through was a small porthole with a view into the snake pit where the crew hustled about in a nest of ropes. In my fatigued state I looked out with squinted eyes but had no way of telling what was happening or how fast we were going. There was a lot of banging and shouting going on, but as one of the winches was right above my head I presumed it was just a regular sail change in testing weather. I closed my eyes and went back to sleep and it was only later I learnt that we had been knocked over by a massive gust and the mast was flat in the water. I had been sleeping on the wall of the boat, effectively under the sea, but the poor folks on the starboard side of the vessel had been launched out of their slumber and caused a pile-up of bodies and luggage in the gangway between their bunks. I also found the cameraman looking a little worse for wear as one of the winches had come loose on impact, struck him, and taken a sizeable chunk out of his leg. There was no doubt that this was a dangerous environment we were operating in and we needed to be fully switched on all of the time.

About a week into the race, we began experiencing technical problems with our navigational and communication equipment. We resorted to using old-school maps and had no idea of our position in relation to the other yachts, giving the impression we were competing against phantoms. We also had to make do with just one twenty-four-hour weather forecast each morning. Not knowing what we were sailing into put us at a considerable disadvantage and led to us hitting squalls, storms and swells that other boats could foresee and avoid. Then one morning we woke up to a total media blackout with no emails going back and forth from Clipper HQ to the boats. That was very strange and put everyone on edge. Rumours began circulating and there were a few hours of uncertainty before the tragic news we all dreaded came through. A man named Andy on the South African boat had been hit on the head by the 500kg boom and killed. It was incredibly sad and, although we were removed from it, it was easy to imagine the pain of sailing with the dead body of a crewmate stored in the back of the vessel. It was also the starkest possible reminder that there are plenty of potentially fatal dangers every time you make a move on these boats. Later on, during the sixth leg of the race, there was another fatality on the same yacht when a woman, Sarah Young, was washed overboard between Qingdao and Seattle. Her lifeless body was recovered but at 1,000 miles from land there was nothing they could do but bury her at sea. If we didn't have the respect due for Mother Nature before, then this was a reminder that every adventure comes with risk. We had all embarked on this journey to experience the world and hoped to learn about ourselves in the process, but the oceans can be indiscriminately hostile and demanded our undivided attention at all times.

I thought of my own family, particularly my mum and sister, who I knew were already anxious about me taking part, when I heard of the tragedies. Part of the experience for me was the isolation and so I wasn't communicating with the outside world until I reached Rio. But I worried about their worry and so when a crewmate came up on deck, excited that she had a weak phone signal as we sailed within range of Cape Verde, I decided to make one quick call to my wife, Lacey. After what just happened to Andy, I wanted someone I loved to hear my voice and know that I was okay.

The worst injury I received arrived not long after that call but it was a mercifully minor incident. There was a problem with a jammed pulley at the top of the mast and its carabiner was beginning to wear. I put a helmet on and was winched up to transfer the sail onto another pulley. Up there, 100 feet high, every gust of wind and sway of the boat is magnified. The furthest I'd been from land in a boat was midway between Holland and the UK in the English Channel, but now I could only see ocean all around. You also get to see the curvature of the Earth from that lofty perspective, which is pretty cool. I loved being there, looking down at what appeared a toy yacht but was also my whole world. The Octagon is a dangerous and unpredictable space to be in, but you are always ready by the time you have to enter, and can always step out of it whenever you please, twenty-five minutes later at the very worst. I couldn't help thinking that I was trapped on this little boat for a month and there were things happening every day that would be impossible to prepare for. I was then snapped out of my temporary reverie by the pain of my finger being caught in the pulley. It took a lot of shouting and screaming into the wind before my crewmates below understood my cries and released the winch so I could extract the precious digit. It was numb and blue but basically all right so I completed the changeover and descended for a well-earned rest.

The most serious situation we faced on our leg took place as we approached the Doldrums, where everything begins to calm down, and our skipper decided to take advantage of the relatively pleasant weather and order a full rig check. As one of the youngest and fittest on board, I normally did that type of thing with another guy called Dhruv who was like a hyperactive spider monkey and always a huge source of energy and entertainment. On this occasion though, we had just finished our shift and retired to bed so someone else volunteered to scale the main mast. Just as I was nodding off, I heard a lot of commotion considering the benign conditions and got out of bed to take a look. I walked to the galley hatch but found it closed, something that only happens in an emergency. So I walked on to the sail locker and peered through the Perspex hatch there to see if I could find out what was happening. Looking up towards the sky I saw the watch leader, John Charles, dangling helplessly from the mast. He was wearing all white and blood was seeping through and quickly dying his shirt a deep scarlet colour. He had been unhooking and rehooking his carabiner from the mast to get over the second set of spreaders, metal arms that stretch out and attach to the shrouds which stabilise the mast, when a freak gust sent him spinning around the mast on the pulley, seventy feet up. As he swung round, he hit the shroud, broke both bones in his forearm, and tore his flesh right down to the muscle tissue under his arm. Such was the impact, both his shoes were also flung off. One was never seen again but I later recovered the other and attached it to the A-Frame at the back of the boat after John had written *ouch!* and signed it with the date and location of where the accident took place.

I sprinted onto deck, where the skipper Peter was already climbing the mast to get John down safely. Others were down below preparing the medical bay in the galley. I helped lower John onto the deck, took his lifejacket off and began to cut through his shirt to see the damage.

'Oh, do you have to?' the battered and bloodied casualty joked with me as I made the first snip. 'It's the first time I've worn this.'

His humour and bravery were unreal considering he was in a pretty bad way. At 1,200 miles from the nearest coast there was no chance of rescue, so we got the paramedics on the phone and they guided us through what needed to be done. Peter was ex-military and trained in field medicine so he stitched John up under the arm with seventeen big ugly crosses and zero cosmetic concern. Meanwhile, I was focused on holding his broken forearm as still as possible and trying to keep him conversational and the mood light. Blood loss was the major fear at this stage and, even if there was something severed inside, there was nothing we could do about it in our crude operating theatre. Once the torn flesh was clamped shut, John got a morphine shot for the pain, but he was remarkably calm and in good spirits throughout the entire harrowing ordeal. Even when Peter and I were trying to realign his snapped radius and ulna and fix a mouldable cast around his arm, he was chatting away, saying, 'Nice job, boys, that looks pretty straight from my angle.' Had it been any other member of the crew, myself included, it would have been a total disaster. I later asked John how he remained so composed. He was a professional sailor, which helped a little, but he confessed to me at the end of the race that he presumed he was dead when he was first dangling seventy feet up with blood flowing freely. When we got him down he knew he wouldn't die and that made it easier to put whatever damage was done into perspective. He spent the next two weeks on antibiotics and painkillers sitting at the back of the boat and was at the helm to take control as we crossed the finishing line in Brazil. In hospital in Rio, surgeons opened him up to check everything and said he was millimetres from a major artery that, had it been nicked, would have meant certain death. They put a metal plate in his arm to hold his fractured bones together and just a few weeks later he was back on board, ready to continue his circumnavigation of the globe.

The month on 'Grace' wasn't easy. Every little issue or annoyance is exaggerated when twenty-five strangers are trapped together in a small space for a long period of time. Everything is exacerbated, especially when fatigue, homesickness, seasickness, and the lack of creature comforts set in. Tempers tend to fray quickly, and accusing fingers are pointed even quicker. It was a big test for me and the whole experience was exhausting, but all the times that I was down and wished I was home were easily made up for by just one of the moments when I was so grateful to be where I was. The night sky over the Atlantic where there is zero light pollution is truly awesome. We could see shooting stars every couple of minutes and you could follow them across the sky for five or ten seconds. I had sneaked a couple of joints on board and I had a smoke one night in the stillness of the Doldrums. Looking heavenwards, there was more light than darkness. It was overwhelming. The phosphorescence in the water was beautiful too. I watched the churning, fluorescent water glowing in the boat's wake and realised that the scene in *Life of Pi* is only slightly exaggerated. A pod of dolphins began following, performing for my attention. They dived under the boat and jumped up the other side to splash down in a multi-coloured explosion of ocean. On another night at the back of the boat I had an almost ceremonial moment, one that had echoes of a ceremony in the MushRoom. It was about not being present in the moment, not living the exact minute I am currently experiencing. I'd spent the first part of the race thinking always about the finishing line, viewing everything through that lens. It was always about how far had we gone, or how many days until Rio. It was just like how I punctuate my life with fight dates, making one year effectively just two or three days. I realised that for too long I had been all about preparing for something in the future and thinking about just getting through days until the goal is reached, when I just needed to relax and enjoy every second as it passes.

We broached twice on the approach into Rio, meaning the boom got snagged by a wave as the mainsail was out at an angle to make the most of the wind direction. This acted as an anchor digging into the sea and caused the boat to turn in a tight circle and drag us onto our side. It is crazy when that happens, everyone on the high side hanging on while the skipper tried to right it. We were a high-tech seventy-foot yacht but we may as well have been a splinter off a match as far as the power of Mother Nature is concerned. Rio de Janeiro was a very cool place to sail into, weaving through the islands, passing the coves and bays, while Christ the Redeemer peered down from on high. I looked back and saw the Irish boat just a mile behind us. A month at sea and 5,200 miles covered, and we end up so close together with our destination in sight, both waiting for a breeze to push us over the finish line first. It was an agonising final hour as the two boats sailed neck and neck the whole way in, but we managed to edge it on this occasion as we gave one of the outlying islands a wider approach and didn't get caught in the wind hole that the peak on the outcrop of land had created on the leeward side. There is a tradition to write something on the sail locker wall upon arrival, and I was first up with the pen in my hand. I had known exactly what I was going to write ever since that night I smoked my joint on the back of the boat in the Doldrums. 'Life is hard at 45,' I scribbled. 'But don't forget to enjoy the ride.'

In Rio we had to hang about for a few days to do a deep clean of the boat and complete any repairs before the next leg. I also had media obligations, going to see Jose Aldo and doing a few TV shows to talk about MMA and my race experience. There was then an awards ceremony and at it they announced that a memorial would take place for Andy. There were a lot of Andrews in the race, at least one on every boat more or less, and we never really learnt each other's surnames. So when we were originally told about Andy's death, no face sprang to mind and I had no recollection of whether I had ever met or spoken with him. It was still incredibly sad, of course, but I felt no direct personal connection. It was only at the awards night that I saw his face on the front of a leaflet giving details of the memorial. He was Andrew Ashman, a paramedic, and I knew him. I had spoken to him several times during training because he was an MMA fan and loved chatting about my fight with St-Pierre. As we were leaving St Katherines Docks in London his boat went past and he pointed over and waved and shouted that we'll have a drink in Rio. Andy was such a nice, friendly and enthusiastic guy. This was his adventure of a lifetime and it ended so tragically for him and his family. It hit me harder then than it had out at sea.

● ● ●

'Grace' may have carried me from London to Rio, but over the past couple of years the good ship UFC has taken me on a truly global journey. I've worked in ten countries across four continents, pit-stopping in Abu Dhabi, Berlin, Dublin, Sydney, Stockholm, Krakow, London, Zagreb, Rotterdam, Hamburg, Manchester, Belfast, Las Vegas, California and Melbourne along the way. The whole UFC package is so polished that it can be transported into any city on the planet for a weekend and run like a well-oiled machine. And now that the vast majority of the mindless opposition to mixed martial arts is dead and buried, we are an accepted and welcomed visitor wherever we go. It is as if stage one, that MMA is a legitimate sport and not some anachronistic freak show of barbarity, of the evolution is complete and we are working through stage two, an educational phase to ensure everyone interested understands the terms and disciplines, and what is going on inside the Octagon. We have made great strides but I can't wait for stage three, when everyone involved is ready for a deeper analysis and appreciation of our great sport.

In the meantime, I just feel lucky to have been embedded in the sport during one of the most dramatic periods in the UFC's history. I've been there to see the end of greatness as Anderson Silva's incredible career limps through its twilight. The Spider is, for me, the pound-for-pound best ever, and it will take a long time for someone to seize that accolade from him. It is always a subjective and rather whimsical debate, but I give him the nod in part because of the overall impact he has had on the sport. I rate the likes of GSP, Jose Aldo, Fedor Emelianenko and Jon Jones very highly too, but I'm not convinced they did as much to truly change the game the way someone like Silva did. The impressive flyweight kingpin Demetrius Johnson is another good example. Mighty Mouse is currently regarded by many as the P4P best, at least in Jones's enforced absence, and I can agree that he is probably the most well-rounded fighter. But I see him taking what has been known to work and perfecting it rather than bringing something totally new to the table. Someone like Randy Couture, on the other hand, most certainly was a revolutionary. He made dirty boxing and clinch work so important, as well as developing the art of ground-and-pound in the modern day. As was B.J. Penn, revolutionising what can be done on your back and proving that the lighter weight classes can be just as big a draw as the heavier fighters. Anderson Silva tops the pile for me because, not only did he change things up, but he did so while winning and dominating the middleweight division for over seven years in a fashion never seen before. The Brazilian was the first to truly highlight how elementary striking was in MMA when he made his UFC debut in 2006 and he then proceeded to use an incredibly languid and fluid style to take advantage of that fact. Many fighters, myself included, invest too much in what works for them but Silva was gifted enough to trust himself to win in so many distinct ways, inspiring other great fighters to try and mimic his spectacular finishes. He never became predictable, and was an expert in using his opponents' predictability against themselves. In my opinion, the Spider is the main man when it comes to the individuals who have been instrumental in raising standards across the board and making the modern-day UFC fighter a genuine master of all trades.

I have also been a cageside witness as two phenomena have become the first mixed martial artists to transcend the sport. My commentating trial run at UFC 170 was only Ronda Rousey's third appearance in the Octagon, but she was already established as a bona fide superstar in American life. Women's MMA had a couple of big names in Gina Carano and Cristiane 'Cyborg' Justino before Ronda, but when Cyborg brutalised

MMA's sweetheart Carano inside a round in 2009, the spectacle turned many fans off. Gina shifted her focus into movies and Cristiane fought only three times in the next three and a half years, so it wasn't until the Ronda Rousey–Meisha Tate rivalry kicked off in 2012 that the women's game received the shot in the arm it so badly needed. Unfortunately for Meisha, her arm took a battering in the process as Rousey nearly ripped it off to claim the Strikeforce bantamweight title. I remember watching it and thinking that if Rousey doesn't bring women to the UFC, then nobody ever will. She burst onto the scene a year later and was just so aggressive and dominant from the off. In winning her first seven inside a round, and five of those inside sixty seconds, there were echoes of Royce Gracie's phenomenal dominance back at the outset of the UFC.

She was untouchable inside the Octagon, but it was what went on outside that made her special. The big thing about Ronda was that she was always so real and it was easy for so many people to connect with her. She reached demographics previously unimaginable for a UFC fighter as, in the only example I can think of, a female athlete who became the first to break through as the trailblazing, mainstream star of a sport. Teenage girls found her inspirational, while soccer moms saw her on *Oprah* and loved her. The fathers and husbands of that fan base then watched her on Jimmy Kimmel and couldn't help falling for Rowdy Rousey too, while the established MMA fans simply appreciated what an astonishing fighter she was. She appealed to entire families in a way that had never been done before by any sportsperson, and that is the key to taking over America. Stardom and Hollywood fame may have changed her, I have no idea, but in the early years at least there was absolutely nothing dislikeable in her character. Lacey and I called in to visit her in Venice Beach one day about a month out from a fight and she was sprawled on the sofa in her PJs watching *South Park* and *Pro Wrestling*. There was no pretence about her, she was a normal cool person to be around, very girly and a little awkward if anything. It just so happened that she had ready access to a full-reptile switch inside her mind and could maul you as soon as look at you. Millions of women worldwide connected with those two sides of her. Both the insecure teenager getting bullied in school and the woman being belittled by an ignorant boss at work identified with Ronda and wished they could tap into their reptiles as she did. It is impossible to overstate how massive she became in such a short space of time. I remember walking past shops in international airports and if there was a rack of ten magazines, Ronda's smiling face could easily be on the front of six or seven of them. Little kids all over the world were begging their mums to dress them up as Ronda for fancy dress parties, and the mums couldn't have been happier to do it. It was all unprecedented for an MMA fighter and, for a year or two, Ronda Rousey basically was the UFC.

As I write today, with Rousey not having fought since her startling defeat at the hands (and feet) of Holly Holm over a year ago, a brash Irishman with a red beard has assumed the mantle of the Octagon's undisputed biggest star. The month after Rousey–Holm did 1.1 million PPVs, Conor McGregor versus Jose Aldo did 1.2 million. McGregor has headlined three cards since, attracting around 5 million PPV buys along the way. The Notorious is a different type of phenomenon, but no less impressive. His swagger and sharp tongue made him more famous and marketable by his third fight than legends like GSP or Silva were in their tenth. He also benefits from the Irish fans, surely the most vociferous in all of sport. Within MMA, the Brazilians are known to be extremely passionate, but only really when it is convenient for them to attend a show. In contrast, the Irish will go above and beyond to fly across an ocean in large numbers to fill an auditorium for a press conference. And when it comes to fight night, I have never experienced anything, in any arena, anywhere in the world like being cageside for a McGregor fight in Dublin. It has all allowed Conor to create the optimum persona to thrive within the modern-day business side of sport, although this money-obsessed alter-ego is beginning to grate within UFC circles. Beyond the hubris, however, there is no denying he is a special fighter. His understanding of range and timing is almost as good as his ability to get inside an opponent's head. More than that, McGregor displays a thirst for knowledge within martial arts and appears to be on a constant quest to introduce new elements into the Octagon and diversify his already versatile attack. This cerebral approach has seen him gravitate towards some of the sharpest minds in the sport, which has evolved his game and greatly expanded his ability as a fighter. His left hand is now as consistent as it is devastating and is totally unique to him in the way he delivers it from a long southpaw stance. And with at least two or three years left at the top of his game, Conor has plenty of time to earn a place within the pantheon of all-time greats.

● ● ●

It is more than four years since I last fought, but I am a better fighter now than then. Four years of intently studying the sport can only improve the most important aspect of any elite mixed martial artist's game: fighting intelligence. Before my enforced layoff, I would pick and choose what I wanted to watch. I looked to specific fighters, my opponents, others with a similar style to my own or one that I saw a benefit in emulating. I'd watch big historical bouts over and over again, and often just the main card of an event. I tended to ignore fighters I considered to be a level or two below me, partly due to a fear of somehow picking up some of their bad habits, integrating what I was seeing into my subconscious, and it having a negative impact on my overall game.

Now, however, I watch absolutely everything, literally hundreds of fights per week. For the first time in my life I'm watching MMA to the point that I want to turn it off and do something else. I regularly find myself awake at 3am or 4am watching bouts that I've already studied and taken notes on earlier that day. I'll fall asleep mid-round and wake a few hours later assuming I was taking nothing in as drowsiness enveloped me. Then, a day or two later in the gym, I'll utilise a move or technique I didn't know I had, one that had seeped quietly into my subconscious throughout a marathon session of scrutinising fight footage. Recently I was researching Jacaré Souza, a guy I consider to be in the top three in the UFC when it comes to the grappling arts. For hours I broke down the techniques he goes to repeatedly and effectively before, without thinking, I used the same transitions and submissions in the gym. Were it not for the fact I was commentating in an upcoming Souza fight, I would never have spent an evening analysing him. Therein lies the beauty of my current role: the broadening scope of what I watch has opened me up to techniques, movement patterns and game-plans that I'd not considered or used before.

When I agreed to take the analyst job, Giff told me that in a year's time I would be viewing the sport through different eyes. I wasn't fully aware what he meant at the time, but I can now say that he was completely right. Today, I see so much more when I watch an MMA bout. I can see the influence that teammates have on one another, particularly the guys coming out of the huge American MMA factories where two or three coaches are working with forty fighters. They tend to have the same strengths and weaknesses and similar game-plans. I've noticed that guys lower down the card don't necessarily make different mistakes to the headliners, it's just that they make those same mistakes more often or at more costly junctures of a fight. It's a little like watching the Nottingham Panthers play in the British ice hockey league and then a top match from the NHL. I see clear patterns forming, guys making the same moves or having the same reactions to what is happening in a fight. Tyron Woodley for example, standing in orthodox stance, feinting with his right hand, throwing a long jab to follow as a range-finder, then landing his bludgeoning overhand right. I watch fighters chronologically and in depth so I can see the development in their game over a career. I have just sat through the entire UFC back catalogue of Woodley's upcoming opponent, Stephen 'Wonderboy' Thompson, three times, back to back. On his debut he knocked out Dan Stittgen with a beautiful head-kick after struggling to land a killer punch, whereas recently his right hand has been finishing most contests. Without having studied his debut, I might think he is all about the right hand and has no secondary option in that position, but I have seen that he uses the exact same footwork for both and so that deadly kick is always there in reserve for when the punches aren't landing sweetly enough. I can see that the average fight IQ of UFC fighters is getting higher every year. When I first watched the UFC there wasn't much strategy, but guys are now setting traps every minute of every round. The increased intelligence is necessary because fighters are so well prepared for one another and at the elite level the physical abilities are often very similar. It's fascinating to find these traps being set on the ground in particular, with fighters punching opponents in a certain way to make them move into the position they want. Just like Nate Diaz did to McGregor in the second round of their first meeting. It is a much more cerebral approach in comparison to the early days of hitting anywhere and everywhere as hard and fast as possible.

Having the opportunity to speak with top coaches like John Danaher has only reinforced my renewed education. I first met John properly when I travelled up to Tristar in Montreal to help GSP in his fight preparations for the Condit and Diaz fights. Our hotel room doors were opposite each other so I was fortunate enough to get a few minutes at the end of each day in conversation with him. I found him to be one of the most fascinating and compelling individuals I had ever met. He is a black belt under the legendary Renzo Gracie and is responsible for the development of some of the best combat athletes in the world. Clearly a very intelligent individual, he has turned his analytical and philosophical mind on the art of grappling. In GSP's corner when we fought, he studied me ahead of the bout and was kind enough to impart some of his observations when we spoke. It forever changed the way I look at the sport of MMA. He and his students, under the banner of The Danaher Death Squad, are changing the sport of submission wrestling. The small but dedicated group of athletes that work with John every day are currently claiming all of the belts, medals and trophies that the grappling world has to offer. I am determined to study under him in the future, but for now I can sit back and watch as his brilliant mind is changing combat sports before my eyes.

I can also see that the evolution of MMA has slowed in recent years. Brazilian jiu-jitsu, ground-and-pound, and sprawl-and-brawl all had their day, but we are now settling down in the middle of a more prolonged era of effective-striking domination. There was a time when guys learnt a bit of everything in order to be able to keep the fight in their preferred range, but modern-day champions are almost as proficient in jiu-jitsu as they are in wrestling and, in turn, striking. The globalisation of sport and the rise of social media has had an effect, with free and easy access to everything at our fingertips. I used to struggle for MMA footage, but now I can watch six shows from six countries in any given weekend. There are probably fewer surprises now, with geographical influences less pronounced. Where once upon a time the average Brazilian fighter was all about jiu-jitsu, the American was a wrestler first and foremost, the Asian fighters had either a more flamboyant and unpredictable or strictly traditional style of martial arts and the European was an ex-kickboxer who learnt gi grappling at the local Gracie Barra, a more integrated approach is now evident as kids have access to specialist MMA gyms from day one. I often wish I could go back in time and, rather than spend thousands of childhood hours marching up and down the village hall practising blocks and kicks and stances, could practise takedown defence, taking a back and sinking a rear-naked choke instead.

As MMA has evolved over the years, it has shed a lot of superfluous techniques as fighters figure out what does and doesn't work inside a cage. But I find it interesting that certain patterns that were once dismissed have later proved to be entirely effective in the right hands. Wonderboy standing side-on, or Conor and his exaggerated long stance, for example. Such positions were once frowned upon in the belief they restricted movement and left a fighter vulnerable to takedowns and low kicks, but Thompson and McGregor have found a way to make them work incredibly well. All you really need is an acute awareness of the dangers involved and a clear strategy for how you are going to handle them. With that in place, Wonderboy is free to knock guys out with spinning head-kicks, and Jon Jones can end opponents with spinning elbows and flying knees. Part of the reason why such moves, once regarded as too high risk, now work is because today's elite fighter is so versatile and has such a deep and varied offence that opponents need to be wary of an almost infinite array of possible attacks. That has actually created a space and a freedom to be more adventurous still and is why Anderson Silva could suddenly pull a front kick to the face out of the bag and put Vitor Belfort to sleep.

It is also a sign that the way forward is to actually look into the past for inspiration. Bruce Lee once said, 'I don't believe in different ways of fighting now. I mean, unless human beings have three arms and three legs, then we will have a different way of fighting. But basically we all have two arms and two legs so that is why I believe there should be only one way of fighting and that is no way.' As well as telling us that we must each strive to find our own optimum way of fighting, Lee was explaining that, somewhere in the long history of martial arts, everything we need to advance has already been done. The secret now is to try and put particular techniques together in a way that works inside the Octagon. I have a Lego analogy I like to use to explain my theory. A jab is your standard Lego brick and is effectively a base and fits with every other piece. But there are plenty of techniques that are much less homogenous. The Von Flue choke, where you force a shoulder into the throat of an opponent when he has made the mistake of holding onto a guillotine as his opponent passes to side control, is a fine example because it only works when the beaten fighter makes the fatal error, or isn't aware of the danger, of failing to release the guillotine. The Von Flue choke isn't one of your regular Lego bricks, but rather a specialist piece, a visor maybe that only connects to one particular helmet on a mini-figure.

Fighters and coaches should now be delving into the martial arts archives in search of specialist Lego pieces and then figuring out how to integrate them into a 2017 MMA contest. My money is on a lot of flying and jumping techniques coming back into play as fighters' timing in the Octagon continues to improve. I feel we will see a revolution in elbow strikes in the clinch in the next few years. It's an obvious hole in the game that is being explored by few fighters in the modern day. Carlos Condit put on a beautiful display in the second round of his bout with Thiago Alves, and that really shows how devastating they can be. I also believe that there is a lot of room to enhance striking inside the Octagon. The high-level strikers competing in the striking-specific arts are still generally better than an MMA exponent, but as the bread-and-butter moves of

MMA continue to be perfected and streamlined, UFC fighters will have more scope in the gym to focus on striking cleaner and harder and more accurately. Finally, as the transitions from one range to another become even more seamless, the more time fighters have in the cage to think and act. Those extra split seconds will be enough for the best of the best to take a chance with a risky or unorthodox attack and be in sufficient control to soon make it look run of the mill. There are movements and patterns that are an absolute given today that the guys at UFC 1 didn't even know about. We will have watched UFC 207 by the end of the year, but imagine what levels will have been reached by UFC 300 or 400, when the top mixed martial artists will be closer to perfection than ever. And the beautiful thing about it all is that, as MMA is still so relatively young, we can watch all these evolutions transpire before our eyes.

● ● ●

I get excited watching it, but nothing can compare to doing it. I have my gumshield in my jacket pocket every time I commentate, but soon I hope to be packing my entire kit before I travel to a UFC event. It is true that the doctor testing me for that last bout with Matt Brown gave me a surgery-or-retire ultimatum, but that was just one opinion and I have always believed that another doctor on another day would see it differently. The UFC door has always been left ajar as far as I am concerned. My contract is still valid, and it states I have three more fights left. I love the sport of mixed martial arts infinitely more than I love my own career and I would never contemplate doing anything to risk the reputation of MMA, but I know I still haven't shown my true capabilities in the Octagon. Far from it, in fact. I still get frustrated watching my younger self in action, often fighting in such a raw and amateurish manner. I could quite easily dissect every one of my fights and highlight all the mistakes I was making along the way. Perhaps one day I will, if only to allow others to learn from my errors and help improve the next generations of fighters.

There was a time when I couldn't think of anything outside my family that I cared about more than the martial arts. But with hindsight I now see that I was being blindly led by the ego of youth and what I actually cared about was myself and my own reputation within the world of martial arts. Today I know that no matter what role I play in the future of the sport, it is important as a martial artist to put the tradition of combat sports before any selfish agenda. It shouldn't really be about being the best fighter in the world, although that is a hell of an achievement and I would have been truly honoured to have ever held that title. The reality of our existence is constantly in flux. As we rise and fall over the years, we have an impact on those around us that will echo through generations. Some, like champions or great musicians, artists and writers, will leave an imprint on millions of individuals around the world, while the influence of others may appear small in comparison. But it is the depth of each individual impact that matters. Although my grandad Derek reached relatively few people during his lifetime, the difference he made in their lives and the lasting impression he left behind is worth a thousand championship belts. To be a champion at life is so much easier than to be a champion at sport, and yet so many fail; even more never even bother to try. Worse still are the champions who are shitty people in real life, and they appear with depressing regularity.

From my time with plant medicine, often in painful and trying circumstances or just plain beaten, I am now clear about what I am trying to achieve while I am on this Earth. I have spent years focused on being destructive, trying to master the art of breaking another person, and yet even within that environment I can see the positive influence I have had on the people that I have been fortunate enough to reach. I'm under no illusions, however, and am not so arrogant as to believe that I am the source of this good energy. Rather, I am simply the conduit for each and every person that has invested in me, just like the many amazing people before me that made efforts to better themselves and were my inspiration. I want to be the continuation of that good energy and do what I can in this lifetime to keep it moving forward.

As we move into a new era with the UFC, the sport of MMA will go from strength to strength. Before the emergence of mixed martial arts, combat systems around the world had become somewhat stagnant. They had been refined as individual styles by many ignorant purists and this led to an unrealistic perspective of real combat and its requirements. Now, within the testing ground that the UFC has established and with each and every MMA show out there providing a safe and fair environment for the new wave of young athletes coming through, we are seeing rapid progress again. The champions of today will be the teachers and examples for future generations.

I truly believe that safe and regulated fighting arenas are a good thing for humankind. We need spaces within which likeminded individuals can explore their fighting skills and that animalistic, raw and quite beautiful side of our nature that connects us to our origin but has no place in modern society. An aggressive or competitive nature is a simple matter of energy, driven by hormones, difficult life experiences or a multitude of other sources, that needs a place to be expelled. When this energy is stifled and suppressed, that is when we see it manifest in a variety of unfavourable behaviours. But as humans, there was a substantial time during our evolution when our very survival depended upon these aggressive tendencies. The martial arts school should be a safe space to confront the struggles we all encounter in life and give us the tools to deal responsibly with the misdirected energy that builds inside us or comes our way from others.

My journey through martial arts was a little more rigorous and demanding than some, but each obstacle I faced forced me to learn, question and evolve. Sweating and bleeding and challenging myself was a big part of my development as a person. Whatever comes next, I at least hope that I have the courage and wisdom to make the right decision at the right time and keep moving forward. My love for the martial arts will drive me to become a better fighter and a better analyst and, regardless of which path I eventually choose, I will continue to improve myself every day.

As this book that you hold in your hands was coming together, I had a constant concern that many of the people that have played a pivotal role in my life would not get the appreciation they deserve within these pages. The truth is it would be impossible to give due credit to everyone that has ever assisted me as I have developed as a martial artist and as a person, but I need to try and quickly cover as many as possible.

My gratitude goes out to all of the coaches, trainers, senseis, shifus, masters, mentors and teammates that have guided me along the way.

The very nature of martial arts is to share knowledge and hope that the next generation can improve it in some way. I know I have benefited greatly from this philosophy. I am also grateful to have fought through the Fertitta years and will always have a lot of appreciation for what Frank, Lorenzo, Dana White and Joe Silva have done for the sport. They invested a lot at the outset and we have all gained from the gamble they took on the early UFC brand. The same goes for every single fighter that has stepped onto the canvas in the Octagon and made their own contribution to the history of the sport. It is not an easy path to walk when for every champion that graces our world, thousands fall painfully short.

Finally, and most importantly, I must give thanks to my family. To my parents who sacrificed so much and worked so hard, and to my two sets of strong and wonderful grandparents. To my grandad Ian for his mellow and somewhat mischievous nature and his penchant for silly costumes, football and long walks in foreign countries. To my nanna Barbara, for her toughness in the face of, well, anything. Her ability to fix, repair, make-do, and figure out the solution to every possible problem that a grandson could present was second to none. To my nanna Doreen with her quiet and caring support and the newly found adventurous side of her character that saw her fly to Vegas at eighty years of age. And to my grandad Derek, my anchor in martial arts and the person that best represented the qualities of loyalty, consistency and hard work. He remains unsurpassable many years after he left us. As much as the martial arts gave to me, none of it would have been possible if it weren't for every person that has guided me safely along the way. I am truly grateful to each and every one of you.

PICTURE CREDITS